教育部"双万计划"一流本科专业建设项目　　　　　　总主编：史宝辉
北京市与在京高校共建项目
中央高校基本科研业务费专项资金（项目编号：2015ZCQ-WY-01）

西方文化基础

（第三版）

Foundations of Western Culture

(3rd Edition)

主　编　南宫梅芳　訾　缨　白雪莲

副主编　李　芝　常　青

编　者（按姓氏拼音排列）
　　　　刘晓希　罗　灿　吕丽塔
　　　　武田田　许景城　姚晓东

图书在版编目(CIP)数据

西方文化基础 / 南宫梅芳，訾缨，白雪莲主编. —3版. —北京：北京大学出版社，2022.1
高等学校本科英语教改新教材
ISBN 978-7-301-32752-4

Ⅰ.①西… Ⅱ.①南…②訾…③白… Ⅲ.①英语—阅读教学—高等学校—教材 ②西方文化—概况 Ⅳ.①H319.4:G

中国版本图书馆CIP数据核字(2021)第257072号

书　　　名	西方文化基础(第三版) XIFANG WENHUA JICHU (DI-SAN BAN)
著作责任者	南宫梅芳　訾　缨　白雪莲　主编
责任编辑	李　颖
标准书号	ISBN 978-7-301-32752-4
出版发行	北京大学出版社
地　　　址	北京市海淀区成府路205号　100871
网　　　址	http://www.pup.cn　新浪微博:@北京大学出版社
电子信箱	evalee1770@sina.com
电　　　话	邮购部 010-62752015　发行部 010-62750672　编辑部 010-62754382
印　刷　者	三河市博文印刷有限公司
经　销　者	新华书店
	787毫米×1092毫米　16开本　13.25印张　418千字 2014年4月第1版　2015年10月第2版 2022年1月第3版　2024年5月第3次印刷
定　　　价	59.00元

未经许可，不得以任何方式复制或抄袭本书之部分或全部内容。
版权所有，侵权必究
举报电话：010-62752024　电子信箱：fd@pup.pku.edu.cn
图书如有印装质量问题，请与出版部联系，电话：010-62756370

第三版前言

当前,我国大学英语教学改革处于一个非常重要的发展阶段。自2017年起,国家大力推进新工科、新文科、新医科、新农科"四新"建设,掀起高等教育"质量革命"。在2018年全国教育大会上,习近平总书记指出,要大力培养掌握党和国家方针政策、具有全球视野、通晓国际规则、熟练运用外语、精通中外谈判和沟通的国际化人才,要有针对性地培养"一带一路"建设急需的懂外语的各类专业技术和管理人才。新时代的外语教育改革发展要立足全球坐标、服务国家战略、培养高质量外语人才。2019年3月,教育部高等教育司司长吴岩在第四届全国高等学校外语教育改革与发展高端论坛上发表了题为"识变、应变、求变——新使命、大格局、新文科、大外语"的讲话,对"新文科""大外语"提出了具体的改革要求。

随着国家需求、社会需求和学生需求的变化,大学英语教学面临着发展的重要时刻,在这一背景下,重新审视大学英语的定位,探索实现大学英语课程教学内容的创新与突破是十分重要的。新形势下的大学英语课程不仅是一门语言基础课程,也是为学生未来的学术研究打基础、拓宽国际化视野、了解世界文化的素质教育课程,兼有专业性和人文性。

在这一思想的指导下,由北京市教学名师史宝辉教授担纲总主编的高等院校本科英语教改新教材系列进行了全面修订,社会反响良好。

该系列教材具有以下创新点:

1. 契合教育部"新文科""大外语"建设的主旨思想,主动融入构建人类命运共同体的大格局,努力提升国家话语能力和行业语言能力。坚持需求导向和目标导向,主动服务国家对外开放战略和"一带一路"建设需求,基于需求进行了优化、调整和升级;牢固树立国家意识、标准意识、质量意识,以培养复合型、应用型的高质量外语人才为目标,将外语教育和国家战略需求紧密结合。

2. 教材以内容为依托,使学生在语言输出实践中了解中、西方语言与文化,学会如何使用流畅、得体的英语构建和表达中、西文化领域的话题,从而实现语言与文化两个层面的输出。

3. 该系列教材融知识性和趣味性于一体,在选材时尽量将历史概述与具体故事相结合,调动学生对阅读的兴趣;图文并茂地提供一种展现中西文化风貌的视觉方式,凸显重要主题,课程内容生动、直观,符合21世纪大学生的认知心理。

本次推出的《西方文化基础(第三版)》在前两版的基础上进行了较大的修订和完善。一方面继续为学生展现西方文化全貌,使学生英语语言技能的提升寓于西方文化基础知识的掌握之中;另一方面,删除了陈旧内容,更新了选篇,并将课程思政元素有机融入教学和练习之中,使学生在了解西方文化的同时,学会鉴别西方文化的根源和本质。内容上,本教材从古希腊、罗马文化开始,以西方现当代文化现象作为终结,展现了西方文化发展的主线。古希腊神话、政治、哲学、戏剧是西方文化和文明发展的摇篮;古罗马人重实用,

大肆修建道路,所以才有了"条条大路通罗马"这样的古话;中世纪文化长期以来为学者和大众所忽视,并简单地将这一漫长的历史时期蒙上"黑暗"这个盖布,但是,在这层"盖布"下却有着意识形态和世俗生活的重大变化:现代意义上的国家逐渐形成、现代意义上的教育有了雏形;文艺复兴则是西方文明的一个拐点:伴随着宗教改革所引起的巨变,以人为本的思想从意大利兴起并迅速蔓延到整个欧洲;随着启蒙时代理性的火种燃遍了整个西方,科学、自由、民主深入人心;浪漫主义和现实主义是继续关注人类和人类社会的时代,不仅是人的理性,更是人类美好的情愫,不仅是个体人的存在,还有丰富复杂、五味杂陈的人类社会;现代主义对人类生存的理解更为深入,不论是艺术、音乐还是建筑,都表现出更加多元、更加个性、更加难以把握的反传统特征……

  西方文化在人类文明的发展进程中贡献了具有特色的思想、政治、经济、意识形态等元素,但是同时应当看到,西方文化在其发展过程中充斥着血腥,每一种新范式的出现都伴随着暴力和对霸权主宰的反叛。在全球化的今天,西方声音对全球的霸权是否还在继续?需要我们在学习西方文化的过程中认真反思。人类文明是丰富多彩和平等的。不同国家和地区在漫长的历史发展进程中所形成的人类文明,都包含着不同地区人民不懈的精神追求,是人类的共同遗产。发端于中国大地的中华文明,也是在与其他文明交流互鉴中发展、演进,成就其辉煌与伟大的。习近平总书记在党的二十大报告中强调:"我们真诚呼吁,世界各国弘扬和平、发展、公平、正义、民主、自由的全人类共同价值,促进各国人民相知相亲,尊重世界文明多样性,以文明交流超越文明隔阂、文明互鉴超越文明冲突、文明共存超越文明优越,共同应对各种全球性挑战。"再一次鲜明地阐明了解决"世界怎么了""人类向何处去"时代之问、世界之问的中国方案。

  《西方文化基础(第三版)》在选篇和练习形式上都做了较大修改。全书分为七个单元,每单元三篇阅读文章,同时增加了四篇当代西方文化的补充阅读。语篇长度、难度适中,附有词汇表和长难句注释。在其姊妹篇《西方文化背景》一书中,有《西方文化基础(第三版)》全部课文的译文和西方文化背景知识词条解释,方便查找和学习。

  为了适应课堂教学和语言操练的需要,每一选篇后都配备了适合的练习;练习形式新颖、规范,以提高学生跨文化交际能力为宗旨,将提高"写"和"说"的能力作为突破目标。练习题的设计原则分为三个层次:第一个层次注重语言和内容的基础理解,第二个层次关注学生的思辨能力发展,第三个层次侧重语言输出能力的培养。

  与教材配套的课堂版教学电子课件制作精美,信息量大,使用便捷,有助于教师的备课和授课工作。在使用过程中,效果良好,受到了任课教师和学生的欢迎。

  本教材读者群广泛,主要读者对象为大专院校非英语专业本科生和研究生,也可供英语专业本科生和其他英语爱好者使用。

  本教材得到了教育部"双万计划"一流本科专业建设项目、北京市与在京高校共建项目、中央高校基本科研业务费专项资金(项目编号:2015ZCQ-WY-01)和北京林业大学教务处的支持。特此感谢上述机构对本项目研发的资助。

编者
2022.1

目 录

Unit 1　Ancient Greek Culture and Wisdom ……………………………… **1**
　　Section A　Greek Mythology ……………………………………………… 1
　　Section B　City-States: Athens and Sparta …………………………… 8
　　Section C　Socrates ……………………………………………………… 14

Unit 2　Roman Empire and Latin Culture …………………………… **24**
　　Section A　History of Roman Empire …………………………………… 24
　　Section B　All Roads Lead to Rome …………………………………… 30
　　Section C　Cleopatra, the Egyptian Queen and Her Love Affairs …… 36

Unit 3　The Middle Ages and the Rise of Modern Europe ………… **46**
　　Section A　The Middle Ages ……………………………………………… 46
　　Section B　The Rise of the States ……………………………………… 53
　　Section C　The Rise of Universities in the Middle Ages …………… 60

Unit 4　Renaissance and Shakespeare ……………………………… **71**
　　Section A　Renaissance …………………………………………………… 71
　　Section B　William Shakespeare ………………………………………… 78
　　Section C　Henry VIII and His Six Wives ……………………………… 84

Unit 5　Enlightenment and the Origin of Modern Science ………… **96**
　　Section A　The Age of Enlightenment …………………………………… 96
　　Section B　On the Shoulders of Giants: Isaac Newton and Modern Science　103
　　Section C　Francis Bacon: Fame and Disgrace ……………………… 108

Unit 6　Romanticism and Realism …………………………………… **119**
　　Section A　Romanticism in Europe ……………………………………… 119
　　Section B　Romanticism in America …………………………………… 127
　　Section C　Realism in Europe …………………………………………… 133

Unit 7 Modernism and Contemporary Western Culture ········ 148
   Section A Modernism and Modernist Movement ················ 148
   Section B The Distinct Character of Contemporary American Culture ··· 156
   Section C How Contemporary American Society Tramples on Principles of Integrity ················ 163

Supplementary Reading ················ 174
   Passage 1 The Toxic Individualism of Pandemic Politics ················ 174
   Passage 2 False Values Conveyed by American Entertainment and Cultural Industries ················ 176
   Passage 3 What Is the Bamboo Ceiling and How Do We Break It? ········ 179
   Passage 4 White-collar Crime ················ 183

Glossary ················ 187

Unit 1

Ancient Greek Culture and Wisdom

导 读

本单元涵盖古希腊神话和城邦国家的基本知识，也涉及古希腊最著名的哲学家苏格拉底等人的基本情况、重要贡献等，旨在使学生对古典文化的代表、西方文化的源头之一古希腊文明有基本认识，为学习西方文化打下良好的基础。

Before You Start

While preparing for this unit, think about the following questions:

1. When we talk about ancient Greece, what comes first into your mind? Interesting stories, the Trojan War or the Olympic Games? Exchange the information you know with your classmates.
2. What do you know about Greek mythology? Can you name any gods, goddesses, or heroes in Greek mythology? Can you tell their stories?
3. Can you introduce any achievement of Socrates, Plato or Aristotle? Why do we say that they made the foundation of western philosophy?

Section A Greek Mythology

① Greek mythology is the body of myths and teachings that belong to the ancient Greeks, concerning their gods and heroes, the nature of the world, and the origins and significance of their own cult and ritual practices. In ancient Greece, stories about gods and goddesses and heroes and monsters were an important part of everyday life. They explained everything from religious rituals to the weather, and they gave meaning to the world people saw around them.

At the center of Greek mythology is the pantheon of deities who were said to live on Mount Olympus, the highest mountain in Greece. ② Olympian gods and goddesses looked like men and women (though they could change themselves into animals and other things) and were—as many myths recounted—vulnerable to human weaknesses and passions.

Zeus was the head of the pantheon, or family of gods. Zeus ruled

Zeus

Poseidon

the sky with his powerful thunderbolt. Many ancient Greeks feared the anger of Zeus during violent thunderstorms. Zeus's wife, Hera, was the goddess of women and marriage.

Poseidon was said to be Zeus's brother and the ruler of the sea. He also had the power to create earthquakes. Greek mariners and fishermen believed that Poseidon would strike the ground with his mighty trident when he was ignored. A trident is a three-pronged spear used by the ancient Greeks both to spear fish and as a weapon. Poseidon might cause shipwrecks with his trident, but he could also create new islands and favor sailors with food and safe travel to other lands.

Another brother named Hades ruled the underworld. The Greeks believed that people passed to Hades's territory when they died, and while they were treated fairly in the underworld, Hades would never allow them to return to the world they once knew.

Greek mythology does not just tell the stories of gods and goddesses, however. Human heroes—such as Heracles, the adventurer who performed 12 impossible labors for King Eurystheus; Pandora, the first woman, whose curiosity brought evil to mankind; and Narcissus, the young man who fell in love with his own reflection—are just as significant. Monsters and "hybrids" (human-animal forms) also feature prominently in the tales: the winged horse Pegasus, the horse-man Centaur, the lion-woman Sphinx and the bird-woman Harpies, etc. Many of these creatures have become almost as well known as the gods, goddesses and heroes who share their stories.

Greek mythology has had an extensive influence on the culture, arts, and literature of Western civilization and remains part of Western heritage and language. ③ Great writers such as Dante, Shakespeare and Milton make frequent references to Greek mythology, so much so that an understanding of Greek myths is necessary to truly appreciate their works. Austrian psychiatrist Freud coined the phrase "Oedipus Complex" based on the myth of Oedipus. ④ An oracle proclaimed that Oedipus would kill his father and marry his mother, and Freud believed that these feelings of jealousy toward the same-sex parent and love for the opposite-sex parent were a phase that all children would go through. ⑤ In general usage, a Trojan horse—just like the one that led to the defeat of Troy—is something that appears desirable but in fact presents a threat. In computer science, a Trojan horse (often called a Trojan for short) is a computer program that looks useful and innocent, such as a free computer game, but allows unauthorized access to your computer. Many consumer products also get

Hades

their names from Greek mythology. ❻ Nike, the sports brand, is the namesake of the goddess of victory, for example. And the famous Amazon river is named after the race of mythical female warriors.

(617 words)

 New Words and Expressions (A)

New Words

New Words	Phonetic Symbols	Meanings
access	[ˈækses]	n. 访问,进入
adventurer	[ədˈventʃərə(r)]	n. 冒险家
Austrian	[ˈɒstrɪən]	adj. 奥地利的
coin	[kɔɪn]	v. 创造,杜撰（新词、新语等）
cult	[kʌlt]	n. 宗教崇拜,宗教信仰
curiosity	[ˌkjʊərɪˈɒsəti]	n. 好奇心
deity	[ˈdeɪəti]	n. 神祇
extensive	[ɪkˈstensɪv]	adj. 广泛的,大量的
heritage	[ˈherɪtɪdʒ]	n. 文化遗产
hybrid	[ˈhaɪbrɪd]	n. 杂交生成的生物体
ignore	[ɪɡˈnɔː(r)]	v. 忽视
innocent	[ˈɪnəsnt]	adj. 无害的
jealousy	[ˈdʒeləsi]	n. 嫉妒
mariner	[ˈmærɪnə(r)]	n. 水手,海员
monster	[ˈmɒnstə(r)]	n. 怪物,妖怪
myth	[mɪθ]	n. 神话
mythology	[mɪˈθɒlədʒi]	n. 神话（总称）
namesake	[ˈneɪmseɪk]	n. 同名者,同名物
oracle	[ˈɒrəkl]	n. 神谕;预言
pantheon	[ˈpænθɪən]	n. 众神
phase	[feɪz]	n. 阶段
philosophy	[fəˈlɒsəfi]	n. 哲学
proclaim	[prəˈkleɪm]	v. 宣称
prominently	[ˈprɒmɪnəntli]	adv. 重要地
psychiatrist	[saɪˈkaɪətrɪst]	n. 精神病学家
recount	[rɪˈkaʊnt]	v. 讲述

reflection	[rɪˈflekʃn]	n. 倒影
religious	[rɪˈlɪdʒəs]	adj. 宗教的
ritual	[ˈrɪtʃuəl]	n. (宗教)仪式
shipwreck	[ˈʃɪprek]	n. 海难
significance	[sɪgˈnɪfɪkəns]	n. 意义
sneaker	[ˈsniːkə(r)]	n. 运动鞋
spear	[spɪə(r)]	n. 矛枪　v. 用矛刺
strike	[straɪk]	v. 猛烈击打
three-pronged	[θriː-prɒŋd]	adj. 有三叉(尖)的
thunderbolt	[ˈθʌndəbəʊlt]	n. (诗/文)雷电,霹雳
trident	[ˈtraɪdnt]	n. 三叉戟,三齿鱼叉
unauthorized	[ʌnˈɔːθəraɪzd]	adj. 未经授权的,未经许可的
underworld	[ˈʌndəwɜːld]	n. 阴间
violent	[ˈvaɪələnt]	adj. 强烈的
warrior	[ˈwɒriə(r)]	n. 武士

Expressions

be named after	以……名字命名
go through	通过,经受
make reference to	提到
so much so that	到这种程度以致
be vulnerable to	易受伤害的;易受影响的
feature prominently	起主要作用,扮演重要角色

Proper Names

Aristotle	亚里士多德,古希腊哲学家和科学家,柏拉图的学生,亚历山大大帝之师,著有《诗学》《修辞学》等。
Centaur	肯陶洛斯,人首马身的怪物。
Dante	但丁,意大利文艺复兴早期的著名诗人,以长诗《神曲》(*Divine Comedy*)留名后世。
Eurystheus	欧律斯特斯,迈锡尼国王,赫拉克勒斯被罚为他做十二件大事。
Freud	弗洛伊德,犹太人,奥地利精神病医生、心理学家、精神分析学家,精神分析学派的创始人。
Hades	哈迪斯,冥王,宙斯的大哥。

Unit 1　Ancient Greek Culture and Wisdom

Harpies	哈皮,希腊神话中的鹰身女妖,传说是堤丰(Typhon)和厄喀德那(Echinda)的四个女儿的总称。
Hera	赫拉,宙斯的姐姐和妻子。
Heracles	赫拉克勒斯,希腊神话中最著名的英雄之一。他完成了十二项被誉为"不可能完成"的伟绩。
Milton	弥尔顿,英国诗人及学者,以其史诗《失乐园》(*Paradise Lost*, 1667)闻名于世。
Mount Olympus	奥林匹斯山,坐落在希腊北部,希腊神话之源。
Narcissus [nɑːˈsisəs]	那喀索斯,美少年,拒绝了仙女厄科的爱,爱上池塘中自己的倒影,最终眷恋而死,化成以其名字命名的水仙花。
Oedipus	俄狄浦斯,底比斯王子,曾破解怪物斯芬克斯之谜,后误杀其父并娶其母为妻,发觉后自刺双目,流浪至死。
Oedipus Complex	恋母情结;俄狄浦斯情结。
Pandora	潘多拉,世界上的第一个女人,主神宙斯命火神用粘土制成。古希腊语中,潘是所有的意思,多拉则是礼物。"潘多拉"即为"拥有一切天赋的女人"。潘多拉下凡时宙斯给潘多拉一个密封的盒子,里面装满了祸害、灾难和瘟疫等,让她送给娶她的男人。潘多拉被好奇心驱使,打开了那只盒子,因而人世间有了所有邪恶,只有希望还留在里面。
Pegasus [ˈpegəsəs]	佩加索斯,有翼的飞马,古希腊神话中缪斯女神的坐骑。
Plato	柏拉图,古希腊哲学家,创办学园,提出理念论和灵魂不朽说,著有30多篇对话和书信等。
Poseidon	波塞冬,海神,掌管海洋、地震及马匹,宙斯的二哥。
Sphinx	斯芬克斯,带翼的狮身女怪,传说常叫过路行人猜谜,猜不出者即遭噬食。
Troy	特洛伊(小亚细亚西北部的古城)。公元前16世纪前后为古希腊人渡海所建,公元前13世纪—前12世纪时,颇为繁荣。
Trojan horse	在古希腊传说中,希腊联军围困特洛伊久攻不下,于是假装撤退,留下一具巨大的中空木马。特洛伊守军把木马运进城中作为战利品。夜深人静之际,木马腹中躲藏的希腊士兵打开城门,特洛伊沦陷。后人常用"特洛伊木马"这一典故,来比喻在敌方营垒里埋下伏兵里应外合的活动。
Trojan War	特洛伊战争。特洛伊战争因世上最漂亮的女人海伦而起,阿伽门农及阿喀琉斯为首的希腊军进攻以帕里斯及赫克托尔为首的特洛伊城,历时十年。
Shakespeare	莎士比亚,英国剧作家、诗人,著有37部戏剧,154首十四行诗和2首长诗。
Socrates	苏格拉底,古希腊著名的思想家、哲学家、教育家、公民陪审员。他和他的学生柏拉图,以及柏拉图的学生亚里士多德被并称为"古希腊三贤"。
Zeus	宙斯,希腊神话中的主神。

Difficult Sentences

① Greek mythology is the body of myths and teachings that belong to the ancient Greeks, concerning their gods and heroes, the nature of the world, and the origins and significance of their own cult and ritual practices.

希腊神话是古希腊人神话和教义的总和,内容涉及神祇和英雄、世界的性质、古希腊人的宗教崇拜和仪式的起源及意义等。

② Olympian gods and goddesses looked like men and women (though they could change themselves into animals and other things) and were—as many myths recounted—vulnerable to human weaknesses and passions.

奥林匹斯众神的外貌看起来与尘世男女一样(尽管他们可以随意变成动物或者其他的形态),而且也正如许多神话所述,具有人类的种种弱点和情感。

③ Great writers such as Dante, Shakespeare and Milton make frequent references to Greek mythology, so much so that an understanding of Greek myths is necessary to truly appreciate their works.

但丁、莎士比亚和弥尔顿等伟大作家经常提及希腊神话,所以想要真正欣赏他们的作品就必须对希腊神话有一定的了解。

④ An oracle proclaimed that Oedipus would kill his father and marry his mother, and Freud believed that these feelings of jealousy toward the same-sex parent and love for the opposite-sex parent were a phase that all children would go through.

神谕宣称,俄狄浦斯会杀父娶母。弗洛伊德认为,这种对同性别父母的嫉妒以及对异性别父母的爱是所有孩子在成长中都要经历的阶段。

⑤ In general usage, a Trojan horse—just like the one that led to the defeat of Troy—is something that appears desirable, but in fact presents a threat.

特洛伊木马一般用以指代那些貌似吸引人,实则潜藏危机的东西,就像导致特洛伊城沦陷的木马一样。

⑥ Nike, the sports brand, is the namesake of the goddess of victory, for example. And the famous Amazon river is named after the race of mythical female warriors.

例如,运动品牌耐克用了胜利女神的名字,而亚马逊河也是以神秘的女战士部族来命名的。

Unit 1 Ancient Greek Culture and Wisdom

Exercises

Task 1 Reading Comprehension

Directions: *Read the passage and choose the best answer to each of the following questions.*

1. Which of the following statements about Greek mythology is true?
    A. Greek mythology is of little importance to modern civilization.
    B. Olympian gods and goddesses never made mistakes because they were all-knowing and morally perfect.
    C. The ancient Greeks used the myths to explain the world of their afterlife.
    D. Human heroes and monsters were important figures in Greek mythology.
2. Who was the head of the Greek pantheon?
    A. Zeus.   B. Poseidon.   C. Hera.   D. Hades.
3. For the Greek mariners and fishermen, _____ could be both a trouble-maker and a helper.
    A. Zeus   B. Pandora   C. Poseidon   D. Heracles
4. Who fell in love with his own reflection in Greek mythology?
    A. Heracles.   B. Centaur.   C. Pandora.   D. Narcissus.
5. According to the passage, if a man has "Oedipus Complex," most probably he would _____.
    A. kill his father
    B. kill his mother
    C. be jealous of his father
    D. be jealous of his mother

Task 2 Vocabulary

Directions: *Complete the following sentences with proper words or phrases from the box. Change the form if necessary. Please note there are more words and phrases than necessary.*

A) shipwreck	B) Greek mythology	C) psychiatrist	D) sneaker	E) heritage
F) feature	G) proclaim	H) pantheon	I) vulnerable to	J) phase
K) territory	L) warrior	M) strike	N) coin	O) trident

1. (1) _____ is the body of traditional tales concerning the gods, heroes, and rituals of the ancient Greeks.
2. The Greek gods and goddesses looked like men and women, and were (2) _____ human weaknesses and passions.
3. The extensive influence of Greek mythology on the world's culture and historic (3) _____ is undeniable.
4. Sigmund Freud, the Austrian (4) _____, (5) _____ "Oedipus Complex" out of Greek mythology to indicate that all children would go through a (6) _____, that is, they would be jealous of the same-sex parent and love the opposite-sex parent.
5. A (7) _____ refers to all the gods of a particular religion, mythology, or tradition.

6. The ancient Greeks believed that Poseidon would (8) _____ the ground with his powerful (9) _____ to cause earthquake. He might also cause (10) _____; that is, he might destroy ships in accidents at sea.

Task 3   Translation

Directions: *Translate the following sentences into English.*
1. 希腊神话的中心是众神的故事，据说他们住在希腊最高的奥林匹斯山上。
2. 宙斯是众神中的主神，他用骇人的雷电主宰天空。
3. 海神波塞冬挥动三叉戟能引发海难和地震，但他也能开辟新的岛屿。
4. 虽然人们在地狱能得到公平对待，但冥王哈迪斯永远不会让他们重返以往熟悉的世界。
5. 希腊神话对西方文明产生了广泛的影响，一直是西方文化遗产和语言的组成部分。

Task 4   Further Development

Directions: *Do you know who Oedipus is? Tell the story of Oedipus to your classmates in 150 words. You may refer to reference books or websites to get more information. The following questions may help you organize your story: What happened to Oedipus when he was born? Did he kill his father on purpose? What happened to him later? When he knew that it was him who brought disasters to his kingdom, what did he do? What's the moral lesson implied in Oedipus's story?*

Section B   City-States: Athens and Sparta

The ancient Greeks shared a common language, culture, and religion. They considered anyone who did not speak Greek a barbarian. Although the Greek people had much in common, they were also very independent of each other. They took great pride in the city-state they belonged to. A city-state was an independently ruled city with its own laws, customs, money and army. A Greek citizen's loyalty was directed to his city-state. ① These city-states often made alliances with other cities, forming into leagues, confederations, or federations while maintaining an independent identity. ② When the very rocky landscape around a city no longer supported the growing population, they sent people to start colonies in other areas along the Mediterranean Sea.

③ The two rivals of ancient Greece that made the most noise and gave us the most traditions were Athens and Sparta. They were close together on a map, yet far apart in what they valued and how they lived their lives.

Ancient Athens

Athens: The Think Tank

The city-state of Athens was the birthplace of many significant ideas. Ancient Athenians were a thoughtful people who enjoyed systematic study of subjects such as science, philosophy, and history, to name a few.

The Athenians placed a heavy emphasis on arts, architecture and literature. ④ The Athenians built thousands of temples and statues that embodied their understanding of beauty. Today the term "classical" is used to describe their enduring style of art and architecture. The Athenians also enjoyed a democratic form of government in which some of the people shared power.

Life was not easy for Athenian women. They did not enjoy the same rights or privileges as males, being nearly as low as slaves in the social system.

Sparta: Military Might

Life in Sparta was vastly different from life in Athens. ⑤ Located in the southern part of Greece on the Peloponnesus peninsula, the city-state of Sparta developed a militaristic society ruled by two kings and an oligarchy, a small group that exercised political control.

Early in their history, a violent and bloody slave revolt caused the Spartans to change their society. A Spartan, Lycurgus, drafted a harsh set of laws that required total dedication to the state from its people. The laws' goal was to train citizens to become hardened soldiers so that they could fight off potential enemies or slave revolts. ⑥ The result was a rigid lifestyle unlike any other in Greece at the time. The devotion of Spartans to developing a military state left little time for the arts or literature.

A Spartan baby had to be hardy and healthy. To test a baby's strength, parents would leave their child on a mountain overnight to see if it could survive on its own until the next morning. By the age of seven, Spartan boys were taken from their families and underwent severe military training. ⑦ They wore uniforms at all times, ate small meals of bland foods, exercised barefoot to toughen their feet, and were punished severely for disobedient behavior. Boys lived away from their families in barracks until the age of 30, even after they were married. Men were expected to be ready to serve in the army until they were 60 years old.

Women, too, were expected to be loyal and dedicated to the state. Like men, women followed a strict exercise program and contributed actively to Spartan society. Although they were not allowed to vote, Spartan women typically had more rights and independence than women in other Greek city-states.

Ancient Sparta

Winning by Losing

The differences between Athens and Sparta eventually led to war between the two city-states. Known as the Peloponnesian War (431BC—404BC), both Sparta and Athens gathered allies and fought on and off for decades because no single city-state was strong enough to conquer the other.

⑧ With war came famine, plague, death and misfortune, but war cannot kill ideas. Despite the eventual military surrender of Athens, Athenian thought spread throughout the region. After temporary setbacks, these notions only became more widely accepted and developed with the passing centuries.

(672 words)

New Words and Expressions (B)

New Words

New Words	Phonetic Symbols	Meanings
alliance	[əˈlaɪəns]	n. 同盟
architecture	[ˈɑːkɪtektʃə(r)]	n. 建筑,建筑风格
barbarian	[bɑːˈbeəriən]	n. 野蛮人
barrack	[ˈbærək]	n. 军营
colony	[ˈkɒləni]	n. 殖民地
confederation	[kənˌfedəˈreɪʃn]	n. 邦联,联盟
conquer	[ˈkɒŋkə(r)]	v. 战胜
dedication	[ˌdedɪˈkeɪʃn]	n. 奉献
democratic	[ˌdeməˈkrætɪk]	adj. 民主的
draft	[drɑːft]	v. 起草
disobedient	[ˌdɪsəˈbiːdiənt]	adj. 不顺从的,不服从的
famine	[ˈfæmɪn]	n. 饥荒
federation	[ˌfedəˈreɪʃn]	n. 联邦
independent	[ˌɪndɪˈpendənt]	adj. 独立的
identity	[aɪˈdentəti]	n. 身份
landscape	[ˈlændskeɪp]	n. 地貌
league	[liːg]	n. 联盟
literature	[ˈlɪtrətʃə(r)]	n. 文学
loyal	[ˈlɔɪəl]	adj. 忠诚的

loyalty	[ˈlɔɪəlti]	n. 忠诚
militaristic	[ˌmɪlɪtəˈrɪstɪk]	adj. 军事主义的
misfortune	[ˌmɪsˈfɔːtʃuːn]	n. 不幸；灾祸，灾难
oligarchy	[ˈɒlɪɡɑːki]	n. 寡头组织
overnight	[ˌəʊvəˈnaɪt]	adv. 通宵，一夜工夫；从夜晚到天明
plague	[pleɪɡ]	n. 瘟疫
polis	[ˈpəʊlɪs]	n. 城邦；城市国家
potential	[pəˈtenʃl]	adj. 潜在的
religion	[rɪˈlɪdʒən]	n. 宗教
revolt	[rɪˈvəʊlt]	n. 起义；叛乱
rigid	[ˈrɪdʒɪd]	adj. 刻板的
rival	[ˈraɪvl]	n. 竞争对手
severe	[sɪˈvɪə(r)]	adj. 严酷的
surrender	[səˈrendə(r)]	n. 投降

Expressions

fight off	击退
have much in common	有很多相似之处
on and off	断断续续地
place emphasis on	重视
take pride in	以……为荣
think tank	思想库，智库

Proper Names

Athens	雅典，被誉为"西方文明的摇篮"，也是欧洲哲学的发源地，对欧洲及世界文化产生过重大影响。雅典诞生了苏格拉底、柏拉图等一大批历史伟人，被称为民主的起源地。
Lycurgus	莱克格斯，传说公元前7世纪斯巴达法典的制定者。
Mediterranean Sea	地中海，世界上最大的陆间海，因介于亚、欧、非三大洲之间而得名。
Peloponnesian War	伯罗奔尼撒战争，是以雅典为首的提洛同盟与以斯巴达为首的伯罗奔尼撒联盟之间的一场战争。这场战争从公元前431年一直持续到前404年，期间双方曾几度停战，最终斯巴达获得胜利。
Peloponnesus peninsula	伯罗奔尼撒半岛，位于希腊南部。
Sparta	斯巴达，古代希腊城邦之一，以其严酷纪律、独裁统治和军事主义而闻名。

Difficult Sentences

① These city-states often made alliances with other cities, forming into leagues, confederations, or federations while maintaining an independent identity.

这些城邦国家一方面保持独立,一方面又常与其他城市结盟,形成联盟、邦联或联邦。

② When the very rocky landscape around a city no longer supported the growing population, they sent people to start colonies in other areas along the Mediterranean Sea.

当城市周围多岩石的地形无法承载日益增长的人口时,他们便会派人沿地中海其他地区开拓新领地。

③ The two rivals of ancient Greece that made the most noise and gave us the most traditions were Athens and Sparta.

在古希腊纷争最多,同时也留下最多传统的两大竞争对手是雅典与斯巴达。

④ The Athenians built thousands of temples and statues that embodied their understanding of beauty.

雅典人建造了数以千计的庙宇和雕像,表现了他们对美的理解。

⑤ Located in the southern part of Greece on the Peloponnesus peninsula, the city-state of Sparta developed a militaristic society ruled by two kings and an oligarchy, a small group that exercised political control.

城邦国家斯巴达位于希腊南部的伯罗奔尼撒半岛上,它发展为军事主义国家,由两个国王和一个寡头政治集团所统治,即由一个小集团实施政治统治。

⑥ The result was a rigid lifestyle unlike any other in Greece at the time. The devotion of Spartans to developing a military state left little time for the arts or literature.

这样做的结果,是斯巴达人形成了一套刻板的生活方式,与当时希腊其他地区的情况全然不同。他们倾力将自己的城邦打造成军事强国,因而无暇研究文学艺术。

⑦ They wore uniforms at all times, ate small meals of bland foods, exercised barefoot to toughen their feet, and were punished severely for disobedient behavior.

他们终年身着军装,每餐吃少量清淡的食物,赤脚训练以使脚板更加坚硬,一旦违背命令将被处以重罚。

⑧ With war came famine, plague, death and misfortune. But war cannot kill ideas.

伴随战争的是饥荒、瘟疫、死亡和不幸,但战争却不能扼杀人们的思想。

Unit 1 Ancient Greek Culture and Wisdom

Exercises

Task 1 Reading Comprehension

Directions: *Read the passage and judge whether the following statements are true (T), false (F) or not given (NG).*

True   if the statement agrees with the information mentioned in the passage
False   if the statement contradicts the information mentioned in the passage
Not Given   if there is no information on this in the passage

1. The city-states shared a common language and often made alliance with other cities, but they were ruled independently.
2. The term "classical" is used to describe Athenian philosophy.
3. The Spartans did not develop arts and literature like the Athenians because they had no time to do so.
4. Sparta became a militaristic society because Spartan men enjoyed their life in the army.
5. An adult Spartan can leave the army and live with his family when he was married.
6. Spartan women had more rights than women in other city-states. For example, they were allowed to vote.
7. The Athenians paid little attention to military training.
8. Though the Spartans were hardened soldiers, they did not win the Peloponnesian War easily.
9. Located in the northern part of Greece, Sparta was ruled by two kings and an oligarchy.
10. When the Athenians were defeated in the Peloponnesian War, their thought also disappeared for ever.

Task 2 Vocabulary

Directions: *Complete the following summary of the passage with proper words from the box. Change the form if necessary.*

apart	undergo	alliance	hardy	despite
confederation	militaristic	classical	democratic	dedicate

City-states in ancient Greece often made (1) _____ with other cities, forming into leagues, (2) _____, or federations while maintaining an independent identity. The city-states of Athens and Sparta were close together on a map, yet far (3) _____ in what they valued and how they lived their lives.

The Athenians placed a heavy emphasis on arts, architecture and literature. Today the term (4) "_____" is used to describe their enduring style of art and architecture. Athenians also enjoyed a (5) _____ form of government in which some of the people shared power.

Sparta developed a (6) _____ society ruled by two kings and an oligarchy. A Spartan baby had to be (7) _____ and healthy. By the age of seven, Spartan boys were

13

taken from their families and (8) _____ severe military training. Women, too, were expected to be loyal and (9) _____ to the state.

The differences between Athens and Sparta eventually led to war between the two city-states. (10) _____ the eventual military surrender of Athens, Athenian thought spread throughout the region.

Task 3 Translation

Directions: *Complete the following sentences by translating the Chinese in brackets into English.*

1. These city-states often made alliances with other cities, while _____（保持独立）.
2. Ancient Athenians were _____（颇具思想性的民族）who studied science, philosophy and history systematically.
3. The Athenians built thousands of temples and statues that _____（表现他们对美的理解）.
4. The hash laws of Lycurgus trained citizens to _____（击退潜在的敌人或造反的奴隶）.
5. Although they were not allowed to vote, Spartan women _____（做出积极贡献）Spartan society.

Task 4 Further Development

Directions: *No other city has contributed more to western civilization than Athens. Please refer to reference books and websites to find more information about this city-state. Choose a topic you are interested in and write a short essay to introduce it to your classmates.*

Section C Socrates

Socrates (470 BC—399 BC) was the wisest philosopher of his time. He was the first of the three great teachers of ancient Greece—the other two being Plato and Aristotle. Today he is ranked as one of the world's greatest moral teachers. His self-control and powers of endurance were unmatched.

Socrates

Socrates was born on the outskirts of Athens in about 470 BC. He studied sculpture, his father's profession, but soon abandoned this work to "seek truth" in his own way. ① His habits were so frugal and his constitution so hardy that he needed only the bare necessities. Although Socrates took no part in the politics of Athens, he would perform civic functions when he was called upon. He was a courageous soldier. During the Peloponnesian War he served

Unit 1 Ancient Greek Culture and Wisdom

as a foot soldier in several engagements and distinguished himself for bravery and remarkable endurance.

In appearance Socrates was short and fat, with a snub nose and wide mouth. ② Despite his unkempt appearance, the Greeks of his day enjoyed talking with him and were fascinated by what he had to say. The young, aristocratic military genius Alcibiades said of him, ③ "His nature is so beautiful, golden, divine, and wonderful within that everything he commands surely ought to be obeyed even like the voice of a god."

Interested in neither money, nor fame, nor power, Socrates wandered along the streets of Athens in the 5th century BC. He wore a single rough woolen garment in all seasons and went barefoot. ④ Talking to whoever would listen, he asked questions, criticized answers, and poked holes in faulty arguments. His style of conversation has been given the name "Socratic dialogue."

Socrates shunned the shallow notion of truth for its own sake. He turned to his conscience for moral truth and enjoyed creating confusion by asking simple questions. He sought to uncover the nature of virtue and to find a rule of life. Favorite objects of his attacks were the Sophists, who charged a fee for their teaching. "Know thyself" was the motto he is thought to have learned from the oracle at Delphi. In knowing oneself he saw the possibility of learning what is really good, in contrast to accepting mere outward appearance.

Socrates's wife, Xanthippe, was notorious in Athens for her sharp tongue and quick temper. ⑤ The sage once jokingly said, "As I intended to associate with all kinds of people, I thought nothing they could do would disturb me, once I had accustomed myself to bear the disposition of Xanthippe."

Socrates did not write any books or papers. The details of his life and doctrine are preserved in the *Memorabilia* of the historian Xenophon and in the dialogues of the philosopher Plato. It was chiefly through Plato and Plato's brilliant disciple Aristotle that the influence of Socrates was passed on to succeeding generations of philosophers.

Socrates, however, was not appreciated by the Athenian mob and its self-serving leaders. ⑥ His genius for exposing pompous frauds made him many enemies. At last, the three of his political foes indicted him on the charge of "neglect of the gods" and "corruption of the young." They were false charges, but politically convenient. He was sentenced to death by drinking hemlock. His parting comments to his judges were simple, as recorded in Plato's

The Death of Socrates

Apology: "The hour of departure has arrived, and we go our ways—I to die, and you to live. Which is better god only knows."

(580 words)

New Words and Expressions (C)

New Words

New Words	Phonetic Symbols	Meanings
abandon	[əˈbændən]	*v.* 放弃
aristocratic	[ˌærɪstəˈkrætɪk]	*adj.* 贵族的,贵族政治的
conscience	[ˈkɒnʃəns]	*n.* 良心
constitution	[ˌkɒnstɪˈtjuːʃn]	*n.* 体质
corruption	[kəˈrʌpʃn]	*n.* 腐败
courageous	[kəˈreɪdʒəs]	*adj.* 勇敢的
disciple	[dɪˈsaɪpl]	*n.* 追随者,弟子
disposition	[ˌdɪspəˈzɪʃn]	*n.* 性情
divine	[dɪˈvaɪn]	*adj.* 神圣的
doctrine	[ˈdɒktrɪn]	*n.* 学说,教义
endurance	[ɪnˈdjʊərəns]	*n.* 忍耐;忍耐力
engagement	[ɪnˈɡeɪdʒmənt]	*n.* 会战
frugal	[ˈfruːɡl]	*adj.* 简朴的
garment	[ˈɡɑːmənt]	*n.* 衣服
hemlock	[ˈhemlɒk]	*n.* 毒芹(汁)
military	[ˈmɪlətri]	*adj.* 军事的
mob	[mɒb]	*n.* 乌合之众
neglect	[nɪˈɡlekt]	*n.* 忽略,忽视
notorious	[nəʊˈtɔːriəs]	*adj.* 臭名昭著的
outskirts	[ˈaʊtskɜːts]	*n.* 郊区
philosopher	[fəˈlɒsəfə(r)]	*n.* 哲学家
pompous	[ˈpɒmpəs]	*adj.* 虚夸的,浮华的
sage	[seɪdʒ]	*n.* 智者
sculpture	[ˈskʌlptʃə(r)]	*n.* 雕刻
succeeding	[səkˈsiːdɪŋ]	*adj.* 以后的
unkempt	[ˌʌnˈkempt]	*adj.* 凌乱的,不整洁的

unmatched	[ˌʌnˈmætʃt]	adj. 无可比拟的
woolen	[ˈwʊlɪn]	adj. 羊毛的

Expressions

associate with	结交，与……交往
be fascinated by	沉迷于
be sentenced to	被判处……
call upon	号召；要求
civic function	公民职责
foot soldier	步兵
pass on to	传承
rank as	把……视为
take part in	参与

Proper Names

Alcibiades	亚西比德，古希腊雅典政客和将领。
Delphi	德尔斐，古希腊城市，因有阿波罗神庙而出名。
Memorabilia	《回忆苏格拉底》
Sophists	智者派，诡辩派，是以传授论术、修辞、伦理学等知识为业的古希腊哲学家。
Xanthippe	占西比，苏格拉底的妻子。
Xenophon	色诺芬，古希腊将领、哲学家，苏格拉底的学生，著有《远征记》《希腊史》《回忆苏格拉底》等。

① His habits were so frugal and his constitution so hardy that he needed only the bare necessities.
他的生活习惯简朴，身强体壮，只需要最基本的生活必需品。

② Despite his unkempt appearance, the Greeks of his day enjoyed being with him to talk with him and were fascinated by what he had to say.
虽然他不修边幅，当时的人们却非常喜欢与他相处，和他交流，并为他所说的话深深着迷。

③ "His nature is so beautiful, golden, divine and wonderful within that everything he commands surely ought to be obeyed even like the voice of a god."

"苏格拉底的本性是如此美好、尊贵而又神圣，因此他所要求的一切人们都理所当然地遵从，就像接受神的旨意一样。"

④ Talking to whoever would listen, he asked questions, criticized answers, and poke holes in faulty arguments. His style of conversation has been given the name "Socratic dialogue."

他与任何愿意倾听的人交谈，提出问题、评点各种回答、指出观点的缺陷和漏洞，这种对话方式被命名为"苏格拉底辩论"。

⑤ The sage once jokingly said, "As I intended to associate with all kinds of people, I thought nothing they could do would disturb me, once I had accustomed myself to bear the disposition of Xanthippe."

这位智者曾经开玩笑地说："我打算和各种人打交道，我觉得只要能忍受占西比的坏脾气，他们不管做什么都不会让我烦恼。"

⑥ His genius for exposing pompous frauds made him many enemies. At last, the three of his political foes indicted him on the charge of "neglect of the gods" and "corruption of the young."

他善于揭穿浮夸骗局的才能使他四面树敌。最终他的三个政治对手以"不敬神祇"和"腐化青年"的罪名对他进行了指控。

Exercises

Task 1 Short Answer Questions

Directions: *Work in pairs to answer the following questions.*

1. Who are the three great teachers of ancient Greece?
2. Why did the Greeks enjoy being with Socrates to talk with him?
3. Can you explain "Socratic dialogue" briefly?
4. How did Socrates understand "Know thyself"?
5. How did Socrates die?

Task 2 Vocabulary

Directions: *Complete the following sentences with proper words from the box. Change the form if necessary. Please note there are more words than necessary.*

A) poke	B) profession	C) converse	D) shun	E) fascinate
F) outskirts	G) welfare	H) upright	I) constitution	J) frugal
K) charge	L) notorious	M) moral	N) pompous	O) claim

1. People who live _____ lives do not spend much money on themselves.
2. Socrates followed his father's _____ of sculpture in which he did not excel.

Unit 1　Ancient Greek Culture and Wisdom

3. To fulfill this difficult task, he must have an extremely strong _____.
4. Socrates took little part in politics, and was content to _____ with his friends alone and not to attempt to convert the populace.
5. Socrates was tried and condemned to death for his _____ that he received guidance from a spirit within him.
6. Socrates believed that people ought to be concerned with the "_____ of their souls" instead of worrying about their families, careers, and political responsibilities.
7. Many people have prejudice against politicians, who are often seen as being _____ and self-serving.
8. When he was on trial, Socrates demonstrated to the jurors that their _____ values were wrong-headed.
9. Socrates was _____ with corrupting the minds of the Athenian youth and subsequently was sentenced to death by drinking a mixture containing poison hemlock.
10. Socrates's wife Xanthippe was _____ for her sharp tongue and bad temper.

Task 3　Translation

Directions: *Complete the following sentences by translating the Chinese in brackets into English.*

1. In the army, Socrates distinguished himself for _____（勇敢和非凡的忍耐力）.
2. Socrates let his hair grow long, Spartan-style, and _____（赤脚穿梭在雅典的大街小巷）, carrying a stick and looking arrogant.
3. Socrates believed the best way for people to live was to focus on the _____ _____（对真理和美德的追求，而不是对物质财富的追逐）.
4. The Socratic Dialogues are a series of dialogues written by Plato and Xenophon _____ _____（以讨论的形式）between Socrates and other persons of his time, or as discussions between Socrates's followers over his concepts.
5. Socrates' genius for _____（揭穿浮夸骗局）made him many enemies and later he was indicted by the three of his political foes.

Task 4　Further Development

Directions: *Write a short summary of the text in 150 words.*

Adages and Proverbs

1. Give me a lever long enough and a fulcrum on which to place it, and I shall move the world.　　　　　　　　　　　　　—Archimedes (287BC—212BC), scientist
  给我一根足够长的杠杆和一个安放杠杆的支点，我就能撬起地球。
  　　　　　　　　　　　　　　　　　　　　　　　　　　　　—阿基米德

19

2. Education is an ornament in prosperity and a refuge in adversity.

　　　　　　　　　　　　　　　—Aristotle (384BC—322BC), scientist and philosopher

教育是顺境中的装饰,逆境中的避难所。　　　　　　　　——亚里士多德

3. The art of living well and the art of dying well are one.

　　　　　　　　　　　　　　　　　　—Epicurus (341BC—270BC), philosopher

活得幸福和死得其所的艺术是一样的。　　　　　　　　——伊壁鸠鲁

4. The only true wisdom is in knowing you know nothing.

　　　　　　　　　　　　　　　　　　— Socrates (470BC—399BC), philosopher

唯一的真知是知道自己一无所知。　　　　　　　　　　——苏格拉底

5. Other men live to eat, while I eat to live.　　　　　　— Socrates

别人为食而生存,我为生存而食.　　　　　　　　　　——苏格拉底

6. At the touch of love everyone becomes a poet.

　　　　　　　　　　　　　　　　　　—Plato (427BC—347BC), philosopher

爱使每个人都变成诗人。　　　　　　　　　　　　　　——柏拉图

7. There are only two people who can tell you the truth about yourself — an enemy who has lost his temper and a friend who loves you dearly.

　　　　　　　　　　　　　　　　　—Antisthenes (444?BC—360BC), philosopher

只有两种人能够告诉你关于你的真实情况——发怒的敌人和真正爱你的朋友。

　　　　　　　　　　　　　　　　　　　　　　　　　——安提西尼

8. Happiness resides not in possessions, and not in gold; happiness dwells in the soul.

　　　　　　　　　　　　　　　　　—Democritus (460BC—370BC), philosopher

幸福不在财富里,不在金子里,幸福在灵魂里。　　　　——德谟克利特

9. There is nothing permanent except change.

　　　　　　　　　　　　　　　　　—Heraclitus (540BC—470BC), philosopher

只有变化是永恒的。　　　　　　　　　　　　　　　　——赫拉克利特

10. Small opportunities are often the beginning of great enterprises.

　　　　　　　　　　　　——Demosthenes (384—322 BC), orator and politician

不起眼的机会往往是伟大事业的开端。　　　　　　　　——狄摩西尼

11. Love is all we have, the only way that each can help the other.

　　　　　　　　　　　　　　　　　—Euripides (480?BC— 406?BC), playwright

爱是我们拥有的一切,是人们帮助他人的唯一途径。　　——欧里庇德斯

12. Success is dependent on effort.　— Sophocles (496BC—406BC), playwright

成功有赖努力。　　　　　　　　　　　　　　　　　　——索福克勒斯

13. I am indebted to my father for living, but to my teacher for living well.

　　　　　　　　　　　　　　　—Alexander the Great (356BC—323BC)

　　我因为父亲而有了生命，因为老师而生活得好。　　　——亚历山大大帝

14. History is philosophy teaching by examples.

　　　　　　　　　　——Thucydides (460BC—395BC), historian and general

　　历史就是用例证讲授的哲学。　　　　　　　　　　　——修昔底德

15. Fast is fine, but accuracy is everything.

　　　　　　　　　　—Xenophon (431BC—355? BC), historian and general

　　快固然好，但精确才决定一切。　　　　　　　　　　——色诺芬

Key to Unit 1 Exercises

导读答案

1. Perhaps what comes first in your mind are the following:

    Names of gods and goddesses, such as Zeus, Athena, etc.

    The Trojan War, the beauty of Helen

    The origin of modern Olympic Games

    Some famous philosophers and scientists, such as Plato, Aristotle, Pythagoras (毕达哥拉斯), Archimedes (阿基米德)

2. You may be familiar with Zeus, his wife Hera and his daughter Athena. Perhaps you know one of the stories of Zeus. He fell in love with Europa, a pretty princess. So he changed himself into a strong bull and when Europa rode on his back, he took the poor girl away from her parents. Later Europa bore three sons for Zeus and the continent of Europe acquired its name from Eruopa, the princess.

3. Through his portrayal in Plato's dialogues, Socrates has become renowned for his contribution to the field of ethics. Plato's Socrates also made important and lasting contributions to the fields of epistemology and logic, and the influence of his ideas and approach remains a strong foundation for much of the western philosophy that followed.

    Plato was a philosopher and a mathematician, student of Socrates, writer of philosophical dialogues, and founder of the Academy in Athens, the first institution of higher learning in the Western world.

    Aristotle was a philosopher and polymath, a student of Plato and teacher of Alexander the Great. His writings covered many subjects, including physics, metaphysics, poetry, theater,

music, logic, rhetoric, linguistics, politics, government, ethics, biology, and zoology. Aristotle's writings were the first to create a comprehensive system of Western philosophy.

Section A

Task 1　Reading Comprehension
1. D　2. A　3. C　4. D　5. C

Task 2　Vocabulary
1. B) Greek mythology　2. I) vulnerable to　3. E) heritage　4. C) psychiatrist　5. N) coined
6. J) phase　　　　　　7. H) pantheon　　8. M) strike　　9. O) trident　　10. A) shipwrecks

Task 3　Translation
1. At the center of Greek mythology is the pantheon of deities who were said to live on Mount Olympus, the highest mountain in Greece.
2. Zeus was the head of the pantheon, who ruled the sky with his powerful thunderbolt.
3. Poseidon might cause shipwrecks and earthquake with his trident, but he could also create new islands.
4. While they were treated fairly in the underworld, Hades would never allow people to return to the world they once knew.
5. Greek mythology has had an extensive influence on Western civilization and remains part of Western heritage and language.

Section B

Task 1　Reading Comprehension
1. T　2. F　3. T　4. NG　5. F　6. F　7. NG　8. T　9. F　10. F

Task 2　Vocabulary
1. alliance　　　　2. confederations　　3. apart　　　　4. classical
5. democratic　　　6. militaristic　　　7. hardy　　　　8. underwent
9. dedicated　　　10. Despite

Task 3　Translation
1. they were independent of each other
2. a thoughtful people
3. embodied their understanding of beauty
4. fight off potential enemies or slave revolts
5. contributed actively to

Unit 1 Ancient Greek Culture and Wisdom

Section C

Task 1   Short answer questions

1. Socrates, Plato, Aristotle.

2. Because he had a beautiful nature.

3. Socrates asked questions, criticized answers and poke holes in faulty arguments.

4. In knowing oneself it is possible for people to learn what is really good.

5. He was sentenced to death by drinking hemlock.

Task 2   Vocabulary

1. J) frugal   2. B) profession   3. I) constitution   4. C) converse   5. O) claim

6. G) welfare   7. N) pompous   8. M) moral   9. K) charged   10. L) notorious

Task 3   Translation

1. bravery and remarkable endurance

2. wandered barefoot along the streets of Athens

3. pursuit of truth and virtue rather than the pursuit of material wealth

4. in the form of discussions

5. exposing pompous frauds

Unit 2
Roman Empire and Latin Culture

 导 读

本单元旨在通过对罗马帝国的历史、政治、经济、文化等各方面的介绍,使学生对西方这一重要时期有基本的了解,开阔视野,能够运用所学西方文化知识及相关的英语表达方式进行文化交流,为今后的深入学习和研究奠定基础。

Before You Start

While preparing for this unit, think about the following questions:
1. What do you know about the Roman Empire, its history, politics, economy, culture and so on?
2. What does "all roads lead to Rome" mean? Do you know why people say so?
3. Have you ever watched any movie about Cleopatra? What do you know about her romance with Julius Caesar and Mark Antony?

Section A   History of Roman Empire

The founding of Rome goes back to the very early days of civilization. It is known as "the eternal city" today. The Romans believed that their city was founded in the year 753 BC, yet modern historians believe it was the year 625 BC.

Early Rome was governed by kings, but after only seven of them had ruled, the Romans took over the power of their own city and ruled themselves. They then instead had a council known as the "*senate*" which ruled over them. From this point on one speaks of the Roman Republic. The word "Republic" itself comes from the Latin words "*res publica*" which mean "public matters" or "matters of state." The senate under the kings had only been there to advise the king. Now the senate appointed a consul, who ruled Rome like a king, but only for one year. ① This was a wise idea, as like that, the consul ruled carefully and not as a tyrant, for he knew that otherwise he could be punished by the next consul, once his term was up.

The Romans were divided into four classes. The lowest class were the slaves. They were owned by other people and had no rights at all. ② The next class were the plebeians. They were free people, but they had little say. The second highest class were the equestrians (sometimes they are called the "knights"). Their name means the "riders," as they were given a horse to ride if they were called to fight for Rome. To be an equestrian you had to be rich. The highest class were the nobles of Rome who were called "patricians." All the real power in Rome lay with them.

The Roman Republic was a very successful government. It lasted from 510 BC until 27 BC—almost 500 years. The greatest challenge the Roman Republic faced was that of the Carthaginians. Carthage was a very powerful city in North Africa which, much like Rome, controlled its own empire. The fight between the two sides was a long one and took place on land and at sea. ③ The most famous incident came when the great Carthaginian general Hannibal crossed the mountain chain of the Alps to the north of Italy with all his troops, including his war-elephants, and invaded Rome. Nevertheless, Rome in the end won and Carthage was completely destroyed in the year 146 BC.

Julius Caesar

Rome's most famous citizen was no doubt Julius Caesar. He was a Roman politician and general who conquered the vast territory of the Gauls to the north of his province in France. In the year 49 BC Caesar crossed the small river between his province and Italy, called the river Rubicon and conquered Rome itself which he then ruled as a dictator. ④ His military campaigns also took him to Egypt where he met the famous Cleopatra. His life was ended as he was infamously murdered in the senate in Rome. So famous and respected was Caesar that a month of the year is still named after him and his heirs today, July (after Julius Caesar). Also the great English poet and playwright Shakespeare wrote a famous play called *Julius Caesar* about his famous murder.

Some of the most famous emperors	
Augustus	Rome's first emperor. He also added many territories to the empire.
Claudius	He conquered Britain.
Trajan	He was a great conqueror. Under his rule the empire reached its greatest extent.
Diocletian	He split the empire into two pieces—western and eastern.
Constantine	He was the first Christian emperor. He united the empire again and chose his capital to be the small town Byzantium, which he renamed Constantinople.
Romulus Augustus	He was the last emperor of Rome, nicknamed Augustulus which means little Augustus.

The Roman Empire in the end was overrun by millions of barbarians from the north and east of Europe. It is believed that huge migrations took place across Europe at least two or three times, where peoples moved to settle in new territories. The great migration proved too much for the Romans to stand. ⑤ Their armies were designed to defeat other armies, not the migrants flooding toward the borders of the empire. The collapse was completed when Rome itself was

conquered by the Visigoth Odoacer and his men in the year AD 476.

However, what is generally referred to as "the Fall of Rome" doesn't include the eastern empire, ⑥ which, with its centre in Constantinople, managed to cling on for almost another thousand years until it was eventually conquered by the Turks under their leader Mohammed II in the year AD 1453.

(769 words)

New Words and Expressions (A)

New Words

New Words	Phonetic Symbols	Meanings
barbarian	[bɑːˈbeərɪən]	n. 野蛮人 adj. 野蛮的
campaign	[kæmˈpeɪn]	n. 战役,运动,活动
collapse	[kəˈlæps]	n. & v. 倒塌,瓦解
conqueror	[ˈkɒŋkərə(r)]	n. 征服者,胜利者
consul	[ˈkɒns(ə)l]	n. 古罗马的执政官
dictator	[dɪkˈteɪtə]	n. 古罗马在紧急情况下任命的有绝对权力的独裁官
equestrian	[ɪˈkwestrɪən]	n. 骑士阶层
eternal	[ɪˈtɜːn(ə)l]	adj. 永恒的,不朽的
flood	[flʌd]	v. 淹没,涌入
historian	[hɪˈstɔːrɪən]	n. 历史学家
infamously	[ˈɪnfəməslɪ]	adv. 臭名昭著地,声名狼藉地
migration	[maɪˈgreɪʃ(ə)n]	n. 迁移,移民
nevertheless	[nevəðəˈles]	adv. 然而,尽管如此
nickname	[ˈnɪkneɪm]	n. 绰号,昵称 v. 给……取绰号
otherwise	[ˈʌðəwaɪz]	adv. & adj. & conj. 否则,不然,另外,在其他方面
patrician	[pəˈtrɪʃ(ə)n]	n. 古罗马的统治阶层成员,贵族
playwright	[ˈpleɪraɪt]	n. 剧作家
plebeian	[plɪˈbiːən]	n. 平民,百姓
senate	[ˈsenət]	n. 古罗马的元老院;参议院
tyrant	[ˈtaɪr(ə)nt]	n. 暴君

Unit 2 Roman Empire and Latin Culture

Expressions

cling on to sth.	坚持某事
have little say	几乎没有发言权
lie with	是……的权利/责任，取决于
refer to as	把……称作/当作

Proper Names

Augustus	奥古斯都（公元前63—公元14），罗马帝国第一代皇帝（公元前27—公元14），恺撒的甥孙、养子、继承人，原名盖乌斯·屋大维（Gaius Octavius）。
Byzantium	拜占庭，古罗马城市，今称伊斯坦布尔。
Carthaginian	迦太基人，从公元前264年起到前146年为止，前后三次和罗马人进行了艰苦的鏖战，延续120年之久，公元前146年最终被罗马人所灭。
Claudius	克劳狄乌斯，（5世纪）罗马十人执政团成员。
Constantine	君士坦丁大帝（288?—337），罗马第一位信仰基督教的皇帝。
Constantinople	君士坦丁堡，为亚欧交通要冲。公元前660年，古希腊人在这里始建拜占庭城。
Diocletian	戴克里先（245—约316），罗马皇帝，曾野蛮地追杀基督教徒。
Gaul	高卢，欧洲一古老地区，包括现在的法国、比利时、卢森堡、荷兰南部、瑞士、德国西南部和意大利北部。
Hannibal	汉尼拔（公元前247—前183），迦太基名将、统帅。
Julius Caesar	尤里乌斯·恺撒（公元前100—前44），罗马共和国末期杰出的军事统帅、政治家，罗马帝国的奠基者，被视为罗马帝国的无冕之皇，有恺撒大帝之称。
Mohammed II	穆罕默德二世，奥斯曼土耳其苏丹，1453年占领君士坦丁堡。
Romulus Augustus	罗慕路·奥古斯都（约463—?），西罗马帝国的最后一位皇帝。
Rubicon	意大利中部的卢比肯河
Trajan	图拉真（约53—117），古罗马皇帝，其统治因大兴土木及怜悯穷人而闻名。
Turk	土耳其人
Visigoth Odoacer	西哥特人奥多亚克（435—493），西哥特人的首领，他于476年废黜罗马帝国的最后一位皇帝罗慕路·奥古斯都，西罗马帝国宣告结束。

 ## Difficult Sentences

① This was a wise idea, as like that, the consul ruled carefully and not as a tyrant, for he knew that otherwise he could be punished by the next consul, once his year was up.

这种做法很明智，可使执政官审慎而不是专制地统治，因为他知道专制的后果是自己期满离任后会受到下一任执政官的惩罚。

② The next class were the plebeians. They were free people, but they had little say at all.

次底层的是平民阶层,他们虽是自由民,但几乎没有发言权。

③ The most famous incident came when the great Carthaginian general Hannibal crossed the mountain chain of the Alps to the north of Italy with all his troops, including his war-elephants, and invaded Rome.

最著名的一次战役是迦太基著名军事统帅汉尼拔率领所有军队和战象,穿越意大利北部的阿尔卑斯山脉入侵罗马。

④ His military campaigns also took him to Egypt where he met the famous Cleopatra.

他因战事前往埃及,并在那里遇到了著名的埃及艳后克利奥帕特拉。

⑤ Their armies were designed to defeat other armies, not entire folks and peoples flooding toward them.

他们建立军队的目的是迎战正规军,而不是为了抵御像潮水般涌入的流民草寇。

⑥ which, with its centre in Constantinople, managed to cling on for almost another thousand years until it was eventually conquered by the Turks under their leader Mohammed II in the year AD 1453.

以君士坦丁堡为中心的东罗马帝国在西罗马帝国灭亡后又坚持了近千年,最终于1453年被穆罕默德二世领导下的土耳其人所灭。

Exercises

Task 1   Reading Comprehension

Directions: Read the passage and choose the best answer to each of the following questions.

1. Which class had the real power in Rome?
    A. The plebeians.　　　　　　　B. The patricians.
    C. The knights.　　　　　　　　D. The slaves.
2. Which of the following statements about Julius Caesar is NOT true according to the passage?
    A. He's probably the most famous citizen in Rome.
    B. He conquered the vast territory of the Gauls.
    C. He conquered Egypt which he then ruled as a dictator in 49 BC.
    D. He conquered Rome itself which he then ruled as a dictator in 49 BC.
3. What was Shakespeare's famous play *Julius Caesar* mainly about?
    A. Caesar's love affair with Cleopatra.
    B. Caesar's dictatorship in Rome.
    C. Caesar's noble origin.
    D. Caesar's being murdered.

Unit 2 Roman Empire and Latin Culture

4. What led to the collapse of the Roman Empire according to the author?
   A. The overwhelming migration from the north and east of Europe.
   B. The overwhelming migration from the south and east of Europe.
   C. The Carthaginian invasion of Roman Empire led by their general Hannibal.
   D. The Turkish invasion of Roman Empire led by their leader Mohammed II.
5. What does "the Fall of Rome" generally refer to?
   A. The fall of the Roman Republic.
   B. The fall of the eastern Roman Empire.
   C. The fall of the western Roman Empire.
   D. The fall of the entire Roman Empire.

Task 2 Vocabulary

Directions: *Complete the following sentences with proper words or phrases from the box. Change the form if necessary. Please note there are more words and phrases than necessary.*

A) appoint	B) lie down	C) aspect	D) respect
E) take over	F) citizen	G) tyrant	H) migration
I) administration	J) overrun	K) challenge	L) flood
M) run	N) murder	O) lie with	

1. Early Rome was governed by kings, but after only seven of them had ruled, the Romans _____ the power of their own city and ruled themselves.
2. Now the senate _____ a consul, who ruled Rome like a king, but only for one year.
3. The Roman consul ruled carefully and not as a _____, for he knew that otherwise he could be punished by the next consul, once his year was up.
4. The Romans were divided into four classes. All the real power in Rome _____ "patricians," the nobles.
5. The greatest _____ the Roman Republic faced was that of the Carthaginians.
6. His life was ended as he was infamously _____ in the senate in Rome.
7. So famous and _____ was Julius Caesar that a month of the year is named after him and his heirs today, that is July.
8. The Roman Empire in the end was _____ by millions of barbarians from the north and east of Europe.
9. It is believed to have happened two or three times in history that huge _____ took place across Europe, where peoples moved to settle in new territories.
10. The Roman armies were designed to defeat other armies, not entire folks and peoples _____ toward them.

Task 3　Translation

Directions: *Translate the following sentences into English.*
1. 现在罗马被称作"永恒之城",其建立可以追溯到早期文明时期。
2. 他们的名字的意思是"骑手",因为如果他们应征作战会得到配发的战马。
3. 罗马和迦太基长期对战,既有陆战也有海战。
4. 事实证明,罗马人无法承受来自欧洲北部和东部的大规模移民。
5. 通常所说的"罗马的衰亡"并不包括东罗马帝国。

Task 4　Further Development

Directions: *Scan the passage and note down the events.*

Year	Event
625 BC	
510 BC	
146 BC	
49 BC	
27 BC	
AD 476	
AD 1453	

Section B　All Roads Lead to Rome

　　It is often said that "all roads lead to Rome," and in fact, they once did. ① The road system of the ancient Romans was one of the greatest engineering accomplishments of its time, with over 50,000 miles of paved road radiating from their center at the miliarius aurem in the Forum in the city of Rome. ② Although the Roman road system was originally built to facilitate the movement of troops throughout the empire, it was inevitably used for other purposes by civilians.

　　③ Of course, the roads were used for trade, as were the waterways surrounding and connecting parts of the Roman Empire to itself and the rest of the known world. The Romans had exceptional nautical technology for their time; ④ however, their network of roads, even with the danger of land travel, was unparalleled in convenience and was often the only choice for travel or shipping goods. The Romans were the first ancient civilization to build paved roads, which did not prevent travel during or after severe weather. ⑤ Indeed, mud or gravel would hinder, if not completely halt many vehicles pulled by animals or other people, not to mention discouraging travelers on foot. Roman engineers, however, did not stop with just paving Roman roads. ⑥ Roads were crowned—that is, they were higher in the middle than on the sides to allow water to run off—and they often had gutters for drainage along the shoulders. Probably the most incredible engineering feat concerning the Roman road system, though, is how well the roads were built. Many are still

The Forum of the ancient Romans

major roads for cars today. Indeed, their road-building methods were unsurpassed until the invention of the macadam in the 19th century. These technological advantages made travel and the shipment of goods across land much easier. Romans shipped lots of goods within the vast expanses of their empire as well as to the rest of the world. Goods were constantly being shipped throughout the empire, depending on the location within the Empire, as well as supply and demand. ⑦ Present-day Great Britain, for example, was a valuable possession to the Romans because of its silver deposits, which were used for jewelry and money. Great Britain also supplied a lot of wool to the rest of the empire. ⑧ From the southeastern corner of the empire, the Romans imported dye for clothing and make-up from the Near East. Over-water transportation usually played a role in imports from the Near East or Africa, from whence they imported Egyptian cotton, or exotic animals for the gladiators to fight. Of course, Rome was connected to the Far East via the Silk Road, the source of silk and other goods imported from Asia. No matter what or from where, if the Romans wanted something exotic, it was probably shipped into Rome.

Though the Romans carefully designed their road network, travel on land was often difficult and dangerous for them. ⑨ Progress was slow compared to today's standards and a person traveling on foot would be lucky to travel 35 miles a day. The richer Romans had more choices as to how they could travel. They could choose to be carried by six to eight men or several mules. Small groups of travelers, such as families, rode in carriages. People in a hurry, such as messengers from the emperor, rode in cisii, a light carriage like a chariot. However, travel for anybody by any mode of transportation was not safe, particularly at night. Roadside inns were strategically located in the countryside at about a day's journey apart. The inns themselves were not safe. Fights broke out. Murders occurred. Whenever possible, a

A Roman Street in Pompeii

traveler stayed with a friend of the family or even a friend of a friend's family.

⑩ The ancient Romans accomplished many feats. They had incredible technological advantages and made advancements that dwarfed those of other civilizations of their time or hundreds of years beyond. It is their advancements we often take for granted that make them one of the most influential peoples around the world today—2000 years after their fall—in more ways than just language.

(688 words)

(Based on http://ancienthistory.about.com/od/romanroads/g/RomanRoads.htm)

New Words and Expressions (B)

New Words

New Words	Phonetic Symbols	Meanings
accomplishment	[əˈkʌmplɪʃ(ə)nt]	n. 成就,技艺
chariot	[ˈtʃærɪət]	n. 二轮战车
civilian	[sɪˈvɪlj(ə)n]	n. & adj. 百姓(的),平民(的)
constantly	[ˈkɒnst(ə)ntli]	adv. 不断地,时常地
crowned	[kraʊnd]	adj. 像王冠的(文中指路中间比两边高的)
deposit	[dɪˈpɒzɪt]	n. 矿床,矿藏
discourage	[dɪsˈkʌrɪdʒ]	v. 阻止,使气馁
drainage	[ˈdreɪnɪdʒ]	n. 排水,排水系统
dwarf	[dwɔːf]	v. 使相形见绌
exceptional	[ɪkˈsepʃ(ə)n(ə)l]	adj. 优越的;异常的;例外的
expanse	[ɪkˈspæns]	n. 宽阔,广阔的区域
exotic	[ɪɡˈzɒtɪk]	adj. 外来的,异国情调的
facilitate	[fəˈsɪlɪteɪt]	v. 促进,帮助,使容易
gladiator	[ˈɡlædɪeɪtə]	n. 古罗马角斗士
gutter	[ˈɡʌtə]	n. 排水沟
halt	[hɔːlt]	v. 停止
incredible	[ɪnˈkredɪb(ə)l]	adj. 难以置信的,惊人的
inevitably	[ɪnˈevɪtəbli]	adv. 不可避免地;必然地
influential	[ˌɪnfluˈenʃ(ə)l]	adj. 有影响的,有势力的
macadam	[məˈkædəm]	n. 碎石;碎石路面
mule	[mjuːl]	n. 骡;倔强之人

nautical	[ˈnɔːtɪk(ə)l]	adj. 航海的,海上的
originally	[əˈrɪdʒɪn(ə)li]	adv. 最初,起初
possession	[pəˈzeʃən]	n. 属地;领地
radiate	[ˈreɪdɪeɪt]	v. 辐射,传播,流露
strategically	[strəˈtiːdʒɪkəli]	adv. 战略性地,战略上
unsurpassed	[ʌnsəˈpɑːst]	adj. 非常卓越的,未被超越的
vast	[vɑːst]	adj. 广阔的,巨大的
vehicle	[ˈviːəkl]	n. 车辆,工具,传播媒介
whence	[wens]	pron. 何处,该处

Expressions

compare to	把……比作,比喻为
be unparalleled in convenience	最为便利
depend on	取决于,依赖,依靠
not to mention	更别提……
play a role in	在……起作用
take for granted	认为……理所当然

Proper Names

miliarius aurem in the Forum	古罗马广场上的金色里程碑。古罗马广场(Forum)是古罗马的城市中心,包括一些罗马最古老与最重要的建筑。

Difficult Sentences

① The road system of the Ancient Romans was one of the greatest engineering accomplishments of its time, with over 50,000 miles of paved road radiating from their center at the miliarius aurem in the Forum in the city of Rome.

古罗马的道路系统是当时最伟大的建筑成就之一,所铺砌的五万多英里的路面以罗马古城金色路标为中心向四周辐射。

② Although the Roman road system was originally built to facilitate the movement of troops throughout the empire, it was inevitably used for other purposes by civilians.

虽然古罗马公路网的建造初衷是为了方便在全国范围内调动军队,但这些道路不可避免地会被市民用于其他目的。

③ Of course, the roads were used for trade, as were the waterways surrounding and connecting parts of the Roman Empire to itself and the rest of the known world.
当然,这些道路和连接罗马帝国各地以及连接已知世界其他地区的环城水路一样,也是用于贸易往来。

④ however, their network of roads, even with the danger of land travel, was unparalleled in convenience and was often the only choice for travel or shipping goods.
尽管陆路交通有其危险之处,但罗马公路的便捷是其他交通方式无法比拟的,因此它往往成为旅行或货运的唯一选择。

⑤ Indeed, mud or gravel would hinder, if not completely halt many vehicles pulled by animals or other people, not to mention discourage travelers on foot.
实际上,土路和砂砾路即便没有完全阻碍牲口车或人力车的行驶,也会对这些车辆的行驶造成困难,更不必说对徒步旅行者的妨碍了。

⑥ Roads were crowned—that is, they were higher in the middle than on the sides to allow water to run off—and they often had gutters for drainage along the shoulders.
公路都有路拱,也就是说,为方便排水,公路中间要比两边高,而且公路两边往往还有排水沟。

⑦ Present-day Great Britain, for example, was a valuable possession to the Romans because of its silver deposits, which were used for jewelry and money.
例如,现在的英国在当时对罗马人而言是举足轻重的属地,因为那里有银矿,白银可用于制作珠宝和钱币。

⑧ From the southeastern corner of the empire, the Romans imported many dyes for clothing, and make-up from the Near East. Over-water transportation usually played a role in imports from the Near East or Africa, from whence they imported Egyptian cotton, or exotic animals for the gladiators to fight.
罗马人从罗马帝国东南地区进口大量的染料,从近东(地中海东部沿岸地区)进口化妆品。当需要从近东或非洲进口埃及的棉花或者用于角斗的奇珍异兽时,水路往往是首选。

⑨ Progress was slow compared to today's standards and a person traveling on foot would be lucky to travel 35 miles a day.
相对现代的标准而言,当时的行进速度可谓十分缓慢,一天能徒步走上35英里就已经算不错的了。

⑩ The ancient Romans accomplished many feats. They had incredible technological advantages and made advancements that dwarfed those of other civilizations of their times or hundreds of years beyond.
古罗马人在许多方面都取得了骄人的业绩。他们有着令人难以置信的技术优势并极大地推进了社会的发展,这就使得同时期或其后几百年的其他文明相形见绌。

Unit 2 Roman Empire and Latin Culture

Exercises

Task 1 Reading Comprehension

Directions: *Read the passage and judge whether the following statements are true (T), false (F) or not given (NG).*

True   if the statement agrees with the information mentioned in the passage
False   if the statement contradicts the information mentioned in the passage
Not Given   if there is no information on this in the passage

1. The ancient Roman road system was built to facilitate the transportation of goods.
2. The ancient Romans had extraordinary nautical technology for their time.
3. The paved roads in the Roman Empire did not prevent travel during or after severe weather.
4. The ancient Roman roads were crowned so that they could be more appealing to the eyes.
5. The ancient Roman roads were so well built that some are still in use today.
6. Great Britain was important to the Roman Empire because of its gold deposits.
7. The goods that the ancient Romans imported from the Near East were of high quality.
8. Rare foreign products could be shipped into the Roman Empire if the Romans really wanted them.
9. Travel on land for the ancient Romans was often safe and interesting.
10. The Roman Empire was much more advanced than other civilizations of their time or hundreds of years after their time.

Task 2 Vocabulary

Directions: *Complete the following sentences with the proper forms of the words given.*

1. The road system of the ancient Romans was one of the greatest engineering _____ (accomplish) of its time.
2. The road system of the Ancient Romans was _____ (parallel) in convenience and was often the only choice for travel or shipping goods.
3. Mud or gravel would _____ (courage) travelers on foot.
4. Probably the most _____ (credit) engineering feat concerning the Roman road system is how well the roads were built.
5. The road-building methods of the Ancient Romans were _____ (surpass) until the invention of the macadam in the 19th century.
6. Thanks to its excellent road system, the goods could be _____ (constant) shipped throughout the Roman Empire.
7. Great Britain was a valuable _____ (possess) to the ancient Romans because of its silver deposits, which were used for jewelry and money.
8. These _____ (technology) advantages made travel and the shipment of goods across land much easier.

9. The ancient Romans had incredible technological advantages and made _____ (advance) that dwarfed those of other _____ (civilize) of their time.
10. It is their advancements that make them one of the most _____ (influence) peoples around the world.

Task 3 Translation

Directions: *Complete the following sentences by translating the Chinese in brackets into English.*

1. Indeed, mud or gravel would hinder, if not completely halt many vehicles pulled by animals or other people, _____ (更别说会阻碍徒步的旅行者).
2. Goods were constantly being shipped throughout the empire, depending on the location within the Empire, _____ (以及供求).
3. Over-water transportation usually _____ (在进口货物方面起着重要的作用) from the Near East or Africa.
4. Of course, Rome _____ (通过丝绸之路与远东相连), the source of silk and other goods imported from Asia.
5. Progress was slow _____ (与今天的标准相比), and a person traveling on foot would be lucky to travel 35 miles a day.

Task 4 Further Development

Directions: *Discuss about the situations in which modern people use the idiom "All roads lead to Rome" and tell the change of its meaning.*

Section C Cleopatra, the Egyptian Queen and Her Love Affairs

① In modern culture, Cleopatra, the last Pharaoh of Ancient Egypt, is an icon of feminine beauty and charisma. Her life and love affairs have been shown in numerous works of art, literature and other media, including Shakespeare's drama *Antony and Cleopatra,* and the film *Cleopatra* (1963). She is typically presented as a great queen who charmed two famous Roman rulers, Julius Caesar and Mark Antony with her surpassing beauty, intelligence and personality.

Born in 69 BC in Alexandria, Cleopatra was a daughter of King Ptolemy XII who descended from a family of Greek origin that ruled Egypt. ② In 51 BC, Ptolemy XII died, thus by his will making 18-year-old Cleopatra and her 10-year-old brother Ptolemy XIII co-rulers of Egypt. Though Cleopatra was married to Ptolemy XIII, she quickly made it clear that she had no intention of sharing power with him. In 48 BC, their relationship completely broke down and Cleopatra was driven out of Egypt by Ptolemy XIII.

Cleopatra was determined to get the throne back and she tried to win Caesar's support. ③

One night, she had herself rolled up in a carpet and secretly carried into the guarded palace to meet Caesar who was a visitor of Ptolemy XIII at that time. That Cleopatra rolled out of the carpet began one of history's greatest love stories. ④ 21-year-old Cleopatra's dramatic appearance surprised and delighted 52-year-old Caesar, and he was immediately captivated by her charm and wit. They became lovers and nine months after their first meeting, she gave birth to their son, Caesarion, which means "little Caesar."

The Statue of Cleopatra

Between 48 BC and 47 BC, Caesar stayed in Egypt; he defeated Ptolemy XIII's army and restored Cleopatra to her throne, with another younger brother Ptolemy XIV as her new co-ruler. In the summer of 46 BC, Cleopatra and Caesarion visited Rome where they lived in a palace built by Caesar in their honor. ⑤ The relationship between Cleopatra and Caesar was obvious to the Romans, and rumors began floating all over the city that Caesar was planning to become king and was going to move the capital to Alexandria. On March 14th, 44 BC, the night before Caesar's death, Cleopatra had a terrible dream that he was about to be murdered. The next morning, she tried to keep him from leaving the palace but failed. Cleopatra fled back to Egypt with Caesarion when she knew Caesar's death. When Ptolemy XIV died, probably poisoned by his elder sister, Cleopatra made Caesarion her co-ruler and successor.

After Caesar's death, two men fought for power in Rome: Mark Antony and Octavian. Mark Antony felt very much attracted to Cleopatra and the Egyptian queen helped him in his battle against Octavian. Antony spent the winter of 41 BC—40 BC with her in Alexandria; Cleopatra gave birth to twins fathered by Antony on 25 December, 40 BC. ⑥ Four years later,

The 1963 movie *Cleopatra* starred famous Hollywood actress Elizabeth Taylor as Cleopatra

Antony visited Alexandria again. This time he renewed his relationship with Cleopatra, married her and made Alexandria his home although he was already married to Octavian's sister Octavia Minor. Antony and Cleopatra had altogether three children.

With the news of Antony's marrying Cleopatra and giving away part of the empire, Octavian became furious. This caused him to convince the Roman Senate to declare war on Egypt. In 31 BC, Cleopatra and Antony's armies faced the Romans in a sea war off the coast of Actium. They fled back to Alexandria after being defeated. In August, 30 BC when Octavian invaded Alexandria, Antony's armies deserted him and joined with Octavian. In despair, Antony committed suicide by stabbing himself with a sword. A short time later Cleopatra let a snake bite her and also died. She was buried with Antony as she wished. ⑦ Her son by Caesar was captured and killed, and her other three children by Antony were spared and taken back to Rome where they were taken care of by Antony's wife, Octavia Minor. With Cleopatra's death, Greek rule came to an end and Egypt became a Roman province.

⑧ More than two thousand years after her death, Cleopatra is still looked upon as the most beautiful, powerful and intelligent Egyptian queen who keeps inciting endless legends and imagination.

(691 words)

New Words and Expressions (C)

New Words

New Words	Phonetic Symbols	Meanings
captivate	[ˈkæptɪveɪt]	*v.* 迷住
charisma	[kəˈrɪzmə]	*n.* 非凡的领导力；魅力
charm	[tʃɑːm]	*v.* 迷住 *n.* 魅力
descend	[dɪˈsend]	*v.* 下降
despair	[dɪˈspeə]	*n.* 绝望
endless	[ˈendlɪs]	*adj.* 无止境的；连续的
furious	[ˈfjʊərɪəs]	*adj.* 狂怒的
imagination	[ɪˌmædʒɪˈneɪʃ(ə)n]	*n.* 想象力
incite	[ɪnˈsaɪt]	*v.* 煽动；激励
intelligence	[ɪnˈtelɪdʒ(ə)ns]	*n.* 智力
invade	[ɪnˈveɪd]	*v.* 侵略
mystique	[mɪˈstiːk]	*n.* 神秘性
numerous	[ˈnjuːm(ə)rəs]	*adj.* 许多的

origin	[ˈɒrɪdʒɪn]	n. 起源, 出身
personality	[pɜːsəˈnælɪti]	n. 个性, 品格
pharaoh	[ˈfɛro]	n. 法老
poison	[ˈpɔɪzn]	v. 投毒
renew	[rɪˈnjuː]	v. 使更新, 复兴
restore	[rɪˈstɔː]	v. 恢复, 修复
roll	[rəʊl]	v. 卷
successor	[səkˈsesə]	n. 继承者
surpassing	[səˈpɑːsɪŋ]	adj. 卓越的, 优秀的
twin	[twɪn]	n. 双胞胎中的一个

Expressions

break down	发生故障, 失败
be driven out of	被赶出
come to an end	结束
commit suicide	自杀
flee back to	逃回
give away	放弃; 泄露; 出卖
have no intention of	无意……
in one's honor	为了纪念; 向……表示敬意
look upon as	视为, 看作

Proper Names

Actium	(地名)希腊的亚克兴
Alexandria	(地名)埃及的亚历山大(埃及北部港市)
Antony and Cleopatra	《安东尼与克利奥帕特拉》,莎士比亚就埃及艳后克利奥帕特拉与安东尼的爱情故事所写的一个悲剧剧本,后被多次改编成电影。
Cleopatra	克利奥帕特拉(公元前69—前30),托勒密王朝的君主,是古埃及最后一位法老,俗称"埃及艳后",其统治时期是埃及的鼎盛时期。
Mark Antony	马克·安东尼(约公元前83—前30),古罗马政治家和军事家。他是恺撒最重要的军队指挥官和管理人员之一。
Octavian	屋大维(公元前63—公元14),罗马帝国的开国君主,元首制的创始人,统治罗马长达40年,是世界历史上最为重要的人物之一。
Octavia Minor	小奥克塔维亚(公元前69—前11),罗马帝国第一任皇帝屋大维同父异母的姐姐,也是马克·安东尼的第四任妻子。

Difficult Sentences

① Few historical figures have modern mystique as strongly as Cleopatra, the last ruler of Ancient Egypt.
现代人感觉最神秘的历史人物当属古埃及的最后一位统治者克利奥帕特拉。

② In 51 BC, Ptolemy XII died, thus by his will making 18-year-old Cleopatra and her 10-year-old brother Ptolemy XIII co-rulers of Egypt.
公元前51年,托勒密十二世去世,根据其遗嘱,18岁的克利奥帕特拉和她10岁的弟弟托勒密十三世共同执政,统治埃及。

③ One night, she had herself rolled up in a carpet and secretly carried into the guarded palace to meet Caesar who was a visitor of Ptolemy XIII at that time.
一天晚上,当恺撒正在托勒密十三世的宫殿作客时,她让人用毯子把自己裹起来秘密地送入戒备森严的宫殿里。

④ 21-year-old Cleopatra's dramatic appearance surprised and delighted 52-year-old Caesar, and he was immediately captivated by her charm and wit.
21岁的克利奥帕特拉戏剧般地出现令52岁的恺撒又惊又喜,顷刻间即为其魅力和智慧所俘获。

⑤ The relationship between Cleopatra and Caesar was obvious to the Romans, and rumors began floating all over the city that Caesar was planning to become king and was going to move the capital to Alexandria.
罗马人注意到了克利奥帕特拉和恺撒之间的关系,整个罗马城开始谣传恺撒要称王并移都亚历山大。

⑥ Four years later, Antony visited Alexandria again. This time he renewed his relationship with Cleopatra, married her and made Alexandria his home although he was already married to Octavian's sister Octavia Minor.
四年以后,安东尼返回亚历山大和克利奥帕特拉重续前缘。尽管安东尼已经娶了屋大维的姐姐小奥克塔维娅,他又与克利奥帕特拉结婚,并在亚历山大安家。

⑦ Her son by Caesar was captured and killed, and her other three children by Antony were spared and taken back to Rome where they were taken care of by Antony's wife, Octavia Minor.
她与恺撒所生的儿子被俘后被杀,她与安东尼所生的三个孩子则被带回罗马,由安东尼的妻子小奥克塔维娅抚养。

⑧ More than two thousand years after her death, Cleopatra is still looked upon as the most beautiful, powerful and intelligent Egyptian queen who keeps inciting endless legends and imagination.

在她死后两千多年,克利奥帕特拉依然被视作最为美丽、最具权势和最富智慧的埃及女王,至今仍轶事流传不断,令人浮想联翩。

Exercises

Task 1   Short Answer Questions

Directions: *Work in pairs to answer the following questions.*
1. What did Cleopatra want to do when her father King Ptolemy XII died?
2. What were the contributing factors to Caesar's being murdered?
3. How many children did Cleopatra have?
4. What happened to Mark Antony when Octavian invaded Alexandria?
5. What happened to Caesarion after the death of Cleopatra?

Task 2   Vocabulary

Directions: *Complete the following summary of the passage with proper words from the box. Change the form if necessary.*

| bite | declare | Egypt | imagine | roll |
| attract | stab | province | captivate | intend |

In modern culture, Cleopatra, the Ancient (1)_____ queen who charmed two famous Roman rulers, Julius Caesar and Mark Antony, is an icon of feminine beauty and charisma.

Cleopatra was a daughter of Egyptian King who by his will made her a co-ruler with her brother. She was driven out of Egypt by him for her obvious (2)_____ to rule alone. To win Caesar's support, Cleopatra had herself (3)_____ up in a carpet and carried into the guarded palace to meet him. (4)_____ by her, Caesar became her lover and restored her to the throne. But he was murdered by the Romans for they feared he might marry her and move the capital to Alexandria. After Caesar's death, Mark Antony and Octavian fought for power in Rome. Though Antony had married Octavian's sister, he was so (5)_____ to Cleopatra that he married her and made Alexandria his home, which caused Octavian to (6)_____ war on Egypt. When Egypt was defeated, Antony (7)_____ himself with a sword and Cleopatra let a snake (8)_____ her. They both died and Cleopatra was buried with Antony as she wished. With Cleopatra's death, Egypt became a Roman (9)_____.

Cleopatra is still looked upon as the most beautiful, powerful and intelligent Egyptian queen who keeps inciting endless legends and (10)_____.

Task 3　Translation

Directions: *Complete the following sentences by translating the Chinese in brackets into English.*

1. Though Cleopatra was married to Ptolemy XIII, she quickly made it clear that she _____ _____ （无意分享）power with him.
2. 21-year-old Cleopatra's dramatic appearance surprised and delighted 52-year-old Caesar, and he _____（立刻被……所俘获）her charm and wit.
3. She was buried with Antony _____（如她所愿）.
4. With Cleopatra's death, Greek rule _____（结束）and Egypt became a Roman province.
5. More than two thousand years after her death, Cleopatra _____（仍被视为）the most beautiful, powerful and intelligent Egyptian queen.

Task 4　Further Development

Directions: *Watch the 1963 epic drama film Cleopatra after class and discuss it with your classmates. You may discuss anything you like, for example, its characters, cast, director, plot, and the reasons why it won four Oscars and so on.*

Adages and Proverbs

1. Veni, vidi, vici. (I came, I saw, I conquered.)
　　　　　　　　　　　　—Julius Caesar (102 BC—44 BC), Roman dictator
　我来到，我看见，我征服。　　　　　　　　　　——尤里乌斯·恺撒
　（公元前47年，恺撒向罗马议会报捷时只用这三个拉丁单词，短小精悍。）

2. It is better to create than to learn! Creating is the essence of life.　　—Julius Caesar
　创造比学习更为重要！生命的精髓在于创造。　　　　——尤里乌斯·恺撒

3. The die is cast.　　　　　　　　　　　　　　　　　　　—Julius Caesar
　木已成舟。　　　　　　　　　　　　　　　　　　——尤里乌斯·恺撒

4. Cowards die many times before their actual deaths.　　　　—Julius Caesar
　懦夫死前已多次历经死亡的恐惧。　　　　　　　　——尤里乌斯·恺撒

5. It is easier to find men who will volunteer to die, than to find those who are willing to endure pain with patience.　　　　　　　　　　　　　　　—Julius Caesar
　易轻生者多，愿承受苦难者少。
　　　　　　　　　　　　　　　　　　　　　　　　——尤里乌斯·恺撒

6. Men willingly believe what they wish.　　　　　　　　　—Julius Caesar
　人总乐于信其所盼。　　　　　　　　　　　　　　——尤里乌斯·恺撒

7. All life is bondage. Man must therefore habituate himself to his condition, complain of

it as little as possible, and grasp whatever good lies within his reach.

　　　　　　　　　　　　—Seneca (4 BC—AD 65), Roman philosopher, statesman

生活无处无束缚。因此个人得适应环境,尽可能少地抱怨,抓住可及的所有美好事物。　　　　　　　　　　　　　　　　　　　　　　　　　——塞内加

8. Love conquers all.　　　　　　　　—Virgil (70 BC—19 BC), Roman poet
　爱能征服一切。　　　　　　　　　　　　　　　　　　　　　——维吉尔

9. Come what may, all bad fortune is to be conquered by endurance.　—Virgil
　不管发生什么事,毅力可以战胜所有厄运。　　　　　　　　　——维吉尔

10. They succeed, because they think they can.　　　　　　　　—Virgil
　　成功的人之所以成功,是因为他们有信念。　　　　　　　　——维吉尔

11. Only the dead can enjoy eternal peace.　　　　　　　　　—Virgil
　　只有死者才能永享安宁。　　　　　　　　　　　　　　　——维吉尔

12. Remember when life's path is steep to keep your mind even.
　　　　　　　　　　　　　　　　—Horace (65 BC—AD 8), Roman poet
　　记住,人生之路险峻时,胸怀要从容平和。　　　　　　　　——贺拉斯

13. Wisdom is not wisdom when it is derived from books alone.　　—Horace
　　只源自书本的智慧称不上是真正的智慧。　　　　　　　　　——贺拉斯

14. A word once uttered can never be recalled.　　　　　　　　—Horace
　　一言既出,驷马难追。　　　　　　　　　　　　　　　　——贺拉斯

15. It's a good thing to be foolishly gay once in a while.　　　—Horace
　　偶尔傻乐一下也未尝不好。　　　　　　　　　　　　　　——贺拉斯

Key to Unit 2 Exercises

导读答案

1. The founding of Rome goes back to the very early days of civilization. Early Rome was governed by kings, but later the Romans took power over their own city and ruled themselves. They then instead had a council known as the "senate" which ruled over them. From this point on one speaks of the Roman Republic. It lasted from 510 BC until 27 BC — almost 500 years.

2. It means different ways of doing things lead to the same result. Probably this idiom has something to do with the history of the Roman Empire.

3. Cleopatra is the last pharaoh of Ancient Egypt. She is typically presented as a great queen who charmed two famous Roman rulers, Julius Caesar and Mark Antony with her surpassing

beauty, intelligence and personality. Her life and love affairs have been shown in numerous works of art, literature and other media, including Shakespeare's drama *Antony and Cleopatra*, and the film *Cleopatra*.

Section A

Task 1   Reading Comprehension
1. B   2. C   3. D   4. A   5. C

Task 2   Vocabulary
1. took over   2. appointed   3. tyrant   4. lay with   5. challenge
6. murdered   7. respected   8. overrun   9. migrations   10. flooding

Task 3   Translation
1. Today, Rome is known as "the eternal city" whose founding goes back to the very early days of civilization.
2. Their name means the "riders," as they were given a horse to ride if they were called to fight for Rome.
3. The fight between Rome and Carthage was a long one and took place on land and at sea.
4. The great migration from the north and east of Europe proved too much for the Romans to stand.
5. What is generally referred to as "the Fall of Rome" doesn't include the eastern Roman Empire.

Task 4   Further Development

Year	Event
625 BC	Rome was founded.
510 BC	The Roman Republic was founded.
146 BC	Rome completely defeated Carthage.
49 BC	Caesar ruled Rome as a dictator.
27 BC	The Roman Republic came to an end.
AD 476	The fall of the western Roman Empire.
AD 1453	The fall of (the eastern) Roman Empire.

Section B

Task 1   Reading Comprehension
1. F   2. T   3. T   4. F   5. T   6. F   7. NG   8. T   9. F   10. T

Task 2   Reading and Blank-Filling
1. accomplishments   2. unparalleled   3. discourage   4. incredible   5. unsurpassed
6. constantly   7. possession   8. technological   9. advancements civilizations
10. influential

Unit 2 Roman Empire and Latin Culture

Task 3 Translation

1. not to mention discouraging travelers on foot
2. as well as supply and demand
3. played an important role in imports.
4. was connected to the Far East via the Silk Road
5. compared to today's standards

Task 4 Further Development

   "All roads lead to Rome" is an idiom that draws its literal meaning from some real situation but has since come to mean something that is often quite different than what it once did. It originally meant that all paths essentially led to the same destination. This is because roads built in Roman Empire were for military use and all the roads spreading out to cover the whole empire eventually led back to the capital city, Rome. But now it means that something is set up so that different methods of doing something will eventually lead to the same result. For example, if a boss says to his secretary, "I don't care if you save the file and then send it to me or copy it and print it out; all roads lead to Rome." He means that he will get what he requires no matter which way the secretary chooses to give it to him. And a person may advise his friend to put down his feet on the earth by saying, "Though all roads lead to Rome, you have to start out at the bottom."

Section C

Task 1 Short Answer Questions

1. She wanted to be the sole ruler of Egypt.
2. The relationship between Caesar and Cleopatra and the rumor that he was planning to become king and going to move the capital to Alexandria.
3. Four children all together, one by Caesar, three by Antony.
4. His armies deserted him and joined with Octavian.
5. He was captured and killed.

Task 2 Vocabulary

1. Egyptian	2. intention	3. rolled	4. Captivated	5. attracted
6. declare	7. stabbed	8. bite	9. province	10. imagination

Task 3 Translation

1. had no intention of sharing
2. was immediately captivated by
3. as she wished
4. came to an end
5. is still looked upon as

Unit 3

The Middle Ages and the Rise of Modern Europe

> 导 读
>
> 本单元旨在通过对中世纪历史、文化教育等方面的介绍,使学生对西方这一重要时期有一基本了解,开阔视野,能够运用所学西方文化知识及相关的英语表达方式进行文化交流,为今后的深入学习和研究奠定基础。

Before You Start

While preparing for this unit, think about the following questions:
1. What do you know about the Middle Ages?
2. Why is this period of time called the "Middle Age" in European history?
3. Do you have the impression that the Medieval period is quite a "dark" period of time? What are the causes for this commonly acquired impression?
4. What do you know about the western universities in their early days?

Section A The Middle Ages

The Middle Ages or Medieval Period (476—1453) is a period in European history lasting from the 5th until the 15th centuries. It began with the collapse of the Western Roman Empire, and was followed by the Renaissance and the Age of Discovery. The Middle Ages is the middle period of the traditional division of Western history into Classical, Medieval, and Modern periods. ① The period is subdivided into the Early Middle Ages, the High Middle Ages, and the Late Middle Ages.

② In the Early Middle Ages, depopulation, de-urbanization, and barbarian invasions, which had begun in Late Antiquity, continued. The barbarian invaders formed new kingdoms in what remained of the Western Roman Empire. In the 7th century North Africa and the Middle East, once part of the Eastern Roman Empire (the Byzantine Empire), became an Islamic Empire after conquest by Muhammad's successors. ③ Although there were substantial changes in society and political structures, the break with Antiquity was not complete. The still sizeable Byzantine Empire survived and remained a major power. The empire's law code, the Code of Justinian, was widely admired later in the Middle Ages. ④ In the West, most kingdoms incorporated extant Roman institutions, while monasteries were founded as Christianity expanded in Western

Europe. The Franks, under the Carolingian dynasty, established an empire covering much of western Europe; the Carolingian Empire endured until the 9th century, when it surrendered to the pressures of invasion—Vikings from the north, the Magyars from the east, and the Saracens from the south.

During the High Middle Ages, which began after AD 1000, the population of Europe increased greatly as technological and agricultural innovations allowed trade to flourish and crop yields to increase. Manorialism and feudalism were two of the ways society was organized in the High Middle Ages. ⑤ The Crusades, first preached in 1096, were military attempts, by western European Christians, to regain control of the Middle Eastern Holy Land from the Muslims. ⑥ Kings became the heads of centralized nation states, reducing crime and violence but making the ideal of a unified Christendom more distant. Intellectual life was marked by scholasticism, a philosophy that emphasized joining faith to reason, and by the founding of universities. The philosophy of Thomas Aquinas, the paintings of Giotto, the poetry of Dante and Chaucer, the travels of Marco Polo, and the architecture of Gothic cathedrals such as Chartres are among the outstanding achievements of this period.

The Medieval Troops

The Late Middle Ages was marked by difficulties and calamities, such as famine, plague, and war, which much diminished the population of Western Europe; between 1347 and 1350, the Black Death killed approximately a third of the European population. ⑦ Controversy, heresy, and differences within the Church paralleled the warfare between states, civil wars, and peasant revolts occurring in the kingdoms. Cultural and technological developments transformed European society, concluding the Late Middle Ages and beginning the Early Modern period.

The most commonly given start date for the Middle Ages is 476. For Europe as a whole, 1500 is often considered to be the end of the Middle Ages, but there is no universally agreed-upon end date; depending on the context, events such as Christopher Columbus's first voyage to the Americas in 1492, the conquest of Constantinople by the Turks in 1453, or the Protestant Reformation in 1517 are sometimes used. English historians often use the Battle of Bosworth Field in 1485 to mark the end of the period. For Spain, dates commonly used are the death of King Ferdinand II in 1516, the death of Queen Isabella I of Castile in 1504, or the conquest of Granada in 1492.

(611 words)

New Words and Expressions (A)

New Words

New Words	Phonetic Symbols	Meanings
Byzantine	[ˈbɪzəntiːn]	adj. 拜占庭式的
Christendom	[ˈkrɪstndəm]	n. 基督教世界；基督教王国
calamity	[kəˈlæməti]	n. 灾难
conclude	[kənˈkluːd]	v. 结束
depopulation	[ˌdiːpɒpjʊˈleɪʃ(ə)n]	n. 人口下降
de-urbanization	[diˈɜː(r)bənaɪˈzeɪʃ(ə)n]	n. 去城镇化
endure	[ɪnˈdjʊə(r)]	v. 忍受；持久
extant	[ekˈstænt]	adj. 尚存的
feudalism	[ˈfjuːdəlɪzəm]	n. 封建制度
heresy	[ˈherəsi]	n. 异教，异端邪说：已立誓信教或受过洗礼的教徒对罗马天主教教义的异议或否认
incorporate	[ɪnˈkɔː(r)pəreɪt]	v. 包含；吸收
Islamic	[ɪzˈlæmɪk]	adj. 伊斯兰教的
manorialism	[məˈnɔːrɪəlɪzəm]	n. 庄园制度
monastery	[ˈmɒnəst(ə)ri]	n. 修道院
parallel	[ˈpærəlel]	v. 与……同时发生
preach	[priːtʃ]	v. 宣扬；布道；训诫
Protestant	[ˈprɒtɪstənt]	n. 新教教徒
revolt	[rɪˈvəʊlt]	n. 暴乱
scholasticism	[skəˈlæstɪsɪzəm]	n. 经院哲学
sizeable	[ˈsaɪzəb(ə)l]	adj. 相当大的
subdivide	[ˌsʌbdɪˈvaɪd]	v. 再分，细分
substantial	[səbˈstænʃ(ə)l]	adj. 实质的，坚实的
succumb	[səˈkʌm]	v. 屈服
Turk	[tɜː(r)k]	n. 土耳其人，突厥人
unified	[ˈjuːnɪfaɪd]	adj. 统一的
yield	[jiːld]	n. 产量

Unit 3　The Middle Ages and the Rise of Modern Europe

Proper Names

Battle of Bosworth Field	博斯沃思原野战役，15世纪后半叶兰开斯特王朝与约克王朝间的内战，也是玫瑰战争中倒数第二场战役。
the Black Death	黑死病，14世纪蔓延于亚欧两洲的鼠疫，造成了数千万人的死亡。
Carolingian dynasty	加洛林王朝，是自公元751年统治法兰克王国的王朝。
Castile	卡斯蒂利亚，西班牙中部和北部一个地区和旧日的王国。从10世纪开始自治，1479年伊莎拉和贝斐迪南结婚后该地并入阿拉贡（Aragon），由此组成了现代西班牙的核心。
Chartres	沙特尔大教堂，法国著名的天主教堂
Chaucer	乔叟，14世纪英国著名诗人，代表作有《坎特伯雷故事集》。
Christopher Columbus	克里斯托弗·哥伦布（1451—1506），意大利航海家、探险家，开辟了横渡大西洋到美洲的航路。
Giotto	乔托，意大利文艺复兴时期杰出的雕刻家，画家和建筑师，被誉为"欧洲绘画之父"。
Code of Justinian	《查士丁尼法典》又称《民法大全》或《国法大全》，是东罗马帝国皇帝查士丁尼一世下令编纂的一部汇编式法典。
Constantinople	君士坦丁堡，是土耳其的城市伊斯坦布尔的旧名，原名为"拜占庭"，罗马帝国皇帝君士坦丁一世于公元330年5月11日定都此地。
Crusades	十字军东征（1096—1291），在罗马天主教教皇的准许下进行的一系列宗教性军事行动，由西欧的封建领主和骑士对地中海东岸的国家以清除异端的名义发动的所谓"正义"战争。
Granada	格拉纳达，西班牙南部一座城市，由摩尔人于8世纪创建，在1238年成为一个独立王国的中心。该城于1492年为卡斯蒂利亚人攻陷，从而结束了摩尔人对西班牙的统治。
High Middle Ages	中世纪鼎盛时期
King Ferdinand II	费迪南德二世（1137—1188），西班牙的莱昂国王，阿方索七世的次子，自称"西班牙人的王"。
Late Antiquity	古典时期晚期
Magyars	匈牙利的马札尔人，原为蒙古族
Muhammad	穆罕默德，伊斯兰教的创立者，也是伊斯兰教徒（穆斯林）公认的伊斯兰教先知。
Marco Polo	马可·波罗，13世纪意大利的旅行家和商人，据称他游历过中国的许多地方。在其口述下，其狱友写下著名的《马可·波罗游记》。

Middle Eastern Holy Land	耶路撒冷，被誉为三大宗教的圣城（犹太教、基督教和伊斯兰教）
Saracens	撒拉逊人，阿拉伯人的古称
Thomas Aquinas	托马斯·阿奎纳（约1225—1274），中世纪经院哲学的哲学家和神学家
Vikings	维京人，泛指北欧海盗，他们从公元8世纪到11世纪一直侵扰欧洲沿海和英国岛屿，其足迹遍及从欧洲大陆至北极广阔疆域，欧洲这一时期被称为"维京时期"（Viking Age）。

Difficult Sentences

① The period is subdivided into the Early Middle Ages, the High Middle Ages, and the Late Middle Ages.

而中世纪也被细分为中世纪早期、中世纪中期和中世纪晚期。

② In the Early Middle Ages, depopulation, de-urbanization, and barbarian invasions, which had begun in Late Antiquity, continued. The barbarian invaders formed new kingdoms in what remained of the Western Roman Empire.

中世纪早期，在古典时期晚期就已开始发生的人口减少、逆城镇化和蛮族入侵等现象仍在继续。在西罗马帝国曾经占据的地方，蛮族入侵者建立了新的王国。

③ Although there were substantial changes in society and political structures, the break with Antiquity was not complete. The still sizeable Byzantine Empire survived and remained a major power.

虽然社会和政治结构上都发生了实质性的变化，但中世纪与古代还没有完全分离。拜占庭帝国领土依旧广阔且仍然作为一种主要势力存在着。

④ In the West, most kingdoms incorporated extant Roman institutions, while monasteries were founded as Christianity expanded in Western Europe.

在西方，大多数国家都采纳了现存的罗马制度法规，与此同时，基督教在西欧传播发展，修道院也随之建立。

⑤ The Crusades, first preached in 1096, were military attempts, by western European Christians, to regain control of the Middle Eastern Holy Land from the Muslims.

第一次十字军东征始于1096年，西欧的基督教徒们希望通过武力手段从穆斯林手中收复中东的圣地。

⑥ Kings became the heads of centralized nation states, reducing crime and violence but making the ideal of a unified Christendom more distant. Intellectual life was marked by scholasticism, a philosophy that emphasized joining faith to reason, and by the founding of universities.

国王成为中央集权国家的元首，犯罪和暴力减少了，但建立统一基督教世界的理想却变

Unit 3　The Middle Ages and the Rise of Modern Europe

得越来越遥远。这一时期文化生活的主要特征是将宗教信仰与理性相结合的经院哲学，以及大学的兴起。

⑦ Controversy, heresy, and differences within the Church paralleled the warfare between states, civil wars, and peasant revolts occurring in the kingdoms. Cultural and technological developments transformed European society, concluding the Late Middle Ages and beginning the Early Modern period.

在这些王国里，教会内部的分歧、论争以及异端邪说时有发生，国家之间的战争、内战和农民起义此消彼长。文化和技术方面的发展改变着欧洲社会，最终宣告了中世纪晚期的终结和早期现代社会的开端。

Exercises

Task 1　Reading Comprehension

Directions: *Read the passage and choose the best answer to each of the following questions.*

1. How long had the Medieval period lasted as commonly believed?
   A. 500 years.
   B. 800 years.
   C. 1,000 years.
   D. 1,500 years.
2. Why is the Medieval period named as the "Middle Ages" in European history?
   A. It is in the middle of the Christian Tradition and Islamic Tradition.
   B. It is in the middle of the Classical period and Modern period.
   C. It is in the middle of the early middle ages and late middle ages.
   D. It is in the middle of the landmass called Eurasia.
3. What is the most significant event occurring in the 7th century Europe?
   A. The Crusades.
   B. The Black Death.
   C. The rise of nation states.
   D. The rise of Islamic power.
4. Which of the following statements about the Early Middle Ages is NOT true?
   A. The population in Europe kept decreasing.
   B. The Byzantine Empire still exerted great power upon European kingdoms.
   C. Both the Western and the Eastern Roman Empires fell by invasion.
   D. The Franks established a great empire in West Europe.

5. What is the fundamental reason for the increase of European population after the 11th century?
   A. Technological and agricultural innovations.
   B. Manorialism and feudalism.
   C. Military attempts.
   D. Centralized power.

Task 2 Vocabulary

Directions: *Complete the following sentences with proper words from the box. Change the form if necessary. Please note there are more words than necessary.*

A) preach	B) depopulation	C) extant	D) endure	E) heritage
F) parallel	G) proclaim	H) context	I) calamity	J) surrender
K) monastery	L) revolt	M) yield	N) given	O) incorporate

1. The tyranny of the Medieval dictator will eventually _____ to the forces of freedom and progress.
2. The _____ by the poor peasants had overthrown the dynasty in the High Middle Ages.
3. The gardens in the _____ are places where the monks can pray and think about their behaviors.
4. Under the reign of Charlemagne, many separate tribes were _____ in the same kingdom.
5. The major function of the Medieval church included not only to _____ over the believers, but also to promote learning and yield works on theology or philosophy.
6. Hardly can anyone _____ the severe tortures by the Church Inquisitor
7. The Crusades had caused great _____ to the Islamic Empire.
8. Medievalists reading and writing about and around authority- related themes lack clear definitions of its actual meanings in the medieval _____.
9. Wars and _____ have been the important adaptive choices in preindustrial society.
10. The Medieval period in the western history _____ Ming dynasty in China.

Task 3 Translation

Directions: *Translate the following sentences into English.*
1. 西方历史将中世纪视为中间时期,在古典时期和现代时期中间。
2. 西方的大多数国家都采纳了现存的罗马制度法规;与此同时,基督教在西欧国家传播发展,修道院也随之建立。
3. 中世纪中期,技术和农业上的创新使得贸易兴盛、农作物增产,因此欧洲人口迅猛增加。
4. 中世纪晚期充满困难和灾祸,例如饥荒、瘟疫和战争,这些灾难都使得西欧人口大幅减少。
5. 公元476年被普遍认为是中世纪的起始时间。

Unit 3　The Middle Ages and the Rise of Modern Europe

Task 4

Directions: *Read the following excerpt and fill in the blanks with words shown in the word box.*

| toll | authority | estimated | symptoms |
| sufferers | abandonment | Black Death | severe |

　　The disease was caused by a bacillus bacteria and carried by fleas on rodents. It was known as the ___1___ because it could turn the skin and sores black while other ___2___ included fever and joint pains. With up to two-thirds of ___3___ dying from the disease, it is ___4___ that between 30% and 50% of the population of those places affected died from the Black Death. The death ___5___ was so high that it had ___6___ consequences on European medieval society as a whole, with a shortage of farmers resulting in demands for an end to serfdom（农奴）, a general questioning of ___7___ and rebellions, and the entire ___8___ of many towns and villages. The worst plague in human history, it would take 200 years for the population of Europe to recover to the level seen prior to the Black Death.

Section B　The Rise of the States

　　The second stage of the Middle Ages was the formative period in the history of the Western states. Kings in France, England and Spain consolidated their power, and set up lasting governing institutions. New kingdoms such as Hungary and Poland, after their conversion to Christianity, became Central European powers. ① Between 1000 and 1300, drastic political, economic, and social change occurred in Europe. Not only did trade revive, cities grow, and a new bourgeois social class emerge, but in several regions kings enforced their power at the expense of the nobility, and strong centralized government was realized in several regions of Europe.

　　② The growth of trade and commerce to national and international scale is one of the impressive achievements of the High Middle Ages. The revitalization of trade and commerce, coupled with a revival of urban life, helped foster the growth of the bourgeoisie, or middle class. Political and economic change, of course, had a direct impact on the culture of the High Middle Ages. In these years, the Church reached the peak of its power, and religion played a crucial role in the development and definition of medieval intellectual life.

　　After the Romans withdrew from England in the fifth century, Germanic tribes known as Anglo-Saxons invaded the island and divided it among more than a dozen hostile tribal kingdoms. ③ Gradually, rivalries among the kingdoms diminished, and the overlordship of the island was held in turn by different rulers. In addition to being a successful warrior, Alfred the Great made

Charlemagne

notable contributions to the creation of a stronger nation. He reorganized the militia of freemen so that some were always ready for battle while the rest tilled the soil, and the ships he built to repel future Viking attacks won for him the title of founder of the English navy. Alfred also advanced the intellectual life of his country, inviting scholars from the Continent to the palace school he founded. He also encouraged monks to keep an account of current affairs, the Anglo-Saxon Chronicle, which continued to be written for hundreds of years after his reign.

For France, the High Middle Ages was also an important era of building foundations for the future. Unlike other rulers, French kings were quite successful in forming the basis of a future absolute monarchy. ④ Charlemagne continued his father's policy towards the papacy and became its protector. He also campaigned against the peoples to his east, forcibly Christianizing them along the way (especially the Saxons), eventually subjecting them to his rule after a protracted war. Charlemagne reached the height of his power in 800 when he was crowned as "Emperor" by the Pope. Called the "Father of Europe," Charlemagne's empire united most of Western Europe for the first time since the Roman Empire. His rule spurred the Carolingian Renaissance, a revival of art, religion, and culture through the medium of the Catholic Church.

⑤ Through his foreign conquests and internal reforms, Charlemagne encouraged the formation of a common European identity. Both the French and German monarchies considered their kingdoms to be descendants of Charlemagne's empire. By the tenth century AD, the process of medieval empire building had reached its height. The German and Frankish kings held great power and prestige. The Germanic king Otto I provided the best example of emergent monarchy.

However, the eleventh century soon witnessed a reversal in church-state relations. Spurred by the reform movement of Cluny, the church underwent a considerable revival. During the pontificate of Innocent III, he made the church stronger and involved in secular issues. ⑥ The long contest for European supremacy between France and England began in this era with the Norman conquest of Anglo-Saxon England.

(617 words)

Unit 3 The Middle Ages and the Rise of Modern Europe

New Words and Expressions (B)

New Words

New Words	Phonetic Symbols	Meanings
absolute	[ˌæbsəˈluːt]	adj. 完全的, 纯粹的
bourgeois	[ˈbʊəʒwɑː]	adj. 资产阶级的
consolidate	[kənˈsɒlɪdeɪt]	v. 巩固, 加强
conversion	[kənˈvɜː(r)ʃ(ə)n]	n. 皈依
crucial	[ˈkruːʃ(ə)l]	adj. 极其重要的
drastic	[ˈdræstɪk]	adj. 激烈的
emergent	[ɪˈmɜːdʒənt]	adj. 新兴的
foster	[ˈfɒstə(r)]	v. 促进, 培养
Frankish	[ˈfræŋkɪʃ]	adj. 法兰克人的
Germanic	[dʒɜː(r)ˈmænɪk]	adj. 日耳曼的
identity	[aɪˈdentɪti]	n. 身份; 特征
impressive	[ɪmˈpresɪv]	adj. 可观的
institution	[ˌɪnstɪˈtjuːʃ(ə)n]	n. 机构, 制度
internal	[ɪnˈtɜː(r)n(ə)l]	adj. 内部的, 内在的
militia	[məˈlɪʃə]	n. 民兵
monarchy	[ˈmɒnə(r)ki]	n. 君主政体
overlordship	[ˈəʊvə(r)ˌlɔː(r)dʃɪp]	n. 封建君主的权位
papacy	[ˈpeɪpəsi]	n. 罗马天主教教皇制度
pontificate	[pɒnˈtɪfɪkeɪt]	n. 教皇的职务或在任期间
protracted	[prəˈtræktɪd]	adj. 旷日持久的
reversal	[rɪˈvɜː(r)s(ə)l]	n. 逆转, 颠倒
revitalization	[ˌriːˌvaɪtəlaɪˈzeɪʃn]	n. 振兴
scale	[skeɪl]	n. 规模, 范围
secular	[ˈsekjʊlə(r)]	adj. 世俗的; 非宗教的
spur	[spɜː(r)]	v. 促进; 推动
supremacy	[sʊˈpreməsi]	n. 霸权
urban	[ˈɜː(r)bən]	adj. 城市的

Expressions

at the expense of	以……为代价
in turn	依次
involve in	卷入；参与
subject... to	使……服从
coupled with	加上

Proper Names

Alfred the Great	阿尔弗雷德大帝，英格兰盎格鲁-撒克逊时期韦塞克斯王朝的国王
Anglo-Saxons	盎格鲁-撒克逊人，日耳曼民族盎格鲁人、撒克逊人和朱特人的一支，5世纪和6世纪居住在英国。
the Carolingian Renaissance	卡洛林文艺复兴，发生在公元8世纪晚期至9世纪，由查理大帝及其后继者在欧洲推行的文艺与科学的复兴运动，被称为"欧洲的第一次觉醒"。卡洛林文艺复兴的标志之一是开始了基督教教义和宗教活动的初步规范工作。
Charlemagne	查理曼(742—814)，法兰克国王(768—814)，罗马灭亡后西欧第一个帝国的创始人
Hungary	匈牙利
Innocent III	英诺森三世(1160—1216)，罗马教皇(1198—1216在位)，在巴黎大学攻读神学。1198年当选教皇。在位期间教廷权势达到历史上的顶峰。
Otto I	奥托一世(912.11.23—973.3.23)，德意志萨克森王朝第二代东法兰克国王(936—973)，兼意大利国王，神圣罗马帝国奠基人和首任皇帝(962—973)，被后世尊称为奥托大帝。
Reform of Cluny	克吕尼改革，是中世纪修道运动中的一系列改革，关注于恢复传统的修道的生活，鼓励艺术，照顾穷人。该运动是因位于法国勃艮第地区的克吕尼隐修院而得名。

Difficult Sentences

① Between 1000 and 1300, drastic political, economic, and social change occurred in Europe. Not only did trade revive, cities grow, and a new bourgeois social class emerge, but in several regions kings enforced their power at the expense of the nobility, and strong centralized government was realized in several regions of Europe.
在1000到1300年间，欧洲经历了政治、经济和社会上的剧变。不仅贸易复苏、城市发展、新兴的资产阶级正在崛起，而且在许多地方，国王牺牲了贵族的利益来强行实施自己的

Unit 3　The Middle Ages and the Rise of Modern Europe

权力,这使得欧洲一些地区出现了强有力的集权政府。

② The growth of trade and commerce to national and international scale is one of the impressive achievements of the High Middle Ages. The revitalization of trade and commerce, coupled with a revival of urban life, helped foster the growth of the bourgeoisie, or middle class.

中世纪中期重大的成就之一就是商业贸易在国家内部和国家之间的增长。商贸活动的重振与城镇生活的复苏为资产阶级(或曰中产阶级)的成长提供了条件。

③ Gradually, rivalries among the kingdoms diminished, and the over-lordship of the island was held in turn by the different rulers. In addition to being a successful warrior, Alfred the Great made notable contributions to the creation of a stronger nation. He reorganized the militia of freemen so that some were always ready for battle while the rest tilled the soil, and the ships he built to repel future Viking attacks won for him the title of founder of the English navy.

王国之间的争斗逐渐消失,对该岛的统治权在不同的统治者之间更迭。阿尔弗雷德大帝不仅是一名骁勇的战士,而且为建立一个强大的国家做出了不可磨灭的贡献。他重新组建了民兵组织,如此一来国内总有一部分自由民随时做好战斗的准备,而其他人则可以照常耕作。他修建的船只在未来抵抗维京人攻击的战役中派上了用场,这为他赢得了英国海军之父的美名。

④ Charlemagne continued his father's policy towards the papacy and became its protector. He also campaigned against the peoples to his east, forcibly Christianizing them along the way (especially the Saxons), eventually subjecting them to his rule after a protracted war.

查理曼大帝延续了其父对教皇的政策,并成为了教皇制的保护者。此外,他还强迫东部的诸民族(尤其是撒克逊人)信奉基督教,发动了旷日持久的战争最终使他们服从自己的管辖。

⑤ Through his foreign conquests and internal reforms, Charlemagne encouraged the formation of a common European identity. Both the French and German monarchies considered their kingdoms to be descendants of Charlemagne's empire.

查理曼大帝对外征战,对内改革,促使欧洲人形成欧洲这一概念。法国与德国的君主政体均将自己的王国视为查理曼帝国的继承者。

⑥ The long contest for European supremacy between France and England began in this era with the Norman conquest of Anglo-Saxon England.

诺曼底公爵征服了盎格鲁-撒克逊英国,英法两国自此为欧洲的霸权展开了旷日持久的争夺。

Exercises

Task 1 Reading Comprehension

Directions: *Read the passage again and judge whether the following statements are true (T), false (F) or not given (NG).*

True   if the statement agrees with the information mentioned in the passage
False   if the statement contradicts the information mentioned in the passage
Not Given   if there is no information on this in the passage

1. Because of the revival of trade and commerce, the bourgeoisies began to take over the power of nobility.
2. In the High Middle Ages, Europeans did business not only with people in their own country, but with those in neighboring countries, too.
3. For most intellectuals in the High Middle Ages, theology was an important part in their work and study.
4. The island of England had been a united nation ever since the Roman Era.
5. Alfred the Great advanced the intellectual life of England by promoting many renowned scholars from the Church.
6. As can be inferred from the text, many European rulers failed in forming the basis of a future absolute monarchy.
7. The Anglo-Saxon England was Christianized by Charlemagne.
8. After the fall of Roman Empire and before the Charlemagne's empire, most of Western Europe had been under feudal separations.
9. In the 900s, popes started to gain more power than kings.
10. Alfred the Great, Charlemagne and Otto I are all powerful kings in Western Europe.

Task 2 Vocabulary

Directions: *Complete the following summary of the passages with proper words from the box. Change the form if necessary.*

| Hungary | emperor | spur | crucial | emerge |
| monarch | converse | center | Germany | revive |

The states arose in Europe as a result of the revival of trade and commerce, and gradually realized (1) _____ governments. During the High Middle Ages, the Western states started to come into beings. New kingdoms such as (2) _____ and Poland, after their (3) _____ to Christianity, became Central European powers. Charlemagne, the father of Europe, built a great (4) _____ in Western Europe and helped to establish a strong Europe. The (5) _____ king Otto I provides the best example of (6) _____ (7) _____. (8) _____ by the reform movement of Cluny, the church underwent a considerable (9) _____. Alfred the

Unit 3　The Middle Ages and the Rise of Modern Europe

Great helped to create a strong nation in England and advanced the intellectual life of his country. Religion played a (10) _____ role in the development and definition of medieval intellectual life.

Task 3　Translation

Directions: *Complete the following sentences by translating the Chinese in brackets into English.*

1. The second stage of the Middle Ages was _____ (形成阶段) in the history of the Western state.
2. After the Romans withdrew from England in the fifth century, Germanic tribes known as Anglo-Saxons invaded the island and divided it among _____ (十几个敌对的部落王国).
3. He also encouraged monks to _____ (记录) current affairs, the Anglo-Saxon Chronicle, which continued to be written for hundreds of years after his reign.
4. His rule _____ (刺激了) the Carolingian Renaissance, a revival of art, religion, and culture through the medium of the Catholic Church.
5. However, the eleventh Century soon witnessed a _____ (翻转) in church-state relations.

Task 4　Further Development

Directions: *Read the following passage on the famous Battle of Hastings, the battle that defined the Norman Conquest. Fill the blanks with the most accurate words. After completing the exercise, write a report on the Battle of Hastings with the information you have searched over the internet.*

　　The Battle of Hastings was to (1)_____ the future of Medieval England. However, the battle took place about seven miles from Hastings—so in many (2)_____ it is misnamed. Why, then was the Battle of Hastings so-called? In 1066, Battle was an important area. Compared to other parts of Sussex, Battle was wealthy. However, the title Battle of Battle would not have worked, and (3)_____ convenience sake, the nearest large town was selected — Hastings. The battle itself was fought (4)_____ the current Battle Abbey — however, the main (5)_____ of the battle concerned Harold's position on Senlac Hill, a short distance from the current abbey. Why was Battle so important? In the 11th century, the coastline of Sussex was different to (6)_____ of today. The coast was nearer to Battle than it is today and the only (7)_____ "road" that linked Hastings to London went through Battle. If Harold had (8)_____ at Battle, William would have great difficulties (9)_____ his campaign. If William won, he would have control of the only (10)_____ "road" to London — the heart of England.

　　1. A. aspect　　　　B. shape　　　　C. figure　　　　D. form
　　2. A. connection　　B. extent　　　　C. respects　　　D. regard
　　3. A. by　　　　　　B. to　　　　　　C. as　　　　　　D. for
　　4. A. by　　　　　　B. to　　　　　　C. as　　　　　　D. for
　　5. A. throw　　　　 B. push　　　　　C. stick　　　　　D. thrust

6. A. that	B. which	C. what	D. where
7. A. main	B. most	C. major	D. more
8. A. held up	B. held out	C. held on	D. held in
9. A. maintaining	B. sustaining	C. preserving	D. obtaining
10. A. smooth	B. steep	C. proper	D. major

Section C The Rise of Universities in the Middle Ages

The Middle Ages of Europe is usually regarded as a "dark period" by many historians, but it is this dark period that gave birth to the university. The European university in the Middle Ages, in terms of educational conception and curricula, inherited from both oriental and western civilization, especially ancient Greece, ancient Rome and Arabian world and characterized the early form of university.

Establishment of the University

The first institutions generally considered to be universities were established in Italy, France, Spain and England in the late 11th and the 12th centuries for the study of arts, law, medicine, and theology. ① These universities evolved from much older Christian cathedral schools and monastic schools, and it is difficult to define the date at which they became true universities. Universities were formalized when they were granted charters. The University of Bologna can trace its origins back to the late 11th century and received its charter in the 12th century.

Other early universities established in Europe include the University of Paris in France and Oxford in England. Before 1500 more than eighty universities were established in Western and Central Europe. During the subsequent Colonization of the Americas the university was introduced to the New World, marking the beginning of its worldwide spread as the center of higher learning everywhere.

Characteristics

② The university of the Middle Ages was not entirely unlike the modern institution that we are familiar with today, in that its ostensible goal was to train the next generation of young minds for a career—in this case, the church.

Initially the universities of the Middle Ages did not have physical facilities such as the campus of a modern university. Classes were taught wherever space was available, such as churches and homes. A university was not a physical space but a collection of individuals banded together as a universitas. Soon, however, some universities (such as Cambridge) began to rent, buy or construct buildings specifically for the purposes of teaching.

Universities were generally structured along three types, depending on who paid the teachers. The first type was in Bologna, where students hired and paid for the teachers. The second type was in Paris, where teachers were paid by the church. The third type, such as Oxford and Cambridge, was predominantly supported by the crown and the state. These structural differences created other characteristics. At the Bologna University the students ran everything—a fact that often put teachers under great pressure and disadvantage. In Paris, teachers ran the school; thus Paris became the premier spot for teachers from all over Europe. In Bologna, where students chose more secular studies, the main subject was law. Latin was the language of instruction throughout the Middle Ages, and beyond.

Curriculum and Degree

University studies took six years for a Master of Arts degree (a Bachelor of Arts degree could be awarded along the way), which entitled a scholar to teach anywhere in Christendom. By the 13th century, almost half of the highest offices and over one-third of the second-highest offices in the Church were occupied by degreed masters. The studies for this were organized by the faculty of arts, where the seven liberal arts were taught: arithmetic, geometry, astronomy, music theory, grammar (the art of reading and writing, focusing on the psalms, other parts of the Bible, and the Latin classics), rhetoric and logic. The primary emphasis was on logic.

A popular textbook for university study was called *The Sentences*; theology students and masters were required to write extensive commentaries on this text as part of their curriculum. ③ Once a Master of Arts degree had been conferred, the student could leave the university or pursue further studies in one of the higher faculties, law, medicine, or theology, the last one being the most prestigious.

Merton College Library, Oxford

④ Courses were not elective: the course offerings were set, and everyone had to take the same courses. There were, however, occasional choices as to which teacher to use.

Social Life

The social life at the medieval university was also quite similar to today's system. ⑤ Their rules and regulations set up provisions against gambling, flamboyant dress, staying up to all hours, and associating with loose women. However, students were afforded the legal protection of the clergy. In

Peterhouse, Cambridge

this way no one was allowed to physically harm them; they could only be tried for crimes in a church court, and were thus immune from any corporal punishment. As a result, this produced many abuses: theft, rape and murder were not uncommon among students. And as much as modern-day professors may complain, 21st-century students who stay up late drinking in pubs are doing no more than following the tradition established by their forebears.

Significance of the Universities during the Middle Ages

❻ The development of universities during the Middle Ages provided and still provides an important center for scholarship and intellectual exchange. It has a profound influence on the modern university and the formation of prototype of higher educational system. The modern disciplines of the sciences are particularly deeply rooted within this academic hierarchy that was initially developed in the Middle Ages.

(956 words)

New Words and Expressions (C)

New Words

New Words	Phonetic Symbols	Meanings
arithmetic	[ˌærɪθˈmetɪk]	n. 算术
astronomy	[əˈstrɒnəmi]	n. 天文学
cathedral	[kəˈθiːdrəl]	n. 主教堂; adj. 天主教的
characterize	[ˈkærɪktəraɪz]	v. 表现……的特色
charter	[ˈtʃɑː(r)tə(r)]	n. 许可证, 执照
confer	[kənˈfɜː(r)]	v. 授予
corporal	[ˈkɔː(r)p(ə)rəl]	adj. 肉体的, 身体的
curriculum	[kəˈrɪkjʊləm]	n. (全部)课程
discipline	[ˈdɪsəplɪn]	n. 学科
entitle	[ɪnˈtaɪt(ə)l]	v. 给予……资格
evolve	[ɪˈvɒlv]	v. 进化, 发展
facility	[fəˈsɪləti]	n. 设备
faculty	[ˈfæk(ə)lti]	n. 大学的院, 系
flamboyant	[flæmˈbɔɪənt]	adj. 华丽的
formalize	[ˈfɔː(r)məlaɪz]	v. 使……正式化; 定型
geometry	[dʒiːˈɒmətri]	n. 几何学
hierarchy	[ˈhaɪəˌrɑː(r)ki]	n. 等级制度; 层次体系

Unit 3 The Middle Ages and the Rise of Modern Europe

intellectual	[ˌɪntəˈlektʃuəl]	adj. 知识的,智力的,脑力的
ostensible	[ɒˈstensəb(ə)l]	adj. 表面上的,貌似的
physical	[ˈfɪzɪk(ə)l]	adj. 物质的,有形的
predominantly	[prɪˈdɒmɪnəntli]	adv. 主要地
premier	[ˈpremɪə(r)]	adj. 首位的,首次的
prototype	[ˈprəʊtətaɪp]	n. 标准,蓝本,典型
provision	[prəˈvɪʒn]	n. 规定,条款
psalm	[sɑːm]	n. 赞美诗
rhetoric	[ˈretərɪk]	n. 修辞
scholarship	[ˈskɒlə(r)ʃɪp]	n. 学问,学识
specifically	[spəˈsɪfɪkli]	adv. 专门地

Expressions

be immune from	不受……的影响
entitle sb. to do sth	使某人有权或有资格做某事
have a profound influence on	对……有极大的影响
give birth to	产生
no more than	不过;只是
stay up late	熬夜
trace...back to...	回溯到

Proper Names

Bologna [bəˈləʊnjə]	博洛尼亚,意大利城市
seven liberal arts	文科七艺:包括语法、修辞和逻辑三艺及算术、几何、天文和音乐四艺
Sentences	【逻辑学】命题
universitas	(拉丁文)联合体

① These universities evolved from much older Christian cathedral schools and monastic schools, and it is difficult to define the date at which they became true universities. Universities were formalized when they were granted charters.

这些大学是从早期的基督教教堂学校和修道院学校发展而来,它们何时成为真正意义上的大学,时间很难确定。大学获得办学许可证后,才能成为正式的教育机构。

② The university of the Middle Ages was not entirely unlike the modern institution that we are familiar with today, in that its ostensible goal was to train the next generation of young minds for a career—in this case, the church.

中世纪的大学与我们所熟悉的现代教育机构并非迥然不同,毕竟它名义上的教学目标是培养下一代,使他们能够为某个事业工作,在中世纪的语境下,这个事业指为教会服务。

③ Once a Master of Arts degree had been conferred, the student could leave the university or pursue further studies in one of the higher faculties, law, medicine, or theology, the last one being the most prestigious.

一旦获得了文学硕士学位,学生可以离开大学,或者在法律、医学、神学中选择一门继续深造,这其中神学最受推崇。

④ Courses were not elective: the course offerings were set, and everyone had to take the same courses. There were, however, occasional choices as to which teacher to use.

学生不能自选课程。大学提供的课程都是固定的,每个人学的课程都一样。不过偶尔会有机会选择任课教师。

⑤ Their rules and regulations set up provisions against gambling, flamboyant dress, staying up to all hours, and associating with loose women. Students were afforded the legal protection of the clergy.

大学的校规规定不许赌博,不得身着奢华服饰,不许熬夜,不许与不正经的妇女有染。学生受教会保护。

⑥ The development of universities during the Middle Ages provided and still provides an important center for scholarship and intellectual exchange. It has a profound influence on the modern university and the formation of prototype of higher educational system. The modern disciplines of the sciences are particularly deeply rooted within this academic hierarchy that was initially developed in the Middle Ages.

中世纪大学的形成发展不仅在当时为学术和思想交流提供了一个重要的阵地,现在也依然如此。它对现代大学和高等教育体系标准的形成具有深远的影响。尤其是现代自然科学学科,深深根植于中世纪发展起来的学术体系当中。

Exercises

Task 1　Short Answer Questions

Directions: *Work in pairs to answer the following questions.*

1. What are the prototypes of univercities?
2. In what language was the textbooks for Medieval university students probably written?
3. Where did the teachers get their salary from?
4. What course would Medieval university students take?
5. After graduation, what kind of job might the students get?

Task 2　Vocabulary

Directions: *Complete the following sentences with proper words based on what are given in the brackets after the sentences. Change the form if necessary.*

(1) In terms of educational conception and curricula, the European university of the Middle Ages is the _____ of both oriental and western civilization. (heir)

(2) When the Americas were _____, the university was introduced to the New World. (colony)

(3) At the Bologna University, students ran the school, and the teachers were put under great _____ . (advantage)

(4) A university graduate who had obtained a Master of Arts degree would be _____ to teach anywhere in Christendom. (title)

(5) Theology students and masters were required to write _____ commentaries on the Sentences. (extend)

(6) Most courses in a university in the Middle Ages were set, but teachers may became _____ exceptions. (occasion)

(7) The rules and regulations set up _____ against gambling and staying up to all hours. (provide)

(8) University students were _____ from any corporal punishment. (immune)

(9) The development of universities during the Middle Ages provided an important center for scholarship and intellectual _____. (exchange)

(10) The modern disciplines of the sciences are particularly deeply rooted within this academic _____. (hierarchical)

Task 3　Translation

Directions: *Complete the following sentences by translating the Chinese in brackets into English.*

1. During the subsequent Colonization of the Americas the university was introduced to the New World, _____ (标志着它全球性的扩张) as the center of higher learning everywhere.

2. Classes were taught _____(无论能够在哪儿找到地方), such as churches and homes.

3. Universities were generally structured along three types, _____ (取决于谁付给教师酬劳).

4. In this way no one was allowed to physically harm them; _____ (他们只会因为犯罪在教会法庭受罚), and were thus immune from any corporal punishment.

5. It _____ (对……具有深远影响) on the modern university and the formation of prototype of higher educational system.

Task 4 Further Development

Directions: Discuss with your classmates and try to finish the table below. The first line is filled.

	Medieval university	Modern western university	Modern Chinese university
Source of Finance	Students/Church/King	Private sector/Government	Government/Private sector/Students
Campus			
Courses			
Degrees			
Career Opportunity			
Student Life			

Adages and Proverbs

1. Dominus illuminatio mea (The Lord is my light)　　　　—Slogan of Oxford
   上主是我的亮光。　　　　——牛津大学校训

2. Hinc lucem et pocula sacra (From here, light and sacred draughts).
   　　　　—Slogan of Cambridge
   此地乃启蒙之所，智识之源。　　　　—— 剑桥大学校训

3. When the words come, they are merely empty shells without the music. They live as they are sung, for the words are the body and the music the spirit.
   ——Hildegard von Bingen, German composer
   当话语出现时，没有音乐，它们只是空壳。它们在被唱的过程中活着，因为歌词是身体，音乐是精神。
   ——圣希尔德加德·冯·宾根

4. Knowledge is power. —Francis Bacon (1561—1626) English essay writer, philosopher and politician, the founder of classic empiricism

Unit 3　The Middle Ages and the Rise of Modern Europe

知识就是力量。　　　　　　　　　　　　　　　　　　——弗兰西斯·培根

5. Nothing is terrible except fear itself.　　　　　　　—Francis Bacon
除了恐惧本身以外,没有任何东西更值得害怕。　　　　——弗兰西斯·培根

6. To have another language is to possess a second soul.
　　　　　　　　—Charlemagne (742—841), the Frankish king in the Medieval time
掌握另一种语言如同获得第二个灵魂。　　　　　　　　——查理曼大帝

7. Friendship is the source of the greatest pleasures, and without friends even the most agreeable pursuits become tedious.　—Thomas Aquinas (1225—1274), Medieval scholar
友谊为无上幸福之源,人若无友,最有趣的探索也会索然无味。　——托马斯·阿奎纳

8. God does not judge you according to your bodies and appearances, but He looks into your hearts and observes your deeds.　　—Muhammad (570—632), Islamic prophet
真主不以肉身样貌鉴人,而是直视内心,考察行为。　　　　——穆罕默德

9. Time and tide wait for no man.　　—Geoffrey Chaucer (1343—1400), English poet
时间如潮水,二者皆不等人(时不我待)。　　　　　　　　——杰弗里·乔叟

10. The human heart is as a frail craft on which we wish to reach the stars.
　　　　　　　　　　　　　　　—Giotto (1266—1337), Italian artist & sculptor
人心如易碎的艺术品,我愿藉此摘星辰。　　　　　　　　　　——乔托

11. Following the light of the sun, we left the Old World.
　　　　　　　　　　　—Christopher Columbus (1451—1506), Italian navigator
追随日光,我们离开了旧世界。　　　　　　　　　　——克里斯托弗·哥伦布

12. [Of the Black Death:] How many valiant men, how many fair ladies, breakfast with their kinfolk and the same night supped with their ancestors in the next world!
　　　　　　　　　—Giovanni Boccaccio (1313—1375), Humanist writer and poet
【黑死病】多少勇敢的绅士和高贵的淑女,清晨还与家人共进早餐,晚上就赴阴曹地府与祖宗们晚宴去了。　　　　　　　　　　　　　　　　——乔万尼·薄伽丘

13. I would rather die than do something which I know to be a sin, or to be against God's will.
　　　　　　　　　　　—Joan of Arc (1412—1431), French military leader
让我行罪恶之事或者违背上帝的旨意,不如让我死了。　　　　——圣女贞德

14. Whatever else the Norman Conquest may or may not have done, it made the old haphazard state of legal affairs forever impossible.　—Edward Jenks, British historian
如果说诺曼征服带来了什么结果的话,那就是它让旧有的松散随意的法治体制荡然无存了。　　　　　　　　　　　　　　　　　　　　　　——爱德华·詹金斯

15. We believe that the very beginning and end of salvation, and the sum of Christianity, consists of faith in Christ, who by His blood alone, and not by any works of ours, has put away sin, and destroyed the power of death.

—Martin Luther (1483—1546), Religious Reformer

我们确信,救赎的开端与结束以及基督教的所有意义都存在于对耶稣的信念。他以他的血消除了罪恶,对抗死亡之威力,而我们什么都没有做。 ——马丁·路德

Key to Unit 3 Exercises

导读答案

1. The Middle Ages is the middle period of the traditional division of Western history into Classical, Medieval, and Modern periods.

2. During most time of the Middle Ages, Europe was involved in continuous wars and religious conflicts. The ordinary people suffered from poverty while the Church censored any products of arts and science. Most importantly, the Late Middle Ages were marked by difficulties and calamities, such as famine, plague, and war, which much diminished the population of Western Europe; between 1347 and 1350, the Black Death killed approximately a third of the European population.

3. The first institutions generally considered to be universities were established in Italy, France, Spain and England in the late 11th and the 12th centuries for the study of arts, law, medicine, and theology. These universities evolved from much older Christian cathedral schools and monastic schools, and it is difficult to define the date at which they became true universities. Universities were formalized when they were granted charters.

Section A

Task 1 Reading Comprehension

1. C   2. B   3. D   4. C   5. A

Task 2 Vocabulary

1. surrender	2. revolt	3. monasteries	4. incorporated	5. preach
6. endure	7. calamity	8. context	9. depopulation	10. paralleled

Task 3 Translation

1. The Middle Ages is the middle period in the view of Western history, between the Classical and Modern periods.

Unit 3 The Middle Ages and the Rise of Modern Europe

2. In the West, most kingdoms incorporated extant Roman institutions, while monasteries were founded as Christianity expanded in Western Europe.
3. During the High Middle Ages, the population of Europe increased greatly as technological and agricultural innovations allowed trade to flourish and crop yields to increase.
4. The Late Middle Ages was marked by difficulties and calamities, such as famine, plague, and war, which much diminished the population of Western Europe.
5. The most commonly given start date for the Middle Ages is 476.

Task 4
1. Black Death   2. symptoms   3. sufferers   4. estimated
5. toll   6. severe   7. authority   8. abandonment

Section B
Task 1 Reading Comprehension
1. F   2. T   3. T   4. F   5. F   6. T   7. F   8. T   9. NG   10. T

Task 2 Vocabulary
1. centralized   2. Hungary   3. conversion   4. empire   5. Germanic
6. emergent   7. monarchy   8. Spurred   9. revival   10. crucial

Task 3 Translation
1. the formative period   2. more than a dozen hostile tribal kingdoms
3. keep an account of   4. spurred   5. reversal/reverse

Task 4 Further development
1. B   2. C   3. D   4. A   5. D   6. A   7. C   8. B   9. B   10. C

Section C
Task 1 Short Answer Questions
1. Christian cathedral schools and monastic schools
2. Latin.
3. Students, the Church or the State.
4. Arithmetic, geometry, astronomy, music theory, grammar (the art of reading and writing, focusing on the psalms, other parts of the Bible, and the Latin classics, rhetoric and logic).
5. A place in the church is ideal.

Task 2 Vocabulary
1. heritage   2. colonized   3. disadvantage   4. entitled   5. extensive
6. occasional   7. provisions   8. immune   9. exchange   10. hierarchy

Task 3 Translation

1. marking the beginning of its worldwide spread
2. wherever space was available
3. depending on who paid the teachers
4. they could only be tried for crimes in a church court
5. has a profound influence

Task 4 Further Development

Direction: discuss with your classmates and try to finish the table below. The first line is filled.

	Medieval university	Modern western university	Modern Chinese university
Source of Finance	*Students/Church/King*	*Private sector/Government*	*Government/Private sector/Students*
Campus	random places	with physical facilities	an allocated piece of walled land
Courses	Arithmetic, geometry, astronomy, music theory, grammar (the art of reading and writing, focusing on the psalms, other parts of the Bible, and the Latin classics, rhetoric and logic	a variety of courses covering almost all areas in human knowledge	a variety of courses covering almost all areas in human knowledge
Degrees	Bachelor/Master/Doctor	Bachelor/Master/Doctor	Bachelor/Master/Doctor
Career Opportunity	church	all kinds of jobs	all kinds of jobs
Student Life	Their rules and regulations set up provisions against gambling, flamboyant dress, staying up to all hours, and associating with loose women.	Churches have no power over modern student life, but students are still regulated by laws and college institutions. The life of college students is much more sophisticated than that of their ancestors.	Students are still regulated by laws and college institutions. The life of college students is much more sophisticated than that of their ancestors.

Unit 4

Renaissance and Shakespeare

导 读

本单元旨在通过对西方文艺复兴、莎士比亚等知识的介绍,使学生对该时期所发生的重要事件有基本的了解,开阔视野,能够运用所学西方文化知识及相关的英语表达方式进行文化交流,并为今后的深入学习和研究奠定基础。

Before You Start

While preparing for this unit, think about the following questions:
1. How much do you know about Renaissance, Humanism, and Shakespeare?
2. What do you know about Henry VIII and his marriages?

Section A Renaissance

"Renaissance," literally meaning "rebirth" in French, was a cultural movement that profoundly affected European intellectual life in the early modern period. Beginning in Italy in the 14th century, and spreading to the rest of Europe by the 16th century, its influence was felt in literature, philosophy, art, music, politics, science, religion, and other aspects of intellectual inquiry. During this period, there was an enormous renewal of interest in and study of classical antiquity.

Yet the Renaissance was more than a "rebirth." It was also an age of new discoveries, both geographical (exploration of the New World) and intellectual. Both kinds of discovery resulted in changes of tremendous importance for Western civilization. ① In science, for example, Copernicus attempted to prove that the sun rather than the earth was at the center of the planetary system, thus radically altering the cosmic world view that had dominated antiquity and the Middle Ages. ② In religion, Martin Luther challenged and ultimately caused the division of one of the major institutions that had united Europe throughout the Middle Ages—the Church. In fact, Renaissance thinkers often thought of themselves as ushering in the modern age, as distinct from the ancient and medieval eras.

③ Humanism gave renewed emphasis to life in this world instead of to the otherworldly, spiritual life associated with the Middle Ages. Renaissance humanists placed great emphasis upon the dignity of man and upon the expanded possibilities of human life in this world. Reviving the study of Greek and Roman history, philosophy, and arts, ④ the Renaissance humanists developed an image of "Man" more positive and hopeful than that of medieval ascetic Christianity. ⑤ Rather than being a miserable sinner awaiting redemption from a pit of fleshly corruption, "Man" was a source of infinite possibilities.

In the terms used in the Renaissance itself, humanism represented a shift from the "contemplative life" to the "active life." ⑥ In the Middle Ages, great value had often been attached to the life of contemplation and religious devotion, away from the world. In the Renaissance, the highest cultural values were usually associated with active involvement in public life, in moral, political, and military action, and in service to the state. Of course, the traditional religious values coexisted with the new secular values; in fact, some of the most important Humanists, like Desiderius Erasmus, were Churchmen. Also, individual achievement, breadth of knowledge, and personal aspiration (as personified by Doctor Faustus) were valued. ⑦ The concept of the "Renaissance Man" refers to an individual who, in addition to participating actively in the affairs of public life, possesses knowledge of and skill in many subject areas. Such figures included Leonardo Da Vinci and John Milton as well as Francis Bacon, who had declared, "I have taken all knowledge to be my province."

Francesco Petrarch

Francesco Petrarch was born in 1304 near Florence and is known as the first great humanist. He was raised in Italy but traveled widely collecting ancient texts. One can see the urban emphasis in his teachings and his emphasis in the experiences of daily life like climbing mountains or traveling. Petrarch was pulled between two worlds, the ideal world of antiquity and his desire to improve the current world. He believed he could learn to make the world a better place by studying classical literature. He, along with other humanists, admired the formal beauty of classical writing. He attempted to share the teachings of classical texts by studying them, and then, imitating them in Latin writings of his own.

Petrarch contributed to a new outlook: one of secular passion and hunger for knowledge. ⑧ This attitude spread, increasing the search for lost works and increasing the number of volumes in circulation, in turn influencing more people with classical ideas. One other major result was a renewed trade in manuscripts and the foundation of public libraries to better enable widespread study. Print then enabled an explosion in the reading and spread of texts.

(649 words)

Unit 4　Renaissance and Shakespeare

New Words and Expressions (A)

New Words

New Words	Phonetic Symbols	Meanings
alter	[ˈɔːltə]	v. 改变，更改
ascetic	[əˈsetɪk]	adj. 苦行的；禁欲主义的
coexist	[ˌkəʊɪɡˈzɪst]	v. 共存；和平共处
contemplative	[kənˈtemplətɪv]	adj. 沉思的；冥想的
cosmic	[ˈkɒzmɪk]	adj. 宇宙的
fleshly	[ˈfleʃli]	adj. 肉体的；肉欲的
infinite	[ˈɪnfɪnət]	adj. 无限的，无穷的
institution	[ˌɪnstɪˈtjuːʃ(ə)n]	n. (社会或宗教等)公共机构；制度；建立
manuscript	[ˈmænjʊskrɪpt]	n. 手稿；原稿
otherworldly	[ˌʌðəˈwɜːldli]	adj. 来世的；超脱尘俗的
personify	[pəˈsɒnɪfaɪ]	v. 使人格化；赋与……以人性
pit	[pɪt]	n. 深坑
planetary	[ˈplænɪt(ə)ri]	adj. 行星的
province	[ˈprɒvɪns]	n. 领域
radically	[ˈrædɪkəli]	adv. 根本上；彻底地
rebirth	[riːˈbɜːθ]	n. 再生；复兴
redemption	[rɪˈdem(p)ʃ(ə)n]	n. 救赎
renewal	[rɪˈnjuːəl]	n. 重新开始，恢复；复兴
revive	[rɪˈvaɪv]	v. 复兴；复活

Expressions

along with	连同……一起；与……一道
attach value to	重视
in turn	依次；反过来；转而
more than	不只是
place emphasis on	重视；强调
refer to	提及，谈到；参考；涉及
usher in	开创；开启

Proper Names

Desiderius Erasmus	德西德里乌斯·伊拉斯谟(1466—1536),中世纪尼德兰(今荷兰和比利时)著名的人文主义思想家和神学家。
Doctor Faustus	浮士德博士,出自《浮士德博士的悲剧》(*The Tragical History of Doctor Faustus*),是英国剧作家克里斯托弗·马洛1588年根据浮士德传说改编的戏剧作品。
Francis Bacon	弗朗西斯·培根(1561—1626),唯物主义哲学家、散文家。
Francesco Petrarch	弗朗西斯克·彼特拉克(1304—1374),意大利学者、诗人、人文主义之父。
Humanism	人文主义
John Milton	约翰·弥尔顿(1608—1674),英国诗人、政论家、民主斗士。
Leonardo Da Vinci	列奥纳多·达·芬奇(1452—1519),天才画家、科学家、发明家。
Martin Luther	马丁·路德(1483—1546),16世纪欧洲宗教改革倡导者,基督教新教路德宗创始人。
Nicolaus Copernicus	尼古拉·哥白尼(1473—1543),波兰天文学家、数学家。

Difficult Sentences

① In science, for example, Copernicus attempted to prove that the sun rather than the earth was at the center of the planetary system, thus radically altering the cosmic world view that had dominated antiquity and the Middle Ages.

例如,在科学领域,哥白尼试图证明太阳是宇宙的中心而非地球,此举彻底改变了主宰古代和中世纪的宇宙世界观。

② In religion, Martin Luther challenged and ultimately caused the division of one of the major institutions that had united Europe throughout the Middle Ages—the Church.

在宗教领域,马丁·路德向统领中世纪欧洲的主要机构之一——教会发出了挑战,并最终导致其分裂。

③ Humanism gave renewed emphasis to life in this world instead of to the otherworldly, spiritual life associated with the Middle Ages.

人文主义开始重新强调现世的生活,而不是中世纪所专注的超世俗生活。

④ the Renaissance humanists developed an image of "Man" more positive and hopeful than that of medieval ascetic Christianity.

与中世纪基督教所提倡禁欲的人的形象相比,文艺复兴时期的人文主义者塑造了一个更加正面,充满希望的"人"的形象。

⑤ Rather than being a miserable sinner awaiting redemption from a pit of fleshly corruption, "Man" was a source of infinite possibilities.

人不再是在腐化堕落的深渊中等待救赎的悲惨罪人,而是具有无限的可能性。

⑥ In the Middle Ages, great value had often been attached to the life of contemplation and religious devotion, away from the world.

中世纪时期,沉思冥想、献身宗教和远离尘世的生活为人们所看重。

⑦ The concept of the "Renaissance Man" refers to an individual who, in addition to participating actively in the affairs of public life, possesses knowledge of and skill in many subject areas.

"文艺复兴人"的概念指除了能积极参与公共事务,还掌握多学科领域知识和技能的人。

⑧ This attitude spread, increasing the search for lost works and increasing the number of volumes in circulation, in turn influencing more people with classical ideas.

这种态度传播开来,寻找遗失作品的力度加大,流通中的书籍数目增加,相应的,受古典思想影响的人也越来越多。

Exercises

Task 1 Reading Comprehension

Directions: *Read the passage and choose the best answer to each of the following questions.*

1. Which of the following statement is true?
   A. Doctor Faustus was a typical Humanist who was ambitious and knowledgeable.
   B. The traditional religious values of the Middle Ages were totally replaced by the new secular values of the Renaissance.
   C. Petrarch endeavored to collect and study the classical texts, but he never tried to follow the example in his own writings.
   D. Renaissance Humanists emphasized the nobility of man and realized man had limited possibilities.

2. Why did Humanism highlight the life in this world rather than the life after death?
   A. Thinking about the life in the other world was too unrealistic.
   B. The renewal of study of classical works made people wiser than before.
   C. The value of "Man" as a source of infinite possibilities was acknowledged.
   D. The Humanists no longer believed in the idea that souls were saved by God.

3. Which of the following was NOT a characteristic of the "Renaissance Man"?
   A. Desiring to possess knowledge of a wide variety of subject areas.
   B. Enjoying the happiness of everyday life.
   C. Being passionate in the finding and studying of classical literature.
   D. Emphasizing one's religious devotion and piety.

4. Which of the following activities are representations of the Humanist life style?
    A. Contemplation; climbing mountains; reading classical literature.
    B. Climbing mountains; reading classical literature; trading manuscripts.
    C. Reading classical literature; trading manuscripts; contemplation.
    D. Climbing mountains; contemplation; trading manuscripts.
5. Who is considered as the first great Humanist?
    A. Desiderius Erasmus.   B. Francesco Petrarch.
    C. Francis Bacon.   D. Martin Luther.

Task 2 Vocabulary

Directions: *Complete the following sentences with proper words from the box. Change the form if necessary. Please note there are more words than necessary.*

A) antiquity	B) circulate	C) cosmic	D) emphasis	E) infinite
F) institution	G) involve	H) intellectual	I) outlook	J) possess
K) rebirth	L) secular	M) shift	N) urban	O) usher

1. Renaissance means the (1)_____ of interest in and study of ancient Greece and Rome from 14th century to mid-17th century.
2. Copernicus dramatically changed the (2)_____ world view by declaring that the sun was the center of the planetary system.
3. Martin Luther was credited with dividing one of the major (3)_____ that had dominated Europe throughout the Middle Ages.
4. Renaissance thinkers often thought of themselves as (4)_____ in the modern age.
5. "Man" was a source of (5)_____ possibilities rather than being a miserable sinner awaiting redemption from a pit of fleshly corruption.
6. Humanism represented a (6)_____ from the contemplative and spiritual life to the active life associated with this world.
7. The highest cultural values were usually associated with active (7)_____ in public life, in moral, political, and military action, and in service to the state.
8. The concept of the "Renaissance Man" refers to an individual who, in addition to participating actively in the affairs of public life, (8)_____ knowledge of and skill in many subject areas.
9. Francesco Petrarch contributed to a new (9)_____: one of secular passion and hunger for knowledge.
10. There was an increase in the search for lost works and the number of volumes in (10)_____, in turn influencing more people with classical ideas.

Task 3 Translation

Directions: *Translate the following sentences into English.*
1. "文艺复兴"是近代早期深刻影响了欧洲知识界的一场文化运动。
2. 文艺复兴时期的思想家们常认为自己迎来了一个与古代和中世纪截然不同的现代时期。
3. 文艺复兴时期的人文主义者强调人的尊严。
4. 在文艺复兴时期,最高的文化价值通常与积极参与公共生活,投身道德、政治和军事行动,以及为国家服务相关。
5. 彼特拉克在两个世界间游弋,一个是理想的古希腊罗马世界,一个是他试图改造的当前世界。

Task 4 Further Development

Directions: *Read the following excerpt from Francis Bacon's essay "Of Studies" and translate the underlined sentences into Chinese. Notice Bacon's reliance on parallel structures throughout this concise essay.*

Of Studies

1   Studies serve for delight, for ornament, and for ability. Their chief use for delight, is in privateness and retiring; for ornament, is in discourse; and for ability, is in the judgment and disposition of business. For expert men can execute, and perhaps judge of particulars, one by one; but the general counsels, and the plots and marshalling of affairs come best from those that are learned.

2   To spend too much time in studies is sloth; to use them too much for ornament is affection; to make judgment wholly by their rules is the humor of a scholar. They perfect nature and are perfected by experience: for natural abilities are like natural plants, that need pruning by study, and studies themselves do give forth directions too much at large, except they be bounded in by experience.

3   Crafty men contemn studies, simple men admire them, and wise men use them, for they teach not their own use; but that is a wisdom without them and above them, won by observation. Read not to contradict and confuse; nor to believe and take for granted; nor to find talk and discourse; but to weigh and consider.

4   Some books are to be tasted, others to be swallowed, and some few to be chewed and digested; that is some books are to be read only in parts; others to be read, but not curiously; and some few to be ready wholly, and with diligence and attention. Some books also may be read by deputy and extracts made of them by others; but that would be only in the less important arguments, and the meaner sort of books; else distilled books are, like common distilled waters, flashy things.

5   Reading makes a full man; conference a ready man; and writing an exact man. And therefore, if a man write little, he had need have a great memory; if he confer little, he had need have a present wit; and if he read little, he had need have much cunning to seem to know that he

doth not.

6 <u>Histories make men wise; poets witty; the mathematics subtle; natural philosophy deep; moral grave; logic and rhetoric able to contend.</u>

7 Abeunt studia in mores. Nay there is no stand or impediment in the wit, but may be wrought out by fit studies: like as diseases of the body may have appropriate exercises. Bowling is good for the stone and reins; shooting for the lungs and breast; gentle walking for the stomach; riding for the head; and the like. So if a man's wit be wandering, let him study the mathematics; for in demonstrations, if his wit be called away never so little, he must begin again. If his wit be not apt to distinguish or find differences, let him study the schoolmen; for they are cymini sectors. If he be not apt to beat over matters, and to call up one thing to prove and illustrate another, let him study the lawyers' cases. So every defect of the mind may have a special receipt.

Section B William Shakespeare

William Shakespeare was an English poet who is considered one of the greatest writers to ever use the English language. He is also the most famous playwright in the world, with his plays being translated into over 50 languages and performed across the globe for audiences of all ages. Known colloquially as "The Bard" or "The Bard of Avon," Shakespeare was also an actor and the creator of the Globe Theatre, a historical theatre that is visited by hundreds of thousands of tourists every year.

Life and Career

Shakespeare was born on April 23, 1564 in Stratford-upon-Avon in Warwickshire, England. He was the son of John Shakespeare, an alderman, and Mary Arden, the daughter of a well-respected farmer. He was one of eight children and lived to be the eldest surviving son of the family. As a commoner, Shakespeare's education was thought to finish at the grammar school level as there is no record of him attending university, which was a luxury reserved for upper-class families.

In 1582, the 18-year-old Shakespeare married Anne Hathaway, who, on the occasion of her wedding, was 26 years old and already with child. Hathaway gave birth to the couple's first child six months later, a daughter named Susanna, with twins, named Hamnet and Judith, following two years later in 1585.

Shakespeare first made his appearance on the London stage, where his plays would be written and performed, around 1592. It was in 1594 that the first known quartos of Shakespeare's plays were published, solidifying his reputation by 1598 when his name became the selling point in new productions.

Shakespeare, along with a group of players that acted in his play, created his own theatre on the River Thames in 1599 and named it the Globe Theatre. After that, a record of property purchases and investments made by Shakespeare showed the playwright had become a very wealthy man, so much so that he bought properties in London and Stratford for himself and his family, as he spent most of his time in London.

Shakespeare died on April 23, 1616, and was buried at the Holy Trinity Church in Stratford two days later, with a curse written on his tombstone to ward off those who would disturb his bones. He was survived by his wife and two daughters. ① Shakespeare had no direct descendants, as both his daughters had children who did not survive to adulthood.

Plays

Shakespeare wrote at least 37 plays that scholars know of, with most of them labeled comedies, histories, or tragedies. From histories written in the late 1580s to the early 1590s, Shakespeare moved into comedies. Among the most well-known are *A Midsummer Night's Dream, Merchant of Venice, As You Like It,* and *Twelfth Night.* Interestingly, two tragedies bookend Shakespeare's comedic era—*Romeo and Juliet* were written at the beginning of the 1590s, and *Julius Caesar* was written at the end of the era. For the last portion of his writing career, Shakespeare focused his work on tragedies and "problem" plays. In this era, which is acknowledged as the playwright's best era, he wrote the works called *Hamlet, Othello, King Lear,* and *Macbeth,* among others. These are the works that are most in production today, both on stage and in film.

Sonnets

Shakespeare's sonnets were a collection of over 150 works that were published late in his life and without any indication of when each of the pieces was composed.② The sonnets have a contrasting set of subjects—one set chronicles the poet's lust for a married woman with a dark complexion, known as "The Dark Lady," while the other describes a conflicted or confused love for a young man, known as the "fair youth." While it is not known or confirmed, many in literature circles believe that the sonnets accurately portray the heart of the poet, leading the public to speculate on Shakespeare's views on sex, marriage, and life.

Shakespeare's Influence

Shakespeare is the master of the iambic pentameter, a form of poetry that is still widely used today. He is the most-read playwright in the Western hemisphere, and the English language is dotted with quotes and phrases that originated from his works, such as "breaking the ice" and "heart of gold." Aside from phrases, it is also common knowledge that he introduced more than

1,700 original words to the English language. In fact, words such as lonely, frugal, dwindle, and more originate from Shakespeare, who transformed English into the populist language that it is today.

(755 words)

New Words and Expressions (B)

New Words

New Words	Phonetic Symbols	Meanings
bard	[bɑːd]	*n.* 诗人
bookend	[ˈbʊkend]	*v.* 放在末尾,置于两端
chronicle	[ˈkrɒnɪkl]	*v.* 按事件发生顺序记载
colloquially	[kəˈləʊkwiəli]	*adv.* 用通俗语,口语地
commoner	[ˈkɒmənə]	*n.* 平民,普通人
complexion	[kəmˈplekʃn]	*n.* 肤色
dot	[dɒt]	*v.* 星罗棋布于;点缀
dwindle	[ˈdwɪndl]	*v.* (逐渐)减少,变小
frugal	[ˈfruːgl]	*adj.* 节俭的
hemisphere	[ˈhemɪsfɪə(r)]	*n.* (地球的)半球
iambic	[aɪˈæmbɪk]	*adj.* 抑扬格的
lust	[lʌst]	*n.* 性欲;强烈的欲望
pentameter	[penˈtæmɪtə(r)]	*n.* 五音步诗行
populist	[ˈpɒpjəlɪst]	*adj.* 平民主义(者)的
quarto	[ˈkwɔːtəʊ]	*n.* 四开本
solidify	[səˈlɪdɪfaɪ]	*v.* 巩固
sonnet	[ˈsɒnɪt]	*n.* 十四行诗
speculate	[ˈspekjuleɪt]	*v.* 猜测

Expressions

ward off	阻挡,防止

Proper Names

A Midsummer Night's Dream	《仲夏夜之梦》,莎士比亚四大喜剧之一,讲述的是一个有情人终成眷属的爱情故事。它是演出次数最多的莎翁喜剧。
As You Like It	《皆大欢喜》,莎士比亚四大喜剧之一,主要描述了被流放的公爵女儿罗瑟琳到森林寻父和她的爱情故事。剧名《皆大欢喜》意味着剧中受迫害的好人最终得到好报,恶人受到感化,有情人喜结良缘。这反映了莎士比亚理想中的以善胜恶的美好境界。
Hamlet	《哈姆雷特》,莎士比亚四大悲剧之一,讲述的是丹麦王子哈姆雷特的叔父克劳狄斯谋害哈姆雷特的父亲,篡取王位,并娶了国王遗孀乔特鲁德,哈姆雷特王子因此向叔父复仇的故事。《哈姆雷特》是莎士比亚所有戏剧中篇幅最长、最负盛名的一部,具有深刻的悲剧意义。该剧复杂的人物性格以及丰富完美的悲剧艺术手法,代表了整个西方文艺复兴时期的最高文学成就。
Julius Caesar	历史剧《裘力斯·凯撒》的剧情围绕古罗马的两个政治党派:凯撒为代表的独裁派和凯歇斯等人为首的共和派之间的斗争展开。
King Lear	《李尔王》,莎士比亚四大悲剧之一,讲述了年事已高的国王李尔王退位后,被大女儿和二女儿赶到荒郊野外,身为法兰西皇后的三女儿率军救父,却被杀死,李尔王伤心地死在她的身旁。
Macbeth	《麦克白》,莎士比亚四大悲剧之一,讲述了利欲熏心的麦克白和麦克白夫人对权力的贪婪,最后被推翻的过程。
Merchant of Venice	《威尼斯商人》,莎士比亚四大喜剧之一,剧情是通过三条线索展开的:一条是鲍西亚选亲;一条是杰西卡与罗兰佐恋爱和私奔;还有一条是"割一磅肉"的契约纠纷。
Othello	《奥赛罗》,莎士比亚四大悲剧之一,讲述奥赛罗是威尼斯公国一员勇将,他与元老的女儿苔丝狄蒙娜相爱。因为两人年纪相差太多,婚事未被准许。两人只好私下成婚。奥赛罗手下有一个阴险的旗官伊阿古,一心想除掉奥赛罗。他挑拨说另一名副将凯西奥与苔丝狄蒙娜关系不同寻常,并伪造了所谓定情信物等。奥赛罗信以为真,在愤怒中掐死了自己的妻子。当他得知真相后,悔恨之余拔剑自刎,倒在了苔丝狄蒙娜的尸体旁边。
Romeo and Juliet	《罗密欧与朱丽叶》讲述了意大利贵族凯普莱特的女儿朱丽叶与蒙太古的儿子罗密欧诚挚相爱,誓言相依,但因两家世代为仇而受到阻挠。为了追求自由爱情,二人不惜以死殉情。爱情最终不但战胜了死亡,并且使两族的世仇消弭于无形。许多学者和评论家从这个意义上称这部作品是乐观主义的悲剧,即人们所说的悲喜剧。
Twelfth Night	《第十二夜》,莎士比亚四大喜剧之一,讲述塞巴斯蒂安和薇奥拉这一对孪生兄妹,在一次海上航行途中不幸遇险,他们俩各自侥幸脱险,流落到伊利里亚。薇奥拉女扮男装给公爵奥西诺当侍童,她暗中爱慕着公爵,但是公爵爱着一位伯爵小姐奥丽维娅。可是奥丽维娅不爱他,反而爱上了代替公爵向自己求爱的薇奥拉。经过一番有趣的波折之后,薇奥拉与奥西诺,奥丽维娅与塞巴斯蒂安双双结成良缘。

Difficult Sentences

① Shakespeare had no direct descendants, as both his daughters had children who did not survive to adulthood.

由于两个女儿的孩子都没能长大成人,所以莎士比亚没有留下直系血脉。

② The sonnets have a contrasting set of subjects—one set chronicles the poet's lust for a married woman with a dark complexion, known as "The Dark Lady", while the other describes a conflicted or confused love for a young man, known as the "fair youth."

这些十四行诗有两组截然不同的主题——一组记录了诗人对一个肤色黝黑、被称为"黑女士"的已婚女子的欲望;而另一组则描绘了对一个青年男子充满矛盾或困惑的爱,这名年轻人被称为"英俊青年"。

Exercises

Task 1   Reading and Note Taking

Notes for William Shakespeare
(1) Birthday: _____ (2) Birth Place: _____
(3) Wife: _____ (4) Children: _____
(5) Education: _____ (6) Occupation: _____
(7) Four great comedies: _____
(8) Four great tragedies: _____
(9) Two subjects of the sonnets: _____
(10) Influence: _____

Task 2   Vocabulary

Directions: Complete the following sentences with proper words from the box. Please note there are more words than necessary.

A) bard	B) chronicle	C) colloquial	D) commoner	E) complexion
F) dot	G) dwindle	H) frugal	I) hemisphere	J) iambic
K) lust	L) playwright	M) solidify	N) sonnet	O) speculate

1. The Dark Lady is a married woman with a dark _____, who is a tempting but degrading object of desire.

2. Shakespeare only learned the basic Latin text and grammar as a _____.

3. Shakespeare was a _____ who got the idea of most of his plays from well-known stories and history.
4. *Romeo and Juliet* _____ the romantic but tragic love story between a young couple from two feuding families.
5. The English language is _____ with quotes and phrases from Shakespeare's works.
6. Shakespeare is one of the most influential writers in the Western _____.
7. Phrases such as "breaking the ice" and "heart of gold" are _____ now, but are also known to have originated in Shakespeare's plays and sonnets.
8. Shakespeare's opinions on sex, marriage, and life are _____ by the public.
9. An introductory series of Shakespeare's _____ celebrates the beauty of a young man and urges him to marry so as to preserve that beauty.
10. In 1594, the first known quartos of Shakespeare's plays were published, _____ his reputation by 1598 when his name became the selling point in new productions.

Task 3 Translation

Directions: *Read the passage again and translate the following sentences into English.*

1. 威廉·莎士比亚是英国诗人和剧作家,他被认为是最伟大的使用英语创作的作家之一。
2. 作为平民,莎士比亚没有上过大学,在当时,上大学是上流社会专属的奢侈。
3. 1594年,第一部已知的莎士比亚戏剧四开本出版,到1598年,他的名字成为新作品的卖点,巩固了他的声誉。
4. 莎士比亚至少写了37部戏剧,其中大部分被称为喜剧、历史剧或悲剧。
5. 莎士比亚晚年出版的十四行诗诗集超过150首作品,没有任何线索表明每首诗是在什么时候创作的。

Task 4 Further Development

Directions: *Read Shakespeare's Sonnet 18 and try to paraphrase it in English.*

Sonnet 18

Shall I compare thee to a summer's day?
Thou art more lovely and more temperate:
Rough winds do shake the darling buds of May,
And summer's lease hath all too short a date:
Sometime too hot the eye of heaven shines,
And often is his gold complexion dimmed,
And every fair from fair sometime declines,
By chance, or nature's changing course untrimmed:
But thy eternal summer shall not fade,
Nor lose possession of that fair thou ow'st
Nor shall death brag thou wander'st in his shade,

When in eternal lines to time thou grow'st,
So long as men can breathe, or eyes can see,
So long lives this, and this gives life to thee.

Section C Henry VIII and His Six Wives

Henry Tudor, the son of Henry VII of England and Elizabeth York, was born on June 28, 1491, in the royal residence, Greenwich Palace. After his brother Arthur died, he became Henry VIII. He married six times, beheaded two of his wives, and was the main instigator of the English Reformation.

Henry VIII

At the age of 17, Henry married his brother's widow Catherine of Aragon, who was the daughter of the Spanish king and queen. ① On February 18, 1516, Queen Catherine bore Henry his first child to survive infancy, Princess Mary. Henry grew frustrated by the lack of a male child and began keeping two mistresses at his beckon. One of his mistresses, Mary Boleyn, introduced him to her sister, Anne Boleyn. Anne and Henry began secretly seeing one another. Henry found a way to officially abandon his marriage with Catherine.

In 1533, Anne Boleyn became pregnant. Henry VIII married her secretly in January of 1533. In August of that year, Anne produced a girl, Elizabeth. Inside the court, Queen Anne suffered greatly from her failure to produce a living male heir. After she miscarried twice, Henry became interested in Jane Seymour, one of Anne's ladies-in-waiting. ② In an all-out effort to leave his unfruitful marriage, Henry contrived an elaborate story that Anne had committed adultery, had incestuous relations and was plotting to murder him. Henry charged three men on account of their adultery with his wife, and then on May 15, 1536, he put her on trial. Anne, regal and calm, denied all charges against her. ③ Four days later, Henry's marriage to Anne was annulled and declared invalid. Anne Boleyn was then taken to the Tower Green, where she was given a private beheading. Within 24 hours of Anne's execution, Jane Seymour and Henry VIII were formally wed.

In October of 1537, Jane Seymour produced Henry's long-hoped-for son. It was a difficult pregnancy. The baby, named Edward, was christened on October 15, and Jane died nine days later from a pregnancy-related infection. Henry considered Jane to be his only "true" wife. He and his court mourned for an extended period of time after her passing.

Three years later, Henry was ready to marry again, mainly to ensure the succession of his

Unit 4 Renaissance and Shakespeare

crown. He inquired in foreign courts about the appearances of available women. Anne, the sister of the Duke of Cleves, was suggested. The German artist Hans Holbein the Younger, who served as the king's official painter, was sent out to create a portrait of her. Henry disapproved of Anne in the flesh and divorced her after six months. She received the title of "The King's Sister" and was given Hever Castle as ample residence.

Within weeks, Henry married the very young Catherine Howard, a first cousin to Anne Boleyn. Henry, 49, and Catherine, 19, started out a happy pair. Henry was now dealing with tremendous weight gain and a bad leg. His new wife gave him zest for life, and he repaid her with lavish gifts. A pretty woman, she began seeking the attention of men of her own age, a tremendously dangerous endeavor for the Queen of England. After an investigation into her behavior, she was deemed guilty of adultery. On February 13, 1542, Henry had her executed on the Tower Green.

Independent and well-educated, Catherine Parr was Henry's last and sixth wife. She was the daughter of Maud Green, a lady-in-waiting to Henry's first wife, Catherine of Aragon. Maud named her daughter after the queen; thus Henry's last wife was named after his first. Parr was a twice-made widow. The two married in 1543. ④ The most well-documented incident of Catherine Parr's life was her effort to ban books, a truly horrible act under her husband's leadership that practically got her arrested. ⑤ When Henry came to admonish her for her brash actions, she submitted to him, saying she was merely looking to create a circumstance when he could teach her the proper way to behave. ⑥ Henry accepted the sentiment, either true or devised, saving her from a brutal end.

On January 28, 1547, at the age of 55, King Henry VIII of England died. He was buried in St. George's Chapel in Windsor Castle alongside his deceased third wife, Jane Seymour. Henry's only surviving son, Edward, inherited the throne, becoming Edward VI. Princesses Mary and Elizabeth waited in succession.

(722 words)

 New Words and Expressions (C)

New Words

New Words	Phonetic Symbols	Meanings
admonish	[əd'mɒnɪʃ]	v. 告诫;劝告
adultery	[ə'dʌlt(ə)ri]	n. 通奸
all-out	['ɔːl'aʊt]	adj. 全部的;竭尽全力的

ample	[ˈæmp(ə)l]	adj. 宽敞的；足够的
annul	[əˈnʌl]	v. 宣告无效；废除
beckon	[ˈbek(ə)n]	n. 召唤
behead	[bɪˈhed]	v. 砍头
brash	[bræʃ]	adj. 无礼的，傲慢的
brutal	[ˈbruːt(ə)l]	adj. 残忍的；不留情面的
chapel	[ˈtʃæp(ə)l]	n. 小礼拜堂，小教堂
commit	[kəˈmɪt]	v. 犯罪，做错事
contrive	[kənˈtraɪv]	v. (常指用欺骗手段) 策划
deceased	[dɪˈsiːst]	adj. 已故的
deem	[diːm]	v. 认为，视作
devise	[dɪˈvaɪz]	v. 设计；想出
endeavor	[ɪnˈdevə]	n. 尝试 vt. 竭力做到
execution	[ˌeksɪˈkjuːʃ(ə)n]	n. 执行，处死
heir	[eə]	n. 继承人；后嗣
infancy	[ˈɪnf(ə)nsi]	n. 婴儿期；初期
incestuous	[ɪnˈsestjʊəs]	adj. 乱伦的
instigator	[ˈɪnstɪɡeɪtə(r)]	n. 煽动者；教唆者
invalid	[ɪnˈvælɪd]	adj. 无效的；站不住脚的
lady-in-waiting	[ˌleɪdɪɪnˈweɪtɪŋ]	n. 侍女；宫女
lavish	[ˈlævɪʃ]	adj. 浪费的；丰富的
miscarry	[mɪsˈkæri]	v. 流产
regal	[ˈriːɡ(ə)l]	adj. 王者的；庄严的
repay	[riːˈpeɪ]	v. 报答；付还
succession	[səkˈseʃ(ə)n]	n. 连续；继位；继承权
zest	[zest]	n. 热情

Expressions

in the flesh	本人

Proper Names

Anne Boleyn	安妮·博林(1507—1536)，亨利八世的第二任妻子，英国王后(1533—1536)，伊丽莎白一世之母。

Anne of Cleves	克利维斯的安妮(1515—1557),亨利八世的第四任妻子,英国王后(1540年1月至7月)。
Aragon	阿拉贡王国(Aragon, Kingdom of 1035—1837),伊比利亚半岛东北部阿拉贡地区的封建王国。
Arthur Tudor	威尔士亲王(1486—1502),亨利八世的哥哥
Catherine Howard	凯瑟琳·霍华德(1520—1542),亨利八世的第五任妻子,英国王后(1540—1542)。
Catherine of Aragon	阿拉贡的凯瑟琳(1485—1536),亨利八世的第一任妻子,英国王后(1509—1533),玛丽一世之母。
Catherine Parr	凯瑟琳·帕尔(1512—1548),亨利八世的第六任妻子,英国王后(1543—1547)。
Edward VI	爱德华六世(1537—1553),都铎王朝第三任君主(1547—1553),英格兰与爱尔兰国王。亨利八世和简·西摩尔之子,也是英格兰首位信奉新教的统治者。
Elizabeth I	伊丽莎白一世(1533—1603),都铎王朝最后一位君主,英格兰与爱尔兰的女王(1558—1603),也是名义上的法国女王。亨利八世和安妮·博林之女。
Henry Tudor	亨利·都铎/亨利八世(1491—1547),都铎王朝第二任君主(1509—1547),英格兰与爱尔兰国王。他是亨利七世与伊丽莎白王后的次子。
Jane Seymour	简·西摩尔(1509—1537),亨利八世的第三任妻子,英国王后(1536—1537),爱德华六世之母。
Mary I	玛丽一世(1516—1558),英格兰和爱尔兰女王(1553—1558),都铎王朝第四任君主,亨利八世和阿拉贡的凯瑟琳之女,丈夫是西班牙国王腓力二世。
Tower Green	格林塔,亦称绿塔,伦敦塔内白塔南部的一小片草地,是安妮·博林和凯瑟琳·霍华德被砍头的地方。

Difficult Sentences

① On February 18, 1516, Queen Catherine bore Henry his first child to survive infancy, Princess Mary. Henry grew frustrated by the lack of a male child and began keeping two mistresses at his beckon.

1516年2月18日,凯瑟琳王后为亨利生下了第一个未夭折的孩子玛丽公主。亨利因久未得子而感到灰心丧气,进而找了两个情人在身边。

② In an all-out effort to leave his unfruitful marriage, Henry contrived an elaborate story that Anne had committed adultery, had incestuous relations and was plotting to murder him.

亨利为了结束这段无果的婚姻无所不用其极,他精心编造了一个故事宣称安妮与他人通奸、乱伦,还意图谋杀自己。

③ Four days later, Henry's marriage to Anne was annulled and declared invalid.

四天之后,亨利和安妮的婚姻被废除并被宣告无效。

④ The most well-documented incident of Catherine Parr's life was her effort to ban books, a truly horrible act under her husband's leadership that practically got her arrested.

史料记载最丰富的就是凯瑟琳·帕尔极力禁书的事件。在她丈夫当政时期,这是个极其可怕的行为,让她几乎被捕。

⑤ When Henry came to admonish her for her brash actions, she submitted to him, saying she was merely looking to create a circumstance when he could teach her the proper way to behave.

当亨利前去警告她这种自以为是的行为时,凯瑟琳屈服了,说自己不过是想找个机会让亨利教她恰当行事而已。

⑥ Henry accepted the sentiment, either true or devised, saving her from a brutal end.

亨利接受了凯瑟琳的解释,不管她的说法是真实的还是编造的,都使她免于残酷的结局。

Exercises

Task 1 Short Answer Questions

Directions: Work in pairs to answer the following questions

1. Of Henry VIII's six marriages, which one was the longest?
2. Why did Henry view Jane Seymour as his only "true" wife?
3. Why did Henry behead two of his wives?
4. Why did Henry divorce Anne of Cleves?
5. Why did most of Henry's wives have a brutal end?

Task 2 Vocabulary

Directions: Complete the following sentences with proper words from the box. Change the form if necessary. Please note there are more words than necessary.

A) ample	B) annul	C) behead	D) brutal	E) commit
F) contrive	G) decease	H) execute	I) heir	J) incident
K) inherit	L) lavish	M) repay	N) succession	O) zest

1. In order to marry Anne Boleyn, Henry found a way to _____ his marriage with Catherine of Aragon.
2. To get rid of his unfruitful marriage, Henry contrived an elaborate story that Anne had _____ adultery, had incestuous relations and was plotting to murder him.
3. Within 24 hours of Anne's _____, Jane Seymour and Henry VIII were formally wed.
4. Jane Seymour gave birth to Henry's only male _____ and died shortly due to a pregnancy-related infection.

Unit 4　Renaissance and Shakespeare

5. Henry remarried after Jane Seymour's death, so as to ensure the _____ of his throne.
6. Anne of Cleves was given Hever Castle as _____ residence after her divorce with Henry.
7. Catherine Howard, who was 30 years younger than Henry, brought him passion, and he _____ her with expensive presents.
8. Henry forgave Catherine Parr for her horrible action of banning books, and thus saved her from a _____ end.
9. Henry VIII and his _____ third wife Jane Seymour were buried together in St. George's Chapel.
10. Henry's only surviving son, Edward, _____ the throne, becoming Edward VI.

Task 3　Translation

Directions: *Complete the following sentences by translating the Chinese in brackets into English.*

1. Inside the court, Queen Anne suffered greatly from _____（她无法诞下男性继承人）.
2. Henry contrived an elaborate story that Anne had committed adultery, but Anne _____（否认了所有针对她的指控）.
3. In October of 1537, Jane Seymour produced Henry's _____（期盼已久的儿子）.
4. Three years later, Henry was ready to marry again, mainly to _____（保证他的王位后继有人）.
5. Henry accepted the sentiment, either true or devised, _____（使她免于残酷的结局）.

Task 4　Further Development

Directions: *Discuss the following questions with your classmates and report your answers to the whole class. You may search the Internet for related information.*

From the passage we can find that Henry VIII was desperate for a male heir. He divorced Catherine of Aragon for pregnant Anne Boleyn because he "grew frustrated by the lack of a male child," but his passion for Anne also died down because of "her failure to produce a living male heir." When Henry finally got his long-hoped-for son with his third wife Jane Seymour, he still desired more sons and married again and again after Jane's death. Why? Was it because he preferred sons to daughters? Or was it because he simply wanted more sons to ensure the succession of his crown?

1. Justice is a temporary thing that must at last come to an end; but the conscience is eternal and will never die.　　　　　　　　—Martin Luther, German theologian

公正是暂时的, 终将消亡, 但良心是永恒的, 且永不消逝。

——马丁·路德（1483—1546）

2. In the country of the blind, the one-eyed man is king.
   　　　　　　　　　　　　　—Desiderius Erasmus, Dutch humanist and theologian
   山中无老虎，猴子称大王。　　　　　　　　　——德西德里乌斯·伊拉斯谟

3. In reading, we converse with the wise; in the business of life, generally with the foolish.　　— Francis Bacon, English philosopher, scientist, and author
   读书时，我们同智者交谈；生活中，我们同愚人交谈。
   　　　　　　　　　　　　　　　　　　　　　——弗朗西斯·培根（1561—1626）

4. Go your own way regardless of what people say.　　—Dante, Italian poet
   走自己的路，让别人说去吧。　　　　　　　　　——但丁（1265—1321）

5. Man has no greater enemy than himself.　　—Francesco Petrarch, Italian Poet
   人最大的敌人是他自己。　　　　　　——弗朗西斯克·彼特拉克（1304—374）

6. Only virtue is eternal fame.　　　　　　— Francesco Petrarch
   只有美德是永恒的名声。　　　　　　　　　　——弗朗西斯克·彼特拉克

7. A kissed mouth doesn't lose its freshness, for like the moon it always renews itself.
   　　　　　　　　　　　　　　　　— Giovanni Boccaccio, Italian poet
   被吻过的嘴唇依然新鲜，就像每天的月亮都是新的。
   　　　　　　　　　　　　　　　　　　　——乔万尼·薄伽丘（1313—1375）

8. Simplicity is the ultimate sophistication.
   　　　　—Leonardo da Vinci, famous Renaissance painter, sculptor, architect from Italy
   至繁归于至简。　　　　　　　　——列奥纳多·达·芬奇（1452—1519）

9. As a well spent day brings happy sleep, so a life well spent brings happy death.
   　　　　　　　　　　　　　　　　　　　　　　—Leonardo da Vinci
   勤劳一日，可得一夜安眠，勤劳一生，可得幸福长眠。　　——列奥纳多·达·芬奇

10. By a small sample we may judge of the whole piece.
    　　　　　　　　　　　　—Miguel de Cervantes Saavedra, Spanish novelist
    见微知著。　　　　　　——米格尔·德·塞万提斯·萨维德拉（1547—1616）

11. Speak the truth and shame the Devil.　　—Francois Rabelais, French humanist writer
    说真话可使魔鬼感到羞愧。　　　　　　——弗朗索瓦·拉伯雷（1493—1553）

12. All that glisters is not gold.　　—William Shakespeare, English playwright and poet
    闪光的并不都是金子。　　　　　　　　——威廉·莎士比亚（1564—1616）

13. Ignorance is the curse of God. Knowledge is the wing wherewith we fly to heaven.
    　　　　　　　　　　　　　　　　　　　　　　　—William Shakespeare

无知乃是上帝的降祸;知识乃人类藉以飞向天堂的翅膀。　　——威廉·莎士比亚

14. The fool doth think he is wise, but the wise man knows himself to be a fool.
—William Shakespeare

愚者自以为聪明,智者却有自知之明。　　　　　　　　——威廉·莎士比亚

15. A light heart lives long.　　　　　　　　　　　　—William Shakespeare

豁达者长寿。　　　　　　　　　　　　　　　　　　——威廉·莎士比亚

Key to Unit 4 Exercises

导读答案

1. Renaissance literally means "rebirth." It refers especially to the rebirth of learning that began in Italy in the fourteenth century, spread to the north, including England, by the sixteenth century, and ended in the north in the mid-seventeenth century (earlier in Italy). During this period, there was an enormous renewal of interest in and study of classical antiquity.

   Humanism is a group of philosophies and ethical perspectives which emphasize the value and agency of human beings, individually and collectively, and generally prefers individual thought and evidence (rationalism, empiricism) over established doctrine or faith (fideism).

   William Shakespeare was an English poet who is considered one of the greatest writers to ever use the English language. He is also the most famous playwright in the world, with his plays being translated into over 50 languages and performed across the globe for audiences of all ages. Known colloquially as "The Bard" or "The Bard of Avon," Shakespeare was also an actor and the creator of the Globe Theatre.

2. Henry VIII (28 June 1491—28 January 1547) was king of England from 21 April 1509 until his death. He was lord, and later king, of Ireland, as well as continuing the nominal claim by the English monarchs to the Kingdom of France. Henry was the second monarch of the Tudor dynasty, succeeding his father, Henry VII.

   His contemporaries considered Henry in his prime to be an attractive, educated and accomplished king. His desire to provide England with a male heir — which stemmed partly from personal vanity and partly because he believed a daughter would be unable to consolidate the Tudor dynasty and the fragile peace that existed following the Wars of the Roses — led to the two things for which Henry is most remembered: his six marriages and the English Reformation. He is frequently characterized in his later life as a lustful,

egotistical, harsh, and insecure king.

His six wives were Catherine of Aragon, Anne Boleyn, Jane Seymour, Anne of Cleves, Catherine Howard, and Catherine Parr.

Section A   Renaissance

Task 1   Reading Comprehension

1. A   2. C   3. D   4. B   5. B

Task 2   Vocabulary

1. K) rebirth   2. C) cosmic   3. F) institutions   4. O) ushering   5. E) infinite
6. M) shift   7. G) involvement   8. J) possesses   9. I) outlook   10. B) circulation

Task 3   Translation

1. "Renaissance" was a cultural movement that profoundly affected European intellectual life in the early modern period.
2. Renaissance thinkers often thought of themselves as ushering in the modern age, as distinct from the ancient and medieval eras.
3. Renaissance Humanists placed great emphasis upon the dignity of man.
4. In the Renaissance, the highest cultural values were usually associated with active involvement in public life, in moral, political, and military action, and in service to the state.
5. Petrarch was pulled between two worlds, the ideal world of antiquity and his desire to improve the current world.

Task 4   Further Development

第1段   读书足以怡情，足以博彩，足以长才。其怡情也，最见于独处幽居之时；其博彩也，最见于高谈阔论之中；其长才也，最见于处世判事之际。

第2段   读书费时过多易惰，文采藻饰太盛则矫，全凭条文断事乃学究故态。

第4段   书有可浅尝者，有可吞食者，少数则须咀嚼消化。换言之，有只须读其部分者，有只须大体涉猎者，少数则须全读，读时须全神贯注，孜孜不倦。

第5段   读书使人充实，讨论使人机智，笔记使人准确。

第6段   读史使人明智，读诗使人灵秀，数学使人周密，科学使人深刻，伦理学使人庄重，逻辑修辞之学使人善辩。

Section B   William Shakespeare

Task 1   Reading Comprehension

(1) April 23, 1564   (2) Stratford-upon-Avon, England
(3) Anne Hathaway   (4) Susanna, Hamnet and Judith

(5) grammar school   (6) poet, playwright, actor

(7) *A Midsummer Night's Dream, The Merchant of Venice, As You Like It, and Twelfth Night*

(8) *Hamlet, Othello, King Lear, and Macbeth*

(9) poet's lust for "the Dark Lady" and his conflicted or confused love for the "fair youth"

(10) Shakespeare is the most-read playwright in the Western Hemisphere, the inventor of the iambic pentameter, and the creator of the Globe Theatre. He introduced more than 1,700 original words to the English language and transformed English into the populist language that it is today.

Task 2 Vocabulary

1. E) complexion   2. D) commoner   3. L) playwright   4. B) chronicles   5. F) dotted
6. I) hemisphere   7. C) colloquial   8. O) speculated   9. N) sonnets   10. M) solidifying

Task 3 Translation

1. William Shakespeare was an English poet and playwright who is considered one of the greatest writers to ever use the English language.

2. As a commoner, Shakespeare didn't attend university, which was a luxury reserved for upper-class families.

3. It was in 1594 that the first known quartos of Shakespeare's plays were published, solidifying his reputation by 1598 when his name became the selling point in new productions.

4. Shakespeare wrote at least 37 plays, with most of them labeled comedies, histories, or tragedies.

5. Shakespeare's sonnets were a collection of over 150 works that were published late in his life and without any indication of when each of the pieces was composed.

Task 4 Further Development

    Sample Answer:

Could I compare you to the days of summer?
You are more lovely and gentler than those days.
The wild wind shakes the favorite flowers of May.
And the duration of summer has a limited period of time.
Sometimes the shinning sun is too hot.
And his gold skin of the face will be dimmed by the clouds.
Every beautiful thing and person will decline from previous state of beauty.
(The beauty) will be stripped of by chance or changes of season in the nature.
But your summer exists forever and will not lose color.
You will never lose your own beauty either.

The Death can't boast that you are under his control.

You grow as time grows in the undying lines of my verse.

As long as men can live in the world with sight and breath,

This poem will exist and you will live in it forever.

Section C Henry VIII and His Six Wives

Task 1 Short Answer Questions

1. His marriage with the first wife Catherine of Aragon was the longest.
2. Henry viewed Jane Seymour as his only "true" wife because she was the only wife that gave birth to a male heir.
3. He believed that they had committed adultery.
4. Henry disliked her for she did not look as beautiful as the portrait of her drawn by the king's official painter.
5. Henry was a capricious and unfaithful husband, who considered his wives as baby machines.

Task 2 Vocabulary

1. annul   2. committed   3. execution   4. heir   5. succession
6. ample   7. repaid   8. brutal   9. deceased   10. inherited

Task 3 Translation

1. her failure to produce a male heir
2. denied all charges against her
3. long-hoped-for son
4. ensure the succession of his crown
5. saving her from a brutal end

Task 4 Further Development

Sample Answer 1:

　　Henry VIII needed a son to be King after him, to establish the still fairly-new Tudor dynasty, and to carry the Tudor name on. It was extremely important in those days; a woman was not considered fit or able to rule by herself. Once Henry did get a son (Edward VI), it became less imperative, but another son or two would have been good to have as spare. Infant mortality was high; Edward could have died early—as, in fact, he did—and another son would have ensured the future of the Tudors.

Sample Answer 2:

　　Henry not only wanted a son, but needed a son. Though a female could succeed to the throne, Henry was worried about the strength of his realm, and the weakness perceived under a female ruler. Additionally, a female wouldn't rule on her own. The Tudor dynasty was new, and

Henry was worried about the loss of the dynasty. A female, as Queen, would be bound to marry and the rule would pass from the Tudors to the family of the husband.

Also, in the 16th century, it was a sign of weakness in a ruler if he couldn't produce a son.

Unit 5

Enlightenment and the Origin of Modern Science

导 读

　　本单元旨在通过对西方启蒙时期的思想家和哲学家、法国大革命、科学与理性等知识的介绍，使学生初步了解启蒙运动的缘起、代表人物与影响，开阔视野，增加文化移入，提高跨文化交际意识，运用所学西方文化知识及相关的英语表达进行跨文化交流，同时为今后实施中华文化"走出去"战略奠定一定基础，增强思想上的敏感性与使命感。

Before You Start

While preparing for this unit, think about the following questions:
1. Do you know any influential figures in the Age of Enlightenment?
2. Share with your class your knowledge of the French Revolution.
3. How do you understand reason, freedom and science as the key words in the period of Enlightenment?

Section A The Age of Enlightenment

　　　John Locke　　　　　David Hume　　　　　Voltaire　　　　Jean-Jacques Rousseau

Unit 5 Enlightenment and the Origin of Modern Science

The Age of Enlightenment (or simply the Enlightenment or Age of Reason) was a cultural movement of intellectuals in the 17th and 18th centuries, first in Europe and later in the American colonies. Its purpose was to reform society with reason, challenge ideas grounded in tradition and faith, and advance knowledge through scientific methods. It promoted science, skepticism and intellectual interchange, and opposed superstition, intolerance and some abuses by church and state.

Originating in about 1650 to 1700, it was sparked by philosophers Baruch Spinoza, John Locke, Pierre Bayle, physicist Isaac Newton, and philosopher Voltaire. The Scientific Revolution is closely tied to the Enlightenment, as its discoveries overturned many traditional concepts and introduced new perspectives on nature and man's place within it. ① The Enlightenment flourished until about 1790—1800, after which the emphasis on reason gave way to Romanticism's emphasis on emotion, and a counter-Enlightenment gained force.

② In France, Enlightenment was based in the salons and culminated in the great Encyclopédie edited by Denis Diderot with contributions by hundreds of leading philosophers (intellectuals) such as Voltaire, Rousseau and Montesquieu. The new intellectual forces spread to urban centers across Europe, notably England, Scotland, the German states, the Netherlands, Russia, Italy, Austria, and Spain, and then jumped the Atlantic into the European colonies, where it influenced Benjamin Franklin and Thomas Jefferson, among many others, and played a major role in the American Revolution. The political ideals of the Enlightenment influenced the American *Declaration of Independence, the United States Bill of Rights* and *the French Declaration of the Rights of Man and of the Citizen.*

The term "Enlightenment" did not come into use in English until the mid-18th century. For Immanuel Kant, Enlightenment was mankind's final coming of age, the emancipation of the human consciousness from an immature state of ignorance. ③ According to historian Roy Porter, the thesis of the liberation of the human mind from the dogmatic state of ignorance that he argues was prevalent at the time is the epitome of what the age of enlightenment was trying to capture. According to Bertrand Russell, however, the enlightenment was a phase in a progressive development, which began in antiquity, and reason and challenges to the established order were constant ideals throughout that time.

④ At that time some intellectual debates revolved around "confessional"—that is Catholic, Lutheran, Reformed (Calvinist), or Anglican issues, and the main aim of these debates was to establish which bloc of faith ought to have the "monopoly of truth and a God-given title to authority." After this date everything thus previously rooted in tradition was questioned and often replaced by new concepts in the light of philosophical reason. ⑤ After the second half of the 17th century and during the 18th century a general process of rationalization and secularization

set in which rapidly overthrew theology's age-old hegemony in the world of study, and thus disputes were reduced to a secondary status in favor of the escalating contest between faith and incredulity.

This period saw the shaping of two distinct lines of enlightenment thought: Firstly the *radical enlightenment*, largely inspired by the one-substance philosophy of Spinoza, which in its political form adhered to "democracy; racial and sexual equality; individual liberty of lifestyle; full freedom of thought, expression, and the press; eradication of religious authority from the legislative process and education; and full separation of church and state."

Secondly the *moderate enlightenment*, which was represented in a number of different philosophical systems, like those in the writings of Descartes, John Locke, Isaac Newton or Christian Wolff, expressed some support for critical review and renewal of the old modes of thought, but in other parts sought reform and accommodation with the old systems of power and faith. ⑥ These two lines of thought were again met by the conservative counter-Enlightenment, encompassing those thinkers who held on to the traditional belief-based systems of thought.

(638 words)

New Words and Expressions (A)

New Words

New Words	Phonetic Symbols	Meanings
bloc	[blɒk]	n. 团体,联盟
dogmatic	[dɒgˈmætɪk]	adj. 教条的;武断的;固执
emancipation	[ɪˌmænsɪˈpeɪʃn]	n. 解放
encompass	[ɪnˈkʌmpəs]	v. 包围;包含
epitome	[ɪˈpɪtəmi]	n. 缩影;典型的人或事
eradication	[ɪˌrædɪˈkeɪʃn]	n. 摧毁,根除
escalate	[ˈeskəleɪt]	v. 逐步上升
hegemony	[hɪˈdʒeməni]	n. 霸权
incredulity	[ˌɪnkrəˈdjuːləti]	n. 怀疑
monopoly	[məˈnɒpəli]	n. 垄断
overturn	[ˌəʊvəˈtɜːn]	v. 推翻;撤销(判决等)
prevalent	[ˈprevələnt]	adj. 流行的,盛行的
romanticism	[rəʊˈmæntɪsɪzəm]	n. 浪漫主义

Unit 5 Enlightenment and the Origin of Modern Science

| secularization | [ˌsekjələraɪˈzeɪʃn] | n. 世俗化 |
| theology | [θiˈɒlədʒi] | n. 神学 |

Expressions

adhere to	遵循；依附；坚持
come into use	投入使用
culminate in sth	终于获得某种结果
gain force	得势，赢得力量
give way to	让位于
hold on to	坚持；信奉
in favor of	偏好；支持
in the light of	鉴于，参照，根据
reduce to	还原；降为
revolve around	围绕
tie to	依靠；迷恋；关联

Proper Names

Baruch Spinoza	巴鲁赫·斯宾诺莎(1632—1677)，西方近代哲学史重要的理性主义者，与笛卡尔和莱布尼茨齐名。
Benjamin Franklin	本杰明·富兰克林(1706—1790)，美国著名政治家、科学家、杰出的外交家与发明家。
Christian Wolff	克里斯蒂安·沃尔夫(1679—1754)，德国博学家、法学家、数学家、启蒙哲学家。
Counter-Enlightenment	反启蒙运动
Declaration of Independence	《独立宣言》
Encyclopédie	《百科全书》
French Declaration of the Rights of Man and of the Citizen	《法国人权宣言》
Immanuel Kant	伊曼努尔·康德(1724—1804)，德国哲学家、天文学家，德国古典哲学的创始人，唯心主义、不可知论者，德国古典美学的奠定者，启蒙运动最后一位主要哲学家。
Isaac Newton	艾萨克·牛顿(1643—1727)爵士，英国皇家学会会长，英国著名的物理学家。

Jean-Jacques Rousseau	让·雅克·卢梭(1712—1778),法国18世纪伟大的启蒙思想家、哲学家、教育家、文学家,18世纪法国大革命的思想先驱,杰出的民主政论家和浪漫主义文学流派的开创者,启蒙运动最卓越的代表人物之一。
John Locke	约翰·洛克(1632—1704),英国哲学家。
Montesquieu	孟德斯鸠(1689—1755),法国政治哲学家、法学家、启蒙思想家;他以《论法的精神》著名,主张立法、行政、司法三权分立可最有效地促进个人自由。
Pierre Bayle	皮埃尔·培尔(1647—1706),法国哲学家、历史评论家,17世纪下半叶最有影响的怀疑论者。
skepticism	怀疑论
The Age of Enlightenment	启蒙时期
Thomas Jefferson	托马斯·杰斐逊(1743—1826),美利坚合众国第三任总统,《美国独立宣言》主要起草人。
Voltaire	伏尔泰(1694—1778),法国启蒙思想家、文学家、哲学家、史学家。

Difficult Sentences

① The Enlightenment flourished until about 1790—1800, after which the emphasis on reason gave way to Romanticism's emphasis on emotion, and a counter-Enlightenment gained force.
启蒙运动的繁荣一直延续到1790—1800年。此后,对理性的尊崇逐渐让位于注重情感的浪漫主义,反启蒙思想风头日劲。

② In France, Enlightenment was based in the salons and culminated in the great Encyclopédie edited by Denis Diderot with contributions by hundreds of leading philosophers (intellectuals) such as Voltaire, Rousseau and Montesquieu.
在法国,启蒙运动的主要阵地是沙龙,收官之作是由德尼·狄德罗主编的巨著《百科全书》。在成书过程中,伏尔泰、卢梭和孟德斯鸠等数百名主要哲学家(学者)都做出了贡献。

③ According to historian Roy Porter, the thesis of the liberation of the human mind from the dogmatic state of ignorance that he argues was prevalent at the time is the epitome of what the age of enlightenment was trying to capture.
历史学家罗伊·波特认为,把人类思想从教条蒙昧的状态中解放出来这一主张,是启蒙时代试图实现目标的集中体现,这一蒙昧状态在当时非常普遍。

④ At that time some intellectual debates revolved around "confessional"—that is Catholic, Lutheran, Reformed (Calvinist), or Anglican issues, and the main aim of these debates was to establish which bloc of faith ought to have the "monopoly of truth and a God-given title to

Unit 5 Enlightenment and the Origin of Modern Science

authority."

那个时期存在一些围绕"忏悔"这个主题的学术争论——那是罗马天主教、路德教、更正教(加尔文教)和圣公会争论的问题,其主要目的是为了确定哪个宗派能够"单独拥有真理和上帝授予的权威"。

⑤ After the second half of the 17th century and during the 18th century a "general process of rationalization and secularization set in which rapidly overthrew theology's age-old hegemony in the world of study" and thus disputes were reduced to a secondary status in favor of the "escalating contest between faith and incredulity."

17世纪下半叶和整个18世纪,"理性化和世俗化总进程的到来,迅速推翻了神学在知识界百年来的统治",因此争论的焦点让位于"逐渐升级的关于信仰和怀疑的争论"。

⑥ These two lines of thought were again met by the conservative counter-Enlightenment, encompassing those thinkers who held on to the traditional belief-based systems of thought.

保守的反启蒙思想者也接受这两条思想,包括那些紧紧追随传统信仰思想体系的思想家们。

Exercises

Task 1 Reading Comprehension

Directions: *Read the passage and choose the best answer to each of the following questions.*

1. According to the passage, which of the following is correct about the movement of Enlightenment?
   A. It placed great emphasis on scientific reasoning and humanity.
   B. It promoted the religious revolutions both in Europe and America.
   C. It fought against intolerance and traditional ideas.
   D. It flourished simultaneously in Europe and America.

2. The Romanticism could possibly fall in the category of _____.
   A. the Scientific Revolution
   B. Classicism
   C. the counter-Enlightenment
   D. moderate enlightenment

3. The expression "in the light of" (Line 5, Paragraph 5) is synonymous with _____.
   A. by way of   B. in relation to   C. for the sake of   D. without

4. Debates about "confessional" gradually lost their position because of the following reasons EXCEPT _____.
   A. the process of rationalization
   B. the presence of secularization
   C. the contest between faith and incredulity
   D. the domination of theology

5. What is the attitude of conservative counter-Enlightenment towards the radical and moderate enlightenment?
   A. Indifferent.   B. Approving.
   C. Hostile.   D. Neutral.

Task 2　Vocabulary

Directions: *Complete the following sentences with proper words or phrases from the box. Change the form if necessary. Please note there are more words and phrases than necessary.*

A) encompass	B) revolve around	C) tie to	D) in favor of
E) spark	F) prevalent	G) horizon	H) abuse
I) isolation	J) in the light of	K) give way to	L) ground

1. No studies _____ all sectors of the counter-Enlightenment movement.
2. The study of Enlightenment must be _____ in a thorough knowledge of the past.
3. The cultural movement of intellectuals _____ the Scientific Revolution in the whole world.
4. Having no other choice, the French government had to _____ these stern demands.
5. The government has set up a working party to look into the problem of power _____.
6. The judge decided _____ the plaintiff.
7. All other tasks must _____ the pivot and must absolutely not interfere with or upset it.
8. The revolution in the American colonies was closely _____ the thought of Enlightenment.
9. Even at that time violation of intellectual property rights was _____ among the offices.
10. Concepts about human beings had changed dramatically _____ the Romanticism.

Task 3　Translation

Directions: *Translate the following sentences into English.*

1. 启蒙运动旨在借助理性进行社会改革，挑战传统观念，借助科学方法推动知识发展。
2. 科技革命与启蒙思想密切相关，其发现推翻了诸多传统观念，引入了人们对自然看法的新视角。
3. 在罗素眼中，启蒙运动不过是改革发展的一个阶段，早在远古时期就开始了。
4. 此后，先前植根于传统的一切遭到了质疑，被哲学理性指导下的新观念所取代。
5. 这些新知识的影响力传播到欧洲大陆的城市中心地带，随后跨越大西洋传播到欧洲的殖民地，极大地影响了包括本杰明·富兰克林和托马斯·杰斐逊在内的许多人，有力推进了美国独立战争的进程。

Unit 5 Enlightenment and the Origin of Modern Science

Task 4 Further Development

Directions: *Retell the passage according to the key words provided in the box.*

Age of reason	featured by	aim at	great changes
uproot	religion	discrepancy	radical Enlightenment
moderate Enlightenment		lose power	Romanticism

Section B On the Shoulders of Giants: Isaac Newton and Modern Science

Much of today's science of physics is based on Newton's discovery of the three laws of motion and his theory of gravity. Newton also developed one of the most powerful tools of mathematics. It is the method we call calculus. ① Late in his life, Newton said of his work: "If I saw further than other men, it was because I stood on the shoulders of giants."

One of those giants was the great Italian scientist, Galileo. Galileo died the same year Newton was born. Another of the giants was the Polish scientist Nicholas Copernicus. He lived 100 years before Newton. Copernicus had begun a scientific revolution. It led to a completely new understanding of how the universe worked. Galileo continued and expanded the work of Copernicus. Isaac Newton built on the ideas of these two scientists and others. He found and proved the answers for which they searched.

Isaac Newton

Isaac Newton was born in Woolsthorpe, England, on December 25, 1642. ② He was born early, small and weak. No one expected him to survive. But he surprised everyone. He had one of the most powerful minds in history. And he lived until he was 84.

Isaac Newton was not a good student. Yet he liked to make things, such as kites and clocks and simple machines. Newton also enjoyed finding new ways to answer questions or solve problems. Strangely, Newton became a much better student after a boy kicked him in the stomach. The boy was one of the best students in the school. ③ Newton decided to get even by getting higher marks than the boy who kicked him. In a short time, Newton became the top student at the school.

Newton left school to help on the family farm. It soon became clear, however, that the boy was not a good farmer. An uncle decided that Newton would do better as a student than as a farmer. So he helped the young man enter Cambridge University to study mathematics. Newton completed his university studies five years later, in 1665, when he was 22 years old.

One day, sitting in the garden, Newton watched an apple fall from a tree. ④ He began to wonder if the same force that pulled the apple down also kept the moon circling the Earth. He believed it was and believed that it could be measured. He called the force "gravity" and began to examine it carefully. ⑤ He decided that the strength of the force keeping a planet in orbit around the sun depended on two things. One was the amount of mass in the planet and the sun. The other was how far apart they were. Newton was able to find the exact relationship between distance and gravity. Newton proved his idea by measuring how much gravity force would be needed to keep the moon orbiting the Earth. He found that his measurement of the gravity force produced was not the same as the force needed. But the numbers were close. Newton did not tell anyone about his discovery. Later, with correct measurements of the size of the Earth, he found that the numbers were exactly the same.

Years later, the British astronomer Edmund Halley visited Newton. He turned to Newton for the answer of the question: What is the path of a planet going around the sun? Newton immediately gave Halley the answer: an egg-shaped path called an ellipse. Halley was surprised and asked for the proof. Newton offered his proof and also showed all of his other scientific work to Halley. Halley said Newton's scientific discoveries were the greatest ever made. He urged Newton to share them with the world. Newton began to write a book that explained what he had done. It was published in 1687. Newton called his book *The Mathematical Principles of Natural Philosophy*. The book is considered the greatest scientific work ever written, where Newton explained the three natural laws of motion. From these three laws, Newton was able to show how the universe worked. He proved it with easily understood mathematics. Scientists everywhere accepted Newton's ideas.

⑥ The leading English poet of Newton's time, Alexander Pope, honored the scientist with these words: "Nature and nature's laws lay hid in night. God said,—'Let Newton be!'—and all was light."

(712 words)

Unit 5 Enlightenment and the Origin of Modern Science

New Words and Expressions (B)

New Words

New Words	Phonetic Symbols	Meanings
calculus	[ˈkælkjələs]	n. 微积分
ellipse	[ɪˈlɪps]	n. 椭圆
expand	[ɪkˈspænd]	v. 拓展,发展
honor	[ˈɒnə(r)]	v. 盛赞
leading	[ˈliːdɪŋ]	adj. 领先的
mass	[mæs]	n. 质量
orbit	[ˈɔːbɪt]	n./v. 轨道;沿轨道运动

Expressions

get even with	报复;与……扯平
gravity force	重力
lead to	导致
of one's time	……时代的
the three laws of motion	三大运动定律
top student	优等生
turn to	向……求助

Proper Names

Cambridge University	剑桥大学,建于1209年,位于英国剑桥市的世界顶级研究型大学。
Edmund Halley	埃德蒙多·哈雷(1656—1742),英国天文学家、地理学家、数学家、气象学家和物理学家。
Galileo Galilei	伽利略·伽利雷(1564—1642),意大利数学家、物理学家、天文学家,科学革命的先驱,近代实验科学的奠基人之一。
The Mathematical Principles of Natural Philosophy	《自然哲学之数学原理》,英国科学家牛顿的代表作。

Difficult Sentences

① Late in his life, Newton said of his work: "If I saw further than other men, it was because I stood on the shoulders of giants."

晚年,当牛顿谈起自己的贡献时说道:"如果说我比其他人看得更远些,那是因为我站在巨人的肩上。"

② He was born early, small and weak. No one expected him to survive. But he surprised everyone. He had one of the most powerful minds in history.

他是个早产儿,个头儿小,身体羸弱。大家都以为他难以存活,但让人吃惊的是,他最终成为历史上最具影响力的思想家之一。

③ Newton decided to get even by getting higher marks than the boy who kicked him.

牛顿下定决心要以更高的分数来报复踹他肚子的那个男孩。

④ He began to wonder if the same force that pulled the apple down also kept the moon circling the Earth.

他开始思索,让苹果落地的力与让月球绕着地球转动的力,是否为同一种力。

⑤ He decided that the strength of the force keeping a planet in orbit around the sun depended on two things. One was the amount of mass in the planet and the sun. The other was how far apart they were.

他认为使行星围绕太阳转动的力由两个因素决定:一是行星和太阳的质量,二是两者之间的距离。

⑥ The leading English poet of Newton's time, Alexander Pope, honored the scientist with these words: "Nature and nature's laws lay hid in night. God said, — 'Let Newton be!' — and all was light."

同时代的英国重要诗人亚历山大·蒲柏,用下面的溢美之词来称赞牛顿:"自然与自然规律隐藏在黑暗中。上帝说:'让牛顿出现吧!'于是世界一片光明。"

Exercises

Task 1 Reading Comprehension

Directions: Read the passage again and judge whether the following statements are true (T), false (F) or not given (NG).

True   if the statement agrees with the information mentioned in the passage
False   if the statement contradicts the information mentioned in the passage
Not Given   if there is no information on this in the passage

1. There is continuity between the research and theories of Copernicus, Galileo and Newton.

Unit 5　Enlightenment and the Origin of Modern Science

2. Copernicus had a different hypothesis about the working mechanism of the universe from his forerunners.
3. When he was a student, Newton was not good at manual and practical work.
4. It was Edmund Halley who helped Newton find the three laws of motion.
5. One of Newton's uncles played an important role in his future life.
6. The insult of his schoolmate had stimulated Newton to become a top student.
7. Newton was cautious and modest in his research career.
8. *The Mathematical Principles of Natural Philosophy* got published easily.
9. In a sense, the fame and publicity of Newton was in debt to Edmund Halley's encouragement.
10. Though Alexander Pope thought highly of Newton's contribution, he did not respect him.

Task 2　Vocabulary

Directions: *Complete the sentences with the words in the brackets in their proper forms.*
1. It is _____ possible, but highly unlikely ever to happen. (theory)
2. I did not ask them, though, as that would show my _____. (ignore)
3. All of these were chance _____ made by scientists engaged in other investigations. (discover)
4. The university conferred on him the _____ degree of Doctor of Laws. (honor)
5. Part of his _____, — and mine —, came from you, the American people, to whom he dedicated his life of public service. (strong)
6. Most of the ceremonies are the _____ from earlier times. (survive)
7. Despite its lack of formal power, the nobility was not _____. (power)
8. D. H. Lawrence was one of the _____ writers of his time. (lead)
9. It turned out that this was a _____ new way of growing rice. (revolution)
10. She sat _____, waiting for their decision. (motion)

Task 3　Translation

Directions: *Complete the following sentences by translating the Chinese in brackets into English.*
1. The firm is looking to _____(开拓海外业务).
2. The landlord played a dirty trick on me, and I swore to _____(报复他).
3. Under given conditions, a bad thing can _____(带来好的结果).
4. The situation was on the edge of slipping out of control, but Mr. Darcy managed to _____(保持在正常范围内).
5. A real bad cold could _____(拖垮你)and leaves you feeling very miserable.

Task 4　Further Development

Directions: *Based on the passage, write a summary about what you have learnt about Isaac Newton.*

Section C Francis Bacon: Fame and Disgrace

Francis Bacon

Francis Bacon (1561—1626) was one of the leading figures in natural philosophy and in the field of scientific methodology in the period of transition from the Renaissance to the early modern era. When Francis Bacon was young, he had displayed talent in many fields. He was educated at home in his early years owing to poor health (which plagued him for the whole life), receiving tuition from a graduate of Oxford. At the age of 12 he entered Trinity College, Cambridge, under the personal tutelage of Dr John Whitgift, future Archbishop of Canterbury. ① It was at Cambridge that he first met Queen Elizabeth, who was impressed by his precocious intellect, and was accustomed to calling him "The Young Lord Keeper."

After his studies at Trinity College, Cambridge and Gray's Inn, Bacon did not take up a post at a university, but tried to start a political career. Although his efforts were not crowned with success during the era of Queen Elizabeth, under James I he rose to the highest political office, Lord Chancellor. Later he fell victim to an intrigue in Parliament and became a scapegoat, losing all his offices and his seat in Parliament, but retained his titles and his personal property. Though Bacon's political career ended up with disgrace, he was still a very influential figure. ② His international fame and influence spread during his last years, when he was able to focus his energies exclusively on his philosophical work, and even more so after his death, when English scientists of the Boyle circle took up his idea of a cooperative research institution in their plans and preparations for establishing the Royal Society.

However, the love life of such a big figure could not be said to be so easy, let alone a smooth and happy marriage. When he was 36, Bacon engaged in the courtship of Elizabeth Hatton, a young widow of 20. Reportedly, she broke off their relationship upon accepting marriage to a wealthier man. Years later, Bacon still wrote of his regret that the marriage to Hatton had not taken place. At the age of 45, Bacon married Alice Barnham, the fourteen-year-old daughter of a well-connected London alderman and Member of Parliament. Bacon wrote two sonnets proclaiming his love for Alice. The first was written during his courtship and the second on his wedding day, 10 May 1606. When Bacon was appointed Lord Chancellor by special Warrant of the King, Lady Bacon was given precedence over all other Court ladies.

③ Reports of increasing friction in his marriage to Alice appeared, with speculation that some of this may have been due to financial resources not being as readily available to her as she was accustomed to having in the past. Alice was reportedly interested in fame and fortune, and when reserves of money were no longer available, there were complaints about where all the money was going. Alice Chambers Bunten wrote in her *Life of Alice Barnham* that, upon their descent into debt, she actually went on trips to ask for financial favors and assistance from their circle of friends. Bacon disinherited her upon discovering her secret romantic relationship with Sir John Underhill. He rewrote his will, which had previously been very generous to her (leaving her lands, goods, and income), revoking it all.

Of course there are different versions about their relationship. Bacon's personal secretary and chaplain, William Rawley, wrote in his biography of Bacon that his inter-marriage with Alice Barnham was one of "much conjugal love and respect," mentioning a robe of honor that he gave to her, and which "she wore unto her dying day, being twenty years and more after his death."

Even worse, there are some rumors about him. The well-connected antiquary John Aubrey noted among his private memoranda concerning Bacon, "He was a pederast." Biographers continue to debate about Bacon's sexual inclinations and the precise nature of his personal relationships. Several authors believe that despite his marriage Bacon was primarily attracted to the same sex. ④ Professor Forker for example has explored the "historically documentable sexual preferences" of both King James and Bacon—and concluded they were all oriented to "masculine love," a contemporary term that seems to have been used exclusively to refer to the sexual preference of men for members of their own gender. The Jacobean antiquarian, Sir Simonds D'Ewes implied there had been a question of bringing him to trial for buggery. ⑤ This conclusion has been disputed by others, who point to lack of consistent evidence, and consider the sources to be more open to interpretation.

⑥ He famously died by contracting pneumonia while studying the effects of freezing on the preservation of meat, bringing him into a rare historical group of scientists killed by their own experiments. At the news of his death, over thirty great minds collected together their eulogies of him, which were then published in Latin. His debts amounted to more than £23,000, equivalent to more than £3 million at current value.

(832 words)

New Words and Expressions (C)

New Words

New Words	Phonetic Symbols	Meanings
alderman	[ˈɔːldəmən]	n. 市府参事,市议员
antiquary	[ˈæntɪkwəri]	n. 研究/收藏、出售/古物的人
buggery	[ˈbʌɡəri]	n. 鸡奸,兽奸
chaplain	[ˈtʃæplɪn]	n. 牧师
conjugal	[ˈkɒndʒəɡl]	adj. 婚姻的,夫妻之间的
descent	[dɪˈsent]	n. 下降;血统
disinherit	[ˌdɪsɪnˈherɪt]	v. 剥夺继承权,剥夺特权
eulogy	[ˈjuːlədʒi]	n. 悼词;颂词
exclusively	[ɪkˈskluːsɪvli]	adv. 专门地;排外地
friction	[ˈfrɪkʃn]	n. 摩擦
intrigue	[ɪnˈtriːɡ]	n. 密谋
memoranda	[ˌmeməˈrændə]	n. 备忘录
pederast	[ˈpedəræst]	n. 鸡奸者
plague	[pleɪɡ]	v. 使痛苦,造成麻烦
pneumonia	[njuːˈməʊniə]	n. 肺炎
precedence	[prɪˈsiːdəns]	n. 优先权
precocious	[prɪˈkəʊʃəs]	adj. 早熟的
revoke	[rɪˈvəʊk]	v. 废除;撤销
scapegoat	[ˈskeɪpɡəʊt]	n. 替罪羊
tutelage	[ˈtjuːtəlɪdʒ]	n. 指导;保护;监护

Expressions

amount to	共计;达到
be crowned with	使圆满;使完美
break off	断交
due to	由于
end up with	以……告终
fall victim to	成为……的牺牲品
give precedence over	给予优先
personal secretary	私人秘书

Unit 5 Enlightenment and the Origin of Modern Science

sexual preference	性取向
take up	从事

Proper Names

Archbishop of Canterbury	坎特伯雷大主教,又称坎特伯雷圣座,继承了圣奥古斯丁的使徒统系,为英格兰牧首,全英国教会的主教长,全世界圣公会的主教长,普世圣公宗精神领袖。
Francis Bacon	弗朗西斯·培根,英国文艺复兴时期最重要的散文家、哲学家。
Gray's Inn	格雷律师学院
James I	詹姆斯一世(1566—1625)。英国国王,1603年到1625年在位。
Robert Boyle	罗伯特·波义耳(1627—1691),英国化学家,物理学家。
Trinity College, Cambridge	剑桥大学三一学院,剑桥大学中规模最大、财力最雄厚、名声最响亮的学院之一。

Difficult Sentences

① It was at Cambridge that he first met Queen Elizabeth, who was impressed by his precocious intellect, and was accustomed to calling him "The Young Lord Keeper."
就是在剑桥,他第一次遇见伊丽莎白女王。女王对他年纪轻轻就展现出的才情赞赏有加,称其为"我年轻的掌玺大臣"。

② His international fame and influence spread during his last years, when he was able to focus his energies exclusively on his philosophical work, and even more so after his death, when English scientists of the Boyle circle took up his idea of a cooperative research institution in their plans and preparations for establishing the Royal Society.
在最后的年月里,他专注于哲学研究。他的国际声誉和影响力广为传扬,在去世后更是如此,那时英国波义耳团体的科学家把他的"建立合作研究机构"的主张,应用于建立英国皇家学会的规划和筹备中。

③ Reports of increasing friction in his marriage to Alice appeared, with speculation that some of this may have been due to financial resources not being as readily available to her as she was accustomed to having in the past.
关于他与爱丽丝婚姻生活中的摩擦的报道越来越多。有猜测说,这可能是因为她不能像从前那样方便地获得钱财,而她早已经适应了先前的那种生活。

④ Professor Forker for example has explored the "historically documentable sexual preferences" of both King James and Bacon—and concluded they were all oriented to "masculine love," a

contemporary term that seems to have been used exclusively to refer to the sexual preference of men for members of their own gender.

举例来说,福克教授研究了历史上有记录的有关詹姆斯国王和培根的"性取向"问题,并认定他们都偏好"男性之爱",当时这一词语专指喜欢同性男子的性取向。

⑤ This conclusion has been disputed by others, who point to lack of consistent evidence, and consider the sources to be more open to interpretation.

但他的这一结论遭到了其他人的怀疑,他们指出西蒙兹的证据相互矛盾,并认为证据来源可以有多种解释。

⑥ He famously died by contracting pneumonia while studying the effects of freezing on the preservation of meat, bringing him into a rare historical group of scientists killed by their own experiments.

他的离世也颇为出名,是在研究冷冻对肉类的防腐作用时感染肺炎而死。这使他成为历史上极少数死于自己实验的科学家。

Exercises

Task 1   Short Answer Questions

Directions: *Work in pairs to answer the following questions.*

1. What can we learn from Paragraph 1 about Bacon's health condition?
2. Why did Bacon lose his power in Parliament?
3. Why was Bacon's love life not easy?
4. What is the focus of the debate about Bacon in Paragraph 6?
5. How did Bacon die?

Task 2   Vocabulary

Directions: *Tell the meanings of the prefixes in the following words in the passage and offer more examples, if possible.*

sample word	precedence	trinity	cooperative	descent	disgrace	inter-marriage
prefix	pre-	tri-	co-	de-	dis-	inter-
sense						
other examples						

Task 3   Translation

Directions: *Translate the following sentences into English.*

1. Francis Bacon felt privileged to be _____ (得到天才人物的教导).
2. Unfortunately, Alice Barnham _____ (成为名利的牺牲品).
3. His desire for power soon _____ (占据绝对优先权).

Unit 5 Enlightenment and the Origin of Modern Science

4. The officer has a house _____ (专门留给他的妻子).
5. Bacon did not _____ (使自己的生活方式适应当时的习俗).

Task 4 Further Development

Directions: *Read the passage again and summarize the fame and disgrace of Bacon on the basis of the text with the help of some key words offered in the box.*

| *fame and influence*: education, political career, death |
| *disgrace and criticisms*: weak, title, marriage, rumor, sexual preference, debt |

Adages and Proverbs

1. Knowledge is power.　　　—Francis Bacon (1561—1626), a British essayist, jurist, philosopher, politician, and the forerunner of classical empiricism
   知识就是力量。　　　　　　　　　　　　　　　　　　——培根

2. Natural abilities are like natural plants that need pruning by study.　— Francis Bacon
   天生的才干，如同天生的植物一样，需要靠学习来修剪。　　——培根

3. The sum of behavior is to retain a man's own dignity, without intruding upon the liberty of others.　　　　　　　　　　　　　　　　　— Francis Bacon
   人的行为准则是，维护自己的尊严，不妨碍他人的自由。　　——培根

4. There is no paradise on earth equal to the union of love and innocence.
   　　—Rousseau (1712—1778), Swiss-French thinker, philosopher and political theorist
   人间最大的幸福莫过于既有爱情又能清白无瑕。　　　　　　——卢梭

5. Patience is bitter, but its fruit is sweet.　　　　　　— Rousseau
   忍耐是痛苦的，但它的果实是甜蜜的。　　　　　　　　　　——卢梭

6. Success often depends upon knowing how long it will take to succeed.
   　　　　　　　　　—Montesquieu (1689—1755), sociologist, thinker
   成功常常取决于知道需要多久才能成功。　　　　　　　　——孟德斯鸠

7. All men are liable to error; and most men are, in many points, by passion or interest, under temptation to it.
   　　　　　　　　　—John Locke (1632—1704), British philosopher
   人都会犯错误，在大多数的情况下，许多的人都是由于欲望或利益的引诱而犯错的。　　　　　　　　　　　　　　　　　　　　　　　　——洛克

8. Freedom is not letting you do whatever you want but teaching you not to do the things you don't want to do.

— Immanuel Kant (1724—1804), philosopher and astronomer

自由不是想做什么,就做什么;自由是教你不想做什么,就可以不做什么。

——康德

9. Prejudices are what fools use for reason.

—Voltaire (1694—1778), a French philosopher, thinker, writer

偏见是愚者思考的方式。 ——伏尔泰

10. All the splendor in the world is not worth a good friend. — Voltaire

人间所有的繁华和富贵抵不上一个好朋友。 ——伏尔泰

11. A long dispute means that both parties are wrong. —Voltaire

持久的争论意味着双方都是错的。 ——伏尔泰

12. Work banishes those three great evils: boredom, vice, and poverty. —Voltaire

工作撵跑三个魔鬼:无聊、堕落和贫穷。 ——伏尔泰

13. Wise men don't need advice. Fools won't take it.

—Benjamin Franklin (1706—1790), statesman, scientist, diplomat

英明的人不需要建议,愚蠢的人不采纳建议。 ——本杰明·富兰克林

14. At twenty years of age, the will reigns; at thirty, the wit; and at forty, the judgment.

— Benjamin Franklin

二十岁时起支配作用的是意志,三十岁时是机智,四十岁时是判断。

——本杰明·富兰克林

15. If I have seen further it is by standing on the shoulders of giants.

—Isaac Newton (1642—1726), English physicist and mathematician

我之所以比别人看得更远,是因为站在巨人的肩膀上。 ——牛顿

Unit 5　Enlightenment and the Origin of Modern Science

导读答案

1. Philosophers such as Baruch Spinoza, David Hume, Denis Diderot, Francis Bacon, John Locke, Immanuel Kant, Pierre Bayle, and Voltaire, Jean-Jacques Rousseau, physicist Isaac Newton, and sociologist Baron de Montesquieu, and so on.

2. The French Revolution was an influential period of social and political upheaval in France that lasted from 1789 until 1799. Inspired by liberal and radical ideas, it profoundly altered the course of modern history, triggering the global decline of theocracies and absolute monarchies while replacing them with republics and democracies.

3. They contribute to the emancipation of human consciousness from an immature state of ignorance by approaching truth and knowledge, rationality and liberation by shaking the established order and dogmas.

Section A　The Age of Enlightenment

Task 1　Reading Comprehension
1. C　2. C　3. A　4. D　5. B

Task 2　Vocabulary
1. encompass　　2. grounded　　3. sparked　　4. give way to
5. abuse　　　　6. in favor of　7. revolve around　8. tied to
9. prevalent　　10. in the light of

Task 3　Translation

1. The purpose of Enlightenment was to reform society with reason, challenge traditional faiths and beliefs, and advance knowledge through scientific methods.

2. The Scientific Revolution is closely tied to the Enlightenment, and its discoveries overturned many traditional ideas by introducing new perspectives on nature.

3. According to Russell, the Enlightenment was no more than a phase in a progressive development which started from the antiquity.

4. Since then, everything previously rooted in tradition was questioned and consequently gave way to new concepts from philosophical reason.

5. The new intellectual forces spread to urban centers across Europe and then jumped the Atlantic into the European colonies, where it influenced Benjamin Franklin and Thomas Jefferson, among many others, and played a major role in the American Revolution.

Task 4 Further Development

1. The Age of Enlightenment is also called <u>Age of Reason</u>. It is <u>featured by</u> appealing to reason, fighting against tradition, <u>aiming at</u> establishing a society of tolerance. Here science and skepticism are highlighted instead of superstition and abuses. To some philosophers like Kant, Russell and Roy Porter, Enlightenment is in opposition to ignorance, a challenge to the dogma, from which human minds can be liberated or emancipated; it was a progressive development in history.

2. <u>Great changes</u> have been brought about by the movement of Enlightenment. New methods are employed to observe the nature, and human beings are seriously taken into consideration. Traditional understandings are <u>uprooted</u> and new concepts are introduced. In the domain of politics, the powerful influence of Enlightenment could be felt at both sides of the Atlantic Ocean. In the sphere of <u>religion</u>, monopoly of truth, theology's hegemony and authority are no more welcomed uncritically, and philosophical reason leads to the process of rationalization and secularization, and a more fierce battle between faith and incredulity comes into being.

3. There are <u>discrepancies</u> in the school of Enlightenment, which find expression well in the differences between the <u>radical Enlightenment</u> and the <u>moderate Enlightenment</u>. The former highlights the doctrine of democracy, equality and freedom, and separation of religion and education and state; while the latter wants to launch criticism, renewal or reform of the old modes of thought, and a compromise with the tradition, both in thoughts and in political systems.

4. After its peak in the late 18th century, the movement of Enlightenment is gradually replaced by the school of <u>Romanticism</u>, which puts great emphasis on emotion, and <u>loses its power</u> in the face of the trend of Counter-Enlightenment.

Section B On the Shoulders of Giants: Isaac Newton and Modern Science

Task 1 Reading Comprehension

1. T   2. T   3. F   4. F   5. T   6. T   7. T   8. NG   9. T   10. F

Task 2 Vocabulary

1. theoretically   2. ignorance   3. discoveries   4. honorary   5. strength
6. survivals   7. powerless   8. leading   9. revolutionary   10. motionless

Task 3 Translation

1. expand its operations overseas
2. get even with him
3. lead to good results

4. keep it in orbit

5. pull you down

Task 4　Further Development

　　Isaac Newton, a genius with brilliant achievements in the fields of mathematics and physics, was modest and cautious in his research career, paying great homage to the scientists before and of his time. From the text, we can learn something else exciting about such a big figure. When he was young, he showed phenomenal competence in manual and practical work. Being clever and determined, once he set a goal, he would not fail himself. He was careful and persistent both in daily life and in his research, and it was these personalities that had pushed him forward to make outstanding accomplishments unapproachable by others.

Section C　Francis Bacon: Fame and Disgrace

Task 1　Short Answer Questions

1. He had a poor health and was troubled and tortured by it for a whole life.
2. He was made a scapegoat of an intrigue in Parliament and lost his offices and his seat in Parliament.
3. His courtship of Elizabeth Hatton was a failure and the latter married a wealthier man, and his marriage with Alice was full of conflicts and rumors.
4. The debates revolved around his sexual inclination, and there were rumors about his masculine love and his committing buggery.
5. He died from pneumonia and was famously killed by his experiment while studying the effects of freezing on the preservation of meat.

Task 2　Vocabulary

sample word	precedence	trinity	cooperative	descent	disgrace	inter-marriage
prefix	pre-	tri-	co-	de-	dis-	inter-
sense	before, in advance	three	together	down, from	reverse; lack	between two or more
other examples	preview presuppose pretest	trifold trilingual triangle	coexist cosign	degrade degenerate decay	disinherit disagree disease	international interplay

Task 3　Translation

1. under the tutelage of a talent
2. fell victim to fame and wealth
3. took precedence over any other considerations

4. reserved exclusively for his wife

5. orient his lifestyle to the customs then

Task 4 Further Development

1. Fame and virtues:

    a. Education: Bacon was intelligent and talented, and went to Trinity College, Cambridge at a very young age.

    b. Political career: His fame came to its peak at the reign of James I, and he was promoted to be Lord Chancellor.

    c. He was very influential in other fields, such as research method and philosophical work, which won him international fame and influence, even more so after his death.

    d. He died in a famous way and the world was impressed by his devotion to his work. He was mourned and praised by great minds of his time.

2. Disgrace and criticisms:

    a. Bacon was not physically strong all his life.

    b. His political career ended with disgrace, and he became a victim and scapegoat in a Parliament struggle, lost all his offices and seat in the Parliament, with his titles and personal properties untouched.

    c. He did not have a happy marriage: first refused by Elizabeth Hatton, and then betrayed by his wife Alice Barnham, who was indulged in fame and fortune, and disloyal to him.

    d. There are some rumors about his sex inclination, or he was accused of committing buggery.

    e. He was in great debt when he died.

Unit 6

Romanticism and Realism

导 读

本单元旨在通过对西方浪漫主义、现实主义等知识的介绍，使学生对西方这一时期所发生的重要事件有基本的了解，开阔视野，能够运用所学西方文化知识及相关的英语表达方式进行文化交流，为今后的深入学习和研究奠定基础。

Before You Start

While preparing for this unit, think about the following questions:

1. Have you ever heard of the terms such as Romanticism, Transcendentalism and Realism?
2. Do you know any romantic or realistic poets, novelists, artists, or musicians? Share your knowledge with your classmates.
3. How much do you know about Charles Dickens? Have a discussion with your partner about his well-known novel *Oliver Twist*.

Section A Romanticism in Europe

① As an artistic, literary, intellectual movement from about 1789 to 1850 in Western civilization, Romanticism emerged as a reaction against rationalist values of the Age of Enlightenment, such as social order, reason and logic. During this period, emphasis was shifted to the importance of the individual's experience in the world and his or her interpretation of that experience, rather than interpretations handed down by the church or tradition.

② The movement was rooted in the German Sturm und Drang movement, which prized intuition and emotion over Enlightenment rationalism. Further, the ideologies and events of the French Revolution (1789—1799) served as the background for Romanticism.

③ The term itself was coined in the 1840s in England, but the movement had been around since the late 18th century, primarily in literature and arts. In England, it was the publication of *Lyrical Ballads*, a collection of poems by William Wordsworth and Samuel Taylor Coleridge, in 1798 that ushered forth the Romantic period. Percy Bysshe Shelley, John Keats, and George Gordon Byron further typified Romanticism. In France, the movement was initiated by great writers like Victor Hugo, who wrote *The Hunchback of Notre Dame*. ④ Although it knew no national boundaries, Romanticism was especially prevalent in Germany, spearheaded by writers like Johann Wolfgang von Goethe, thinkers like Georg Friedrich Wilhelm Hegel, and musicians like Richard Wagner.

⑤ Embodied strongly in literature, visual arts, and music, Romanticism praised individualism, subjectivism, irrationalism, imagination, and nature—emotion over reason and senses over intellect. Usually, Romanticism is typically characterized by the following features.

Love of Nature

⑥ The Romanticists greatly emphasized the importance of nature and the primal feelings of awe, apprehension and horror felt by man when approaching the sublimity of it. This was mainly because of the industrial revolution which had shifted life from peaceful, serene countryside towards chaotic cities, transforming man's natural order. ⑦ Nature was not only appreciated for its visual beauty, but also worshipped for its ability to help the urban man find his true identity.

Emotions over Rationality

Unlike the age of Enlightenment, which focused on rationality and intellect, Romanticism placed human emotions, feelings, instinct, and intuition above everything else. ⑧ While the poets in the era of rationality advocated reason and logic, the Romantic writers trusted their emotions and feelings to create poetry. Praising emotion and feeling, Goethe declared, "Feeling is everything." William Wordsworth announced that poetry should be "the spontaneous overflow of powerful feelings." The emphasis on emotions also spread to the music created in that period, and can be observed in the compositions made by musicians like Richard Wagner, Ludwig van Beethoven, Robert Schumann, etc.

Individualism

Another important characteristic of Romanticism was individualism, an interest in the unique traits of each person. The Romanticists' desire to follow their inner drives led them to rebel against middle-class conventions. ⑨ Long hair, beards, and outrageous clothing served to reinforce the individualism that young Romanticists were trying to express.

Supernatural and Medieval Past

Romantic literatures were also featured by the use of the supernatural. Romanticists were interested in the supernatural and included it in their works. Besides, many Romanticists showed a passionate interest of the medieval past. While artists painted images of Gothic ruins and buildings, architects replicated its style in both private and public buildings. ⑩ The revival of Gothic architecture left European countryside adorned with pseudo-medieval castles and cities decorated with grandiose neo-Gothic cathedrals, city halls, parliament buildings, and even railway stations.

(579 words)

New Words and Expressions (A)

New Words

New Words	Phonetic Symbols	Meanings
adorn	[əˈdɔːn]	v. 装饰,使生色
approach	[əˈprəʊtʃ]	v. 接近,着手处理
boundary	[ˈbaʊndri]	n. 边界
chaotic	[keɪˈɒtɪk]	adj. 混乱的
convention	[kənˈvenʃn]	n. 惯例
embody	[ɪmˈbɒdi]	v. 体现,使具体化
grandiose	[ˈgrændiəʊs]	adj. 宏伟的
individualism	[ˌɪndɪˈvɪdʒuəlɪzəm]	n. 个体主义
intuition	[ˌɪntjuˈɪʃn]	n. 直觉(力)
ideology	[ˌaɪdɪˈɒlədʒi]	n. 意识形态,思想意识
initiate	[ɪˈnɪʃieɪt]	v. 开始
medieval	[ˌmediˈiːvl]	adj. 中世纪的
neo-Gothic	[ˌniːəʊˈgɒθɪk]	adj. 新哥特式的
outrageous	[aʊtˈreɪdʒəs]	adj. 惊人的;反常的
overflow	[ˌəʊvəˈfləʊ]	v. 充满,洋溢
parliamentary	[ˌpɑːləˈmentri]	adj. 议会的
passionate	[ˈpæʃənət]	adj. 热情的
primal	[ˈpraɪml]	adj. 原始的,主要的
pseudo-	[ˈsjuːdəʊ]	comb. 表示"假","伪"
rationalism	[ˈræʃnəlɪzəm]	n. 理性主义
rebel	[ˈrebl]	v. 反叛,反抗
reinforce	[ˌriːɪnˈfɔːs]	v. 加强,加固
replicate	[ˈreplɪkeɪt]	v. 复制
revival	[rɪˈvaɪvl]	n. 复兴,复活
spontaneous	[spɒnˈteɪniəs]	adj. 自发的,自然的
subjectivism	[səbˈdʒektɪvɪzəm]	n. 主观主义
sublimity	[səˈblɪməti]	n. 崇高,庄严

supernatural	[ˌsuːpəˈnætʃərəl]	*adj.* 超自然的
transform	[trænsˈfɔːm]	*v.* 改变
trait	[treɪt]	*n.* 特性，特点
unique	[juˈniːk]	*adj.* 独特的
usher	[ˈʌʃə(r)]	*v.* 迎接；开辟
worship	[ˈwɜːʃɪp]	*v.* 崇拜，尊敬

Expressions

be featured by	以……为特征
rather than	而不是
rebel against	反叛；反抗

Proper Names

Enlightenment	启蒙运动
Gothic architecture	哥特式建筑，11世纪下半叶起源于法国，13—15世纪流行于欧洲的一种建筑风格，在当代普遍被称作"法国式"。其特点是尖塔高耸、尖形拱门、大窗户及绘有圣经故事的花窗玻璃。
Georg Friedrich Wilhelm Hegel	黑格尔(1770—1831)，著名的德国古典唯心主义哲学家。
George Gordon Byron	乔治·戈登·拜伦(1788—1824)，英国浪漫主义诗人。他的诗歌塑造了一批"拜伦式英雄"。
Johann Wolfgang von Goethe	约翰·沃尔夫冈·冯·歌德(1749—1832)，德国小说家，剧作家，诗人，思想家，自然科学家，博物学家，是德国和欧洲最重要的作家之一。
John Keats	约翰·济慈(1795—1821)，杰出的英诗作家之一，浪漫派的主要成员。
Ludwig van Beethoven	路德维希·凡·贝多芬(1770—1827)，德意志古典音乐作曲家，钢琴演奏家，被人们尊称为"乐圣"。
Percy Bysshe Shelley	珀西·比西·雪莱(1792—1822)，英国文学史上最有才华的抒情诗人之一。
Richard Wagner	理查德·瓦格纳(1813—1883)，德国作曲家，是19世纪欧洲最著名的浪漫派作曲家之一。
Robert Schumann	罗伯特·舒曼(1810—1856)，德国作曲家，音乐评论家，19世纪德奥浪漫主义音乐的典型代表。
Samuel Taylor Coleridge	塞缪尔·泰勒·柯勒律治(1772—1834)，英国浪漫主义诗人，"湖畔派诗人"之一。

Unit 6 Romanticism and Realism

Sturm und Drang【德】= storm and stress	狂飙(突进)运动,18世纪70—80年代在德国发生的一场文学运动。这个时期是文艺形式从古典主义向浪漫主义过渡的阶段。狂飙运动在政治上追求自由,反对专制暴政;在文学上崇尚感情,反对古典主义,歌颂自然,其杰出代表为歌德和席勒。
The Hunchback of Notre Dame	《巴黎圣母院》,法国浪漫主义作家雨果的代表作。
William Wordsworth	威廉·华兹华斯(1770—1850),英国浪漫主义诗人,"湖畔派诗人"之一。

Difficult Sentences

① As an artistic, literary, intellectual movement from about 1789 to 1850 in Western civilization, Romanticism emerged as a reaction against rationalist values of the Age of Enlightenment, such as social order, reason and logic.

大约1789年到1850年间,西方文明史上出现了浪漫主义,它是与"启蒙时代"重社会秩序、推理和逻辑等理性主义价值观所相反的一种艺术、文学和学术思潮。

② The movement was rooted in the German Sturm und Drang movement, which prized intuition and emotion over Enlightenment rationalism. Further, the ideologies and events of the French Revolution (1789—1799) served as the background for Romanticism.

该思潮源于德国狂飙运动,颂扬直觉和情感,反对"启蒙时代"的理性主义价值观。此外,法国大革命(1789—1799)及其意识形态是浪漫主义产生的背景。

③ The term itself was coined in the 1840s, in England, but the movement had been around since the late 18th century, primarily in literature and arts.

浪漫主义一词诞生于19世纪40年代的英国,但浪漫主义运动在18世纪末期就已开始,最初体现在文学和艺术领域。

④ Although it knew no national boundaries, Romanticism was especially prevalent in Germany, spearheaded by artists like Johann Wolfgang von Goethe, thinkers like Georg Friedrich Wilhelm Hegel and musicians like Richard Wagner.

虽然浪漫主义跨越国界,但它在德国格外盛行,尤以艺术家歌德、思想家黑格尔、音乐家瓦格纳等为领军人物。

⑤ Embodied strongly in literature, visual arts, and music, Romanticism praised individualism, subjectivism, irrationalism, imagination and nature—emotion over reason and senses over intellect.

浪漫主义文学、视觉艺术和音乐极力宣扬个体主义、主观主义、非理性主义、想象力、情感和自然——情感凌驾于理智之上,感觉凌驾于智力之上。

⑥ The Romanticists greatly emphasized the importance of nature and the primal feelings of awe, apprehension and horror felt by man when approaching the sublimity of it.

浪漫主义者极其重视自然的重要性以及自然的崇高美所产生的最初的敬畏、忧虑和恐惧。

⑦ Nature was not only appreciated for its visual beauty, but also worshipped for its ability to help the urban man find his true identity.

自然不仅因其视觉之美被欣赏,同时也因它有助于城市人寻找到内心真实的自我而受到崇敬。

⑧ While the poets in the era of rationality advocated reason and logic, the Romantic writers trusted their emotions and feelings to create poetry.

启蒙主义时期的诗人提倡理智与逻辑,而浪漫主义作家则依靠他们的情感和感觉进行诗歌创作。

⑨ Long hair, beards, and outrageous clothing served to reinforce the individualism that young Romanticists were trying to express.

年轻的浪漫主义者留长发、蓄胡须和穿着稀奇古怪的服装来强化他们试图表现的个体主义。

⑩ The revival of Gothic architecture left European countryside adorned with pseudo-medieval castles and cities decorated with grandiose neo-Gothic cathedrals, city halls, parliamentary buildings, and even railway stations.

哥特式建筑的复兴使欧洲的乡村处处可见模仿中世纪的城堡,城市里也到处可见高大宏伟的新哥特式建筑:教堂、市政厅、议会大厦,甚至火车站。

Exercises

Task 1　Reading Comprehension

Directions: Read the passage and choose the best answer to each of the following questions.

1. Nature was greatly favored by Romanticists on the grounds that
   A. it could lead the romantists to appreciate its intrinsic beauty.
   B. it could render chaotic cities tranquil and peaceful.
   C. it could offer them awe, apprehension, horror and sublimity.
   D. it could help the countrymen to respect it and find their true identity.

2. Which of the following does Romanticism value most?
   A. Ration.　　B. Emotion.　　C. Reason.　　D. Will.

3. The article mentions Goethe's and Wordsworth's attitudes towards emotion and feeling primarily to ＿＿＿＿.
   A. broaden the application of what emotions and feelings are in romanticists' eyes
   B. demonstrate the similarity between those two poets' attitudes
   C. make a distinction between them in their attitudes towards emotion and feeling
   D. provide an additional illustration of the importance of emotions in romanticists' eyes

Unit 6 Romanticism and Realism

4. Which of the following is correct about individualism preferred by romanticists?
   A. It is interesting to romanticists in the sense that it is one unique and inescapable trait of each man.
   B. It is a way of romanticists to follow their inner drives to lead them to rebel against noble and elite traditions.
   C. It is an important feature of Romanticism leading young romanticists to rebel against traditions of dressing and wearing.
   D. It is favored by young romanticists to display long hair, beards, tattoos and outrageous clothes.
5. Which of the following architectures might NOT be attractive to Romantic architects?

   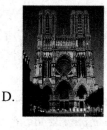

A.   B.   C.   D.

Task 2   Vocabulary

Directions: *Select a proper word or expression from what are listed in the box below for each sentence and change the form when/where necessary. Please note that there are more words and phrases than necessary.*

A) adorn	B) revival	C) reinforce	D) parliamentary	E) grandiose
F) medieval	G) trait	H) overflow	I) convention	J) embody
K) initiate	L) transform	M) worship	N) chaotic	O) rebel against

1. This policy is aimed to _____ the self-developments of small and medium-sized enterprises.
2. The Nobel-prize winning novel revived his _____ memories of the happy countryside moments.
3. It's just a social _____ that women don't grow beards.
4. Since inhabiting in the idyllic place two years ago, he has _____ his living mode and thinking pattern.
5. The leader of the country advocated his people to get united and _____ the foreign invaders.
6. His constructive proposal has been _____ in this draft resolution.
7. The _____ of the protagonist in this film aroused a heated discussion among fans.
8. During the past two decades, the economic _____ has always been one of the key development goals of this country.

9. Because of the great contribution to the social harmony and peace, he was _____ by the whole nation.
10. When entering the exhibition hall, I was greatly attracted by the wall _____ with Van Gogh's paintings.

Task 3 Translation

Directions: *Translate the following sentences into English.*
1. 尽管浪漫主义一词诞生于19世纪40年代的英国，但是英国浪漫主义运动是以华兹华斯和柯勒律治合著的《抒情歌谣集》出版为开端的。
2. 与启蒙时期专注理性和智力不同，浪漫主义将人类情感、感觉、本能和直觉置于一切之上。
3. 德国浪漫主义作家歌德歌颂情感与感觉，宣称"感觉就是一切"。
4. 浪漫主义者从心所欲，不满并反抗中产阶级的社会习俗。
5. 浪漫主义建筑师倾向于在建造公共和私人建筑上模仿哥特式风格。

Task 4 Further Development

Directions: *Read the following poem by Percy Bysshe Shelley, and discuss it with your group members in terms of why you like or dislike it. During the discussion, please try to incorporate what you have learned from the text above about Romanticism. After the discussion, please choose one representative to report to the whole class in around 150 words what your group has come to agreement with.*

Love's Philosophy

By Percy Bysshe Shelley

The fountains mingle with the river
And the rivers with the ocean,
The winds of heaven mix for ever
With a sweet emotion;
Nothing in the world is single;
All things by a law divine
In one spirit meet and mingle.
Why not I with thine?—

See the mountains kiss high heaven
And the waves clasp one another;
No sister-flower would be forgiven
If it disdained its brother;
And the sunlight clasps the earth
And the moonbeams kiss the sea:
What is all this sweet work worth
If thou kiss not me?

Unit 6   Romanticism and Realism

Section B   Romanticism in America

"The universe is composed of Nature and the Soul.
Spirit is present everywhere. Nature is the symbol of spirit."

① The lines above quoted from *Nature* by Ralph Waldo Emerson are the new voice the new world was thrilled to hear, and an apt description of the trend of Romanticism in America.

The European Romantic movement reached America in the early 19th century. ② Like European romanticists, American romanticists enthusiastically embraced nature, imagination, emotion, and individuality instead of formality, order and authority. However, they demonstrated their own peculiar traits by tinting it with American color and came into being the American Transcendentalism. ③ Developed in the 1830s and 1840s in New England, Transcendentalism was in essence a romantic idealism and a literary, political, philosophical and intellectual movement.

Ralph Waldo Emerson (1803—1882), an American essayist, lecturer, and poet, led the Transcendentalist movement. The United States had won its independence from Britain just twenty-two years before Emerson was born. But it had yet to win its cultural independence. It still took its traditions from other countries, mostly from Western Europe. Emerson wanted more cultural independence, and was not happy about the materialism-oriented life of his time. ④ Thus, he, together with other intellectuals founded the transcendentalist club in Cambridge, Massachusetts, on September 8, 1836 to start a movement as a protest against the general state of culture and society, and in particular, the state of intellectualism at Harvard University and the doctrine of the Unitarian church taught at Harvard Divinity School.

Ralph Waldo Emerson

Emerson gradually moved away from the religious and social beliefs of his contemporaries, formulating and expressing the philosophy of Transcendentalism in his 1836 essay *Nature*. The publication of *Nature* is usually considered as a ground-breaking work and the watershed moment. *Nature*'s voice pushed American Romanticism into a new phase, the one of New England Transcendentalism, the summit of American Romanticism, exerting a tremendous impact on intellectual thinking in America.

Transcendentalism emphasized mostly spirit or the Oversoul as the most important thing in the universe. ⑤ The Oversoul was an all-pervading power of God, omnipresent and omnipotent, from which all things came and of which all were a part. It existed in nature and man alike and constituted the chief element of the universe.

Moreover, what Transcendentalists offered is their fresh perception of nature as symbolic of the Spirit or God. Transcendentalism suggests that we can only understand reality through studying nature. ⑥ Nature was, to them, not purely matter. It was alive, filled with God's overwhelming presence. It was the garment of the Oversoul. Therefore, it could exercise a healthy and restorative influence on the human mind. Just as Emerson wrote in his *Nature*, ⑦ "Go back to nature, sink yourself, back into its influence, and you'll become spiritually whole again." The natural implication of all this was, of course, that things in nature tended to become symbolic, and the physical world was a symbol of the spiritual.

Furthermore, Transcendentalists stressed the importance of the individual and self-reliance. To them, the individual was the most important element of society. ⑧ As the regeneration of society could only come about through regeneration of the individual, his perfection, his self-culture and self-improvement, and not the crazy effort to get rich, should become the first concern of his life. The ideal type of man was the self-reliant individual. Emerson and Henry David Thoreau were telling people to depend on themselves for spiritual perfection if they cared to make the effort. Because in their opinion, the individual soul communed with the Oversoul and was therefore divine. In a speech called "Self-Reliance" Emerson told his listeners, ⑨ "Believe your own thoughts, believe that what is true for you in your private heart is true for all men." Emerson agreed that society urged us to act carefully but this as he admitted also restricted our freedom of action: "It is always easy to agree," and "yet nothing is more holy than the independence of your own mind. Let a person know his own value. Have no regrets. Nothing can bring you peace but yourselves."

⑩ Speaking words of self-dependence, self-reliance—a new language of freedom, he was the first to bring a truly American spirit. Emerson's words shaping the Romanticism in America has had a lasting impact on American life even until the present day.

(712 words)

New Words and Expressions (B)

New Words

New Words	Phonetic Symbols	Meanings
all-pervading	[ˈɔːl pəˈveɪdɪŋ]	*adj.* 普及的,普遍传播的
apt	[æpt]	*adj.* 恰当的;有……倾向的
authority	[ɔːˈθɒrəti]	*n.* 权威,权力

enthusiastically	[ɪnˌθjuːzɪˈæstɪkli]	adv. 热心地，满腔热情地
essence	[ˈesns]	n. 本质，实质
formulate	[ˈfɔːmjuleɪt]	v. 规划，明确地表达
ground-breaking	[ˈɡraʊndˌbreɪkɪŋ]	adj. 独创的，开拓性的
idealism	[aɪˈdiːəlɪzəm]	n. 理想主义
intellectualism	[ˌɪntəˈlektʃʊəlɪzəm]	n. 理智主义
materialism	[məˈtɪərɪəlɪzəm]	n. 唯物主义，物质主义
omnipresent	[ˌɒmnɪˈpreznt]	adj. 无处不在的
omnipotent	[ɒmˈnɪpətənt]	adj. 无所不能的，全能的
Oversoul	[ˈəʊvəsəʊl]	n. 超灵
peculiar	[pɪˈkjuːlɪə(r)]	adj. 特殊的，独特的
restorative	[rɪˈstɔːrətɪv]	adj. 有助于复元的
regeneration	[rɪˌdʒenəˈreɪʃn]	n. 再生，重生
thrilled	[θrɪld]	adj. 非常兴奋的，极为激动的
tint	[tɪnt]	v. 着色
tremendous	[trəˈmendəs]	adj. 巨大的
watershed	[ˈwɔːtəʃed]	n. 分水岭，转折点

Expressions

commune with	与……谈心，亲密交谈
in essence	本质上
self-culture	自我修养

Proper Names

Henry David Thoreau	亨利·戴维·梭罗(1817—1862)，美国作家、超验主义者、哲学家。
Transcendentalism	超验主义，美国的浪漫主义
Unitarian	唯一神派的

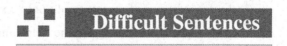

Difficult Sentences

① The lines above quoted from *Nature* by Ralph Waldo Emerson are the new voice the new world was thrilled to hear, and an apt description of the trend of Romanticism in America.
这段话引自拉尔夫·瓦尔多·爱默生作品《论自然》，它表达了新世界盼望听到的新声音，

也是对美国浪漫主义趋势的准确描述。

② Like European romanticists, American romanticists enthusiastically embraced nature, imagination, emotion, and individuality instead of formality, order and authority.

和欧洲浪漫主义者一样,美国浪漫主义者崇尚自然、想象、情感和个人主义,反对形式、秩序和权威。

③ Developed in the 1830s and 1840s in New England, Transcendentalism was in essence a romantic idealism and a literary, political, philosophical and intellectual movement.

超验主义发展于19世纪30年代和40年代的新英格兰,本质上是浪漫理想主义,同时也是一场文学、政治、哲学和思想运动。

④ Thus, he, together with other intellectuals founded the transcendentalist club in Cambridge, Massachusetts, on September 8, 1836 to start a movement as a protest against the general state of culture and society, and in particular, the state of intellectualism at Harvard University and the doctrine of the Unitarian church taught at Harvard Divinity School.

因此,1836年9月8日,他与其他几位学者在马萨诸塞州堪布里奇市创立了超验主义俱乐部。这一思潮的兴起,是出于对当时美国社会和文化的不满,特别是哈佛大学的理性主义学风以及哈佛神学院所倡导的唯一神论。

⑤ The Oversoul was an all-pervading power of God, omnipresent and omnipotent, from which all things came and of which all were a part.

超灵是上帝赋予的一种无所不能、无处不在的力量,滋生万物,是万物之本。

⑥ Nature was, to them, not purely matter. It was alive, filled with God's overwhelming presence. It was the garment of the Oversoul.

对他们而言,自然并不是单纯的物质,它是鲜活的,存在着无所不能的上帝。自然是超灵的表象。

⑦ "Go back to nature, sink yourself, back into its influence, and you'll become spiritually whole again." The natural implication of all this was, of course, that things in nature tended to become symbolic, and the physical world was a symbol of the spiritual.

"重返自然,沉浸其中,感受它的影响,你会在精神上重新变得完整。"其含义就是自然界中的事物具有象征性,而物质世界是精神的象征。

⑧ As the regeneration of society could only come about through regeneration of the individual, his perfection, his self-culture and self-improvement, and not the crazy effort to get rich, should become the first concern of his life.

社会的复兴只能通过个人的改造来实现,因此个人生活的第一要旨就是自我学习,自我改进,自我完善,而不是疯狂地追求富裕的物质生活。

⑨ "Believe your own thoughts, believe that what is true for you in your private heart is true for

all men."

"相信你自己的想法,要相信你的内心告诉你正确的事对人类来说也必然是正确的。"

⑩ Speaking words of self-dependence, self-reliance—a new language of freedom, he was the first to bring a truly American spirit.

爱默生宣扬自主和自立的新型自由言论使他成为真正美国精神的开拓者。

Exercises

Task 1 Reading Comprehension

Directions: *Read the passage and judge whether the following statements are true (T), false (F) or not given (NG).*

True   if the statement agrees with the information mentioned in the passage

False   if the statement contradicts the information mentioned in the passage

Not Given   if there is no information on this in the passage

1. New York was the birthplace of Transcendentalism.
2. The transcendentalist club in Cambridge, Massachusetts, on September 8, 1836 was set up to fight for the cultural independence from Western European influences.
3. Emerson's philosophy of Transcendentalism was formulated and expressed in his 1836 essay *Nature*, whose publication was usually considered as a ground-breaking work and the watershed moment.
4. The garment of the Oversoul refers to Nature.
5. The difference of American Romanticism from European Romanticism lies in the fact that it values the Oversoul and nature as the symbol of spirit.
6. In the eyes of Transcendentalists social reality can only be comprehended via studying nature.
7. Henry David Thoreau, inspired and encouraged by Emerson, came to practice self-reliance in Walden.
8. It can be concluded that Emerson's Nature values the physical world more than the spiritual world.
9. The individual was regarded the most important element of society, for the regeneration of the society can help regenerate the individual.
10. The first concern of the individual's life was his spiritual perfection, his self-culture and self-improvement, rather than the crazy pursuit of material life.

Task 2 Vocabulary

Directions: *Read the following dialogue and complete it with words and phrases from the box. Change the form if necessary. Do not use any of the words more than once.*

| A) restore | B) condemn | C) permeate with | D) self-reliant | E) self-perfection |
| F) omnipotence | G) regenerate | H) commune with | I) omnipresence | J) essence |

(*This is a conversation between a student and a professor about transcendentalist beliefs.*)

Vanilla: Professor Woolsey, may I ask a question about your lecture on Transcendentalism this morning? I don't think I understand transcendentalist beliefs on Nature, the Oversoul, and (1) _____ very well.

Professor Woolsey: Well, Emerson and other transcendentalists believe that nature is not purely matter, but is alive, (2) _____ God's overwhelming presence. Nature in their eyes was a healthy and (3) _____ remedy to the human mind.

Vanilla: But does that mean nature and God or the Oversoul are actually the same thing?

Professor Woolsey: Strictly speaking, we cannot say so. According to transcendentalist beliefs, nature is the garment of the Oversoul or God. And the Oversoul, (4) _____ and (5) _____, an all-pervading power of God, is the most important thing in the universe.

Vanilla: Ok. I understand. The Oversoul is the (6) _____ element of the universe in the eyes of Transcendentalist.

Professor Woolsey: Transcendentalists also believed the individual soul could (7) _____ the Oversoul, and was thus divine. Correspondingly, they encouraged the individual to be spiritually self-reliant, (8) _____, self-cultured and self-improved, which was the first concern of life. Besides, they (9) _____ the individual's crazy efforts for material life, because they didn't want a corrupted society as the (10) _____ of the society came from the renewing of the individual.

Vanilla: I think those transcendentalist beliefs are much clearer to me now after you explained it to me. Thank you, Professor Woolsey!

Professor Woolsey: You're welcome!

Task 3 Translation

Directions: *Translate the following sentences into English.*
1. 爱默生诞生前22年，美国脱离英国统治，获得政治独立，却未获得文化独立。
2. 爱默生对当时物质至上的生活感到极为不满。
3. 对于他们而言，自然不仅是单纯的物质，而且鲜活的生命体，充溢着无所不能的上帝。
4. 超验主义强调个人主义、自立和自我净化的重要性。
5. 爱默生的思想为美国浪漫主义奠定了基础，对美国人民的生活有着深远的影响。

Task 4 Further Development

Directions: *An introductory sentence for a brief summary of the passage is provided below. Complete the summary by selecting the FOUR answer choices that express the most important ideas in the passage. Some sentences do not belong to the summary because they express ideas that are minor ideas*

Unit 6 Romanticism and Realism

in the passage.

Introductory Sentence: Transcendentalism is a unique trend of Romanticism in America.
Answer Choices   A. Like European romanticists, American romanticists also enthusiastically embraced nature, imagination, emotion, and individuality instead of formality, order and authority.   B. American romanticists demonstrated their own peculiar traits by tinting it with American color and came into being the American Transcendentalism, which was developed in the 1830s and 1840s in New England.   C. It was led by Ralph Waldo Emerson, an American essayist, lecturer, and poet, who founded the transcendentalist club in Cambridge, Massachusetts, on September 8, 1836 to start a movement as a protest against the general state of culture and society, and in particular, the state of intellectualism at Harvard University and the doctrine of the Unitarian church taught at Harvard Divinity School.   D. *Nature*'s voice pushed American Romanticism into a new phase, the phase of New England Transcendentalism, the summit of American Romanticism, exerting a tremendous impact on intellectual thinking in America.   E. Emerson and Henry David Thoreau were telling people to depend on themselves for spiritual perfection if they cared to make the effort. Because in their opinion, the individual soul communed with the Oversoul and was therefore divine.   F. Transcendentalism laid emphasis mostly on spirit or the Oversoul as the most important thing in the universe, offered a fresh perception of nature as symbolic of the Spirit or God, and stressed the importance of the individual and self-reliance.   G. Speaking words of self-dependence, self-reliance—a new language of freedom, he was the first to bring a truly American spirit.

Section C Realism in Europe

① Realism, literally, is always related to some form of reality and takes on various meanings depending on the context in which the term is used. Literary realism or realist literature is one of the conspicuous forms of Realism. It begins with nineteenth-century Russian literature and extends to late nineteenth and early twentieth century literature in other western countries. It is the trend towards depictions of contemporary life and society as it was. ② In the spirit of general "realism," realist authors chose to depict everyday activities and experiences, instead of a romanticized or similarly stylized presentation.

Lev Nikolayevich Tolstoy

Honoré de Balzac

Charles Dickens

Realism began earlier in the 19th century in Russia than elsewhere in Europe and took a more classical form. Lev Nikolayevich Tolstoy (1828—1910) is considered to have been one of the world's greatest realistic novelists. ③ *War and Peace*, first published in 1869, is acknowledged as one of the greatest novels of all time and peak of realist fiction and is generally thought to be remarkable for its dramatic breadth and unity. ④ It describes in graphic detail events surrounding the French invasion of Russia, and the impact of the Napoleonic era on Tsarist society. All this is seen through the eyes of five Russian aristocratic families. The vast and thick book includes 580 characters, among which many are historical. The story moves from the court to the battlefields, family life to headquarters of Napoleon.

Honoré de Balzac (1799—1850) is remembered as one of the founders of realism in European literature. ⑤ His well-known *La Comédie Humaine* stands as a unique literary monument to individual genius and a remarkable landmark of an era because of his keen observation and multivolume panoramic description of French society. In 1832, Balzac got the idea for an enormous series of books that would paint a panoramic portrait of "all aspects of society." When the idea struck, he raced to his sister and proclaimed, "I am about to become a genius." He was right. ⑥ In *La Comédie Humaine*, Balzac frequently regretted the loss of a pre-Revolutionary society of honor which had now become a society dominated by money. He satirized the attempts of talented but poor youth to achieve social success. He also mocked the heredity of nobles and aspiration of people of good blood to a title. He revealed the coldness and indifference between human beings in the immoral and corrupted society. All the characters he created are impressively vivid and typical. ⑦ One of his characters, Goriot in *Le Père Goriot*, has deeply imprinted readers' mind as a representative of mammonism.

The Victorian period (1837—1901) in Britain witnessed the flourish of realist novels. Due to the rapid industrialization, there were many social, political and economic problems associated with it. ⑧ For example, society saw the abuses of government and industry, and the suffering of the poor who were not profiting from England's economic prosperity. ⑨ Novelists in Britain reacted to reveal the dark society and corrupted bourgeois middle-class by writing stories to help create sympathy for the poor working class and promote change. Charles Dickens

(1812—1870) was such a writer. ⑩ Having emerged on the literary scene in the 1830s, he dominated the first part of Victoria's reign and is deemed to be one of the greatest realist novelists in Britain. During his lifetime he viewed situations on the streets and wrote about real-life situations of the poor people of London. Stories such as *Oliver Twist* encouraged people to push Parliament to change laws to protect the poor.

(587 words)

New Words and Expressions (C)

New Words

New Words	Phonetic Symbols	Meanings
acknowledge	[əkˈnɒlɪdʒ]	v. 承认
aspiration	[ˌæspəˈreɪʃn]	n. 渴望, 抱负
battlefield	[ˈbætlfiːld]	n. 战场
corrupted	[kəˈrʌptɪd]	adj. 腐败的
conspicuous	[kənˈspɪkjuəs]	adj. 显著的, 显而易见的
contemporary	[kənˈtemprəri]	adj. 当代的, 同时代的
deem	[diːm]	v. 认为, 视作, 相信
dominate	[ˈdɒmɪneɪt]	v. 控制, 支配
emerge	[ɪˈmɜːdʒ]	v. 出现, 形成
enormous	[ɪˈnɔːməs]	adj. 巨大的
flourish	[ˈflʌrɪʃ]	v. 繁荣, 兴旺
graphic	[ˈɡræfɪk]	adj. 图表的, 形象的
headquarters	[ˈhedˈkwɔːtəz]	n. 总部
heredity	[həˈredəti]	n. 遗传(性)
impressively	[ɪmˈpresɪvli]	adv. 令人难忘地
imprint	[ɪmˈprɪnt]	v. 使留下印象
immoral	[ɪˈmɒrəl]	adj. 不道德的, 邪恶的
indifference	[ɪnˈdɪfrəns]	n. 漠不关心, 冷淡
industrialization	[ɪnˌdʌstrɪəlaɪˈzeɪʃn]	n. 工业化
invasion	[ɪnˈveɪʒn]	n. 侵略
landmark	[ˈlændmɑːk]	n. 地标, 里程碑
literally	[ˈlɪtərəli]	adv. 字面上, 逐字地
mammonism	[ˈmæmənɪzəm]	n. 拜金主义

mock	[mɒk]	v. 嘲弄
multivolume	[ˌmʌltɪˈvɒljuːm]	adj. 多卷的
panoramic	[ˌpænəˈræmɪk]	adj. 全景的
peak	[piːk]	n. 山峰,最高点
portrait	[ˈpɔːtreɪt]	n. 肖像,描写
prosperity	[prɒˈsperəti]	n. 繁荣,成功
reign	[reɪn]	n./v. 统治
remarkable	[rɪˈmɑːkəbl]	adj. 卓越的,值得注意的
romanticize	[rəʊˈmæntɪsaɪz]	v. 使浪漫化
satirize	[ˈsætəraɪz]	v. 讽刺
witness	[ˈwɪtnəs]	v. 目击;n. 目击者

Expressions

be deemed to	被认为
profit from	从……获利,获益
take on	呈现

Proper Names

Goriot	高老头戈里奥,《高老头》中的人物。
La Comédie Humaine	《人间喜剧》,巴尔扎克的作品,全面反映19世纪法国的社会生活,写出一部法国的社会风俗史。
Le Père Goriot	《高老头》,巴尔扎克《人间喜剧》中的篇章
Napoleonic	拿破仑一世的
Oliver Twist	《雾都孤儿》,英国小说家狄更斯的小说
Tsarist	沙皇式的

Difficult Sentences

① Realism, literally, is always related to some form of reality and takes on various meanings depending on the context in which the term is used.

从字面上看,现实主义常常与某种现实的形式相关,并根据该词的语境呈现出不同的含义。

② In the spirit of general "realism," realist authors chose to depict everyday activities and experiences, instead of a romanticized or similarly stylized presentation.

Unit 6　Romanticism and Realism

本着现实主义的精神，现实主义作家笔下描绘的是日常生活和经历，而不是呈现浪漫想象的或类似非写实的东西。

③ *War and Peace*, first published in 1869, is acknowledged as one of the greatest novels of all time and peak of realist fiction and is generally thought to be remarkable for its dramatic breadth and unity.

《战争与和平》首次出版于1869年，被公认为史上最伟大的小说之一，同时也是现实主义小说的巅峰之作，因其戏剧性的广度和统一性而为人们所知。

④ It describes in graphic detail events surrounding the French invasion of Russia, and the impact of the Napoleonic era on Tsarist society.

这部小说围绕着法国入侵俄国这一历史，生动详尽地描摹了该历史事件，以及拿破仑时代对沙皇社会的影响。

⑤ His well-known *La Comédie Humaine* stands as a unique literary monument to individual genius and a remarkable landmark of an era because of his keen observation and multivolume panoramic description of French society.

他著名的《人间喜剧》既是一座独一无二、展现个人天才的文学丰碑，也是那个时代的里程碑，这都源于他对法国社会的敏锐洞察力和多卷本的全景化描绘。

⑥ In *La Comédie Humaine*, Balzac frequently regretted the loss of a pre-Revolutionary society of honor which has now become a society dominated by money.

在《人间喜剧》中，巴尔扎克常常痛惜，法国社会丢失了革命前的高尚品质，因为他所处的社会充满着铜臭味。

⑦ One of his characters, Goriot in *Le Père Goriot*, has deeply imprinted readers' mind as a representative of mammonism.

《高老头》中高老头这一人物形象作为拜金主义的代表已深深印刻在读者心中。

⑧ For example, society saw the abuses of government and industry, and the suffering of the poor who were not profiting from England's economic prosperity.

比如说，政府滥用职权，工业流弊横行，穷苦人民生活在水深火热中，未能从英国繁荣经济中获得利益。

⑨ Novelists in Britain reacted to reveal the dark society and corrupted bourgeois middle-class by writing stories to help create sympathy for the poor working class and promote change.

英国小说家通过小说来揭露社会的黑暗，资本主义中产阶级的堕落，以期能引发社会对贫苦工人阶级的同情，促使改革。

⑩ Having emerged on the literary scene in the 1830s, he dominated the first part of Victoria's reign and is deemed to be one of the greatest realist novelists in Britain.

19世纪30年代他开始在英国文坛崭露头角，在维多利亚前期的文坛独领风骚，被认为是英国最伟大的现实主义小说家之一。

Exercises

Task 1   Short Answer Questions

Directions: *Work in pairs to answer the following questions.*

1. When and where did literary Realism emerge?
2. What themes did realist literature represent?
3. What is the masterpiece of Tolstoy mentioned in the passage?
4. Why is Balzac considered as one of the founders of realism in European literature?
5. What contribution did Dickens's novel make to the social change?

Task 2 Vocabulary

Directions: *Complete the following sentences with proper words or phrases from the box. Change the form if necessary. Please note there are more words and phrases than necessary.*

A) battlefield	B) invade	C) dominate	D) satire
E) emerge	F) reign	G) portrayal	H) aspire
I) profit from	J) panoramic	K) remark	L) imprint
M) prosperous	N) witness	O) corruption	

1. Thanks to the effective reform policies, the country has achieved _____ economic results.
2. His account of the car crash incident approximates to that of other _____.
3. Ecocriticism is a(n) _____ literary theory which aims to represent the relationship between literature and environment.
4. It is reported that many veterans could not well _____ this new medical welfare program.
5. In the Genesis of the Bible, God grants humans the _____ over the nonhuman beings.
6. Without peace, no sustainable development and _____ could be fulfilled.
7. When he was a boy, Thomas nursed a(n) _____ to be a musician.
8. A(n) _____ roof system was established in this modern architecture so that people could better observe the starry sky in the night.
9. Since there are many morally _____ officials, the government is adopting strict and tough _____ measures to punish them.
10. The poet in his poetry employed many rhetorical devices to _____ the immoral _____ of the rural regions in various ways and guises.

Task 3   Translation

Directions: *Complete the following sentences by translating the Chinese in brackets.*

1. More and more people _____ (极力呼吁) the government to reform the unequal social welfare.

2. Since Bird Nest attracts tourists from all over the world, it is now becoming a _____ (特色的国家标志性建筑).
3. It is this _____ (引人入胜、妙趣横生的描述) of the protagonist in this novel that makes the novelist achieve global fame.
4. No effective medicine has been invented to cure this _____ (流行病).
5. One of the national prosperities is featured by the sincere respect for _____ (传统经典文化).

Task 4   Further Development
Exercise A   Oral English Practice
Directions: Look at the following diagram and try to search for information related to the questions listed and then report to your classmates what you know about the orphan Oliver Twist in the novel *Oliver Twist*.

Exercise B   Writing Practice
Directions: The following is taken from an email written by the recruiting director of the Association of World Literature in University Q.

Over the past five years, there has been a 15 percent decline in the size of the average students enrolling in the Association of World Literature. In spite of increased advertising, we are attracting fewer and fewer students to enroll, causing the popularity of our Association to decrease significantly. We must take action to attract new members. The best way to do so is by instituting a "Honoré de Balzac" program this semester. Two years ago the nearby University P

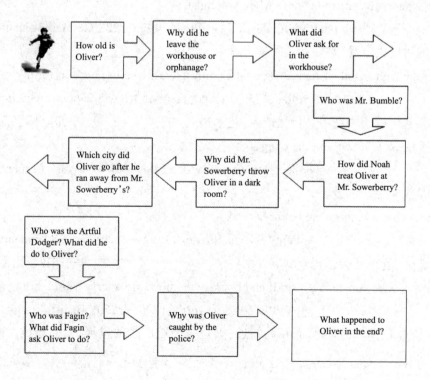

started a "Charles Dickens" program, and its size of members has increased 20 percent since then. If we start a "Honoré de Balzac" program, we can predict that the size of members and the popularity will increase, too.

1. Read the text about Honoré de Balzac and Charles Dickens again and the email above.
2. Please first identify the thesis statement, claim or recommendation, and evidence for it.
3. Then use the knowledge of what you have learned in this unit to write a 300-word response, in which you discuss what questions would need to be answered in order to decide whether the recommendation is likely to have the predicted result. Be sure to explain how the answers to these questions would help to evaluate the recommendation.

Thesis Statement/Claim/Recommendation:
_____

Evidences:
_____
_____

Essay Writing:
_____
_____

Adages and Proverbs

1. Enjoy when you can, and endure when you must.
   — Johann Wolfgang von Goethe (1749—1832), German Romantic poet
   能做的时候去享受，必须做的时候去忍耐。——歌德

2. Art is the right hand of nature. The latter only gave us being, but the former made us men.   —Friedrich Schiller (1759—1805), German Romantic poet and philosopher
   艺术是自然的得力助手。自然造人，艺术塑人。   ——弗里德里希·席勒

3. Friendship is love without his wings.
   —George Gordon Byron (1788—1824), British Romantic poet
   友谊是没有羽翼的爱。   ——乔治·拜伦

4. If winter comes, can spring be far behind?
   — Percy Bysshe Shelley (1792—1822), British Romantic poet
   冬天来了，春天还会远吗？   ——珀西·比希·雪莱

5. Dreams, books, are each a world; and books, we know, are a large world, both pure and good.   —William Wordsworth (1770—1850), British Romantic poet
   梦与书属于不同的世界，而我们知道，书是一个更广阔的世界，它们既纯洁而又美

Unit 6 Romanticism and Realism

好。　　　　　　　　　　　　　　　　　　　　　　　——威廉·华兹华斯

6. To most men, experience is like the stern light of a ship which illuminates only the track it has passed.　　—Samuel Taylor Coleridge (1772—1834), British Romantic poet
对于大多数人,经验像是船上的尾灯,只照亮船驶过的航道。
　　　　　　　　　　　　　　　　　　　　　　　——萨缪尔·柯勒律治

7. Have a heart that never hardens, a temper that never tires, a touch that never hurts.
　　　　　　　　　　　—Charles Dickens (1812—1870), British Realistic novelist
拥有一颗心,永远柔软,一种脾性,永不厌倦,一种触碰,不含伤害。
　　　　　　　　　　　　　　　　　　　　　　　——查尔斯·狄更斯

8. Dare and the world always yields. If it beats you sometimes, dare it again and again and it will succumb.
　　　　　　　　—William Makepeace Thackeray (1811—1863), British Realistic novelist
大胆挑战,世界总会让步。如果有时候你被它打败了,不断地挑战,它总会屈服的。
　　　　　　　　　　　　　　　　　　　　　　　——威廉·萨克雷

9. A compliment is something like a kiss through a veil.
　　　　　　　　　　　　　　　　—Victor Hugo (1802—1885), French writer
赞誉就像是透过面纱的亲吻。　　　　　　　　　　　——维克多·雨果

10. There is no such thing as a great talent without great will-power.
　　　　　　　　　　—Honoré de Balzac (1799—1850), French Realistic novelist
没有伟大的意志力,便没有雄才大略。　　　　　　——奥诺雷·德·巴尔扎克

11. Ideal is the beacon. Without ideal, there is no secure direction; without direction, there is no life.　　　　—Leo Tolstoy (1828—1910), Russian Realistic novelist
理想是指路明灯。没有理想,就没有坚定的方向;没有方向,就没有生活。
　　　　　　　　　　　　　　　　　　　　　　　——列夫·托尔斯泰

12. The landscape belongs to the man who looks at it.
　　　　—Ralph Waldo Emerson (1803— 1882), American Transcendentalist and philosopher
风景属于看风景的人。　　　　　　　　　　　　　——拉尔夫·沃尔多·爱默生

13. A great man is always willing to be little.　　　　— Ralph Waldo Emerson
伟大的人物总是愿意当小人物的。　　　　　　　——拉尔夫·沃尔多·爱默生

14. It is not enough to be industrious, so are the ants. What are you industrious for?
　　　　　　　　　　—Henry David Thoreau (1817—1862), American writer, philosopher
光勤劳是不够的,蚂蚁也是勤劳的.要看你为什么而勤劳。　　——亨利·大卫·梭罗

15. Don't part with your illusions. When they are gone you may still exist, but you have ceased to live.　　　　—Mark Twain (1835—1910), American Realistic novelist

> 不要放弃你的幻想。当幻想没有了以后，你还可以生存，但是你虽生犹死。
>
> ——马克·吐温

Key to Unit 6 Exercises

导读答案

1. Romanticism was an artistic, literary, intellectual movement from about 1789 to 1850 in Western civilization. It aimed to fight against rationalist values of the Age of Enlightenment, such as social order, reason and logic. It praised individualism, subjectivism, irrationalism, imagination, emotions and nature-emotion over reason and senses over intellect. This period saw many famous romantic figures such as William Wordsworth, Percy Bysshe Shelley, George Gordon Byron, Goethe, Richard Wagner, Ludwig van Beethoven, and so on.

   Transcendentalism was developed in the 1830s and 1840s in New England and was in essence a romantic idealism and a literary, political, philosophical and intellectual movement which was led by Ralph Waldo Emerson. It emphasized mostly spirit or the Oversoul as the most important thing in the universe, offered a fresh perception of nature as symbolic of the Spirit or God, and stressed the importance of the individual and self-reliance.

   Realism began with nineteenth-century French literature and extended to late-nineteenth and early-twentieth-century literature in other western countries. Although different countries had different features, Realism was the trend towards depictions of contemporary life and society as it had been. This period saw many famous realistic figures such as Lev Nikolayevich Tolstoy, Honoré de Balzac, Charles Dickens etc.

2. The Romantic figure worth mentioning is Percy Bysshe Shelley. Shelley, born on 4 August 1792 and died on 8 July 1822, is one of the major English Romantic poets and is critically regarded as among the finest lyric poets in the English language. He is the poet of the famous line "If Winter comes, can Spring be far behind?" at the end of his Ode to the Western Wind. His wife is also a famous literary figure whose masterpiece is *Frankenstein*.

   The Realistic figure worth mentioning is Charles Dickens. Dickens (1812—1870), emerging on the literary scene in the 1830s, and dominating the first part of Victoria's reign, is thought to be one of the greatest realist novelists in Britain. He wrote vividly about London life and struggles of the poor, and showed great sympathy towards the lower class, which can be seen in one of his masterpieces *Oliver Twister*. His other novels such as *David Copperfield*, *A Tale of Two Cities*, *Great Expectations* etc. are favorably accessible to readers of all classes.

Unit 6 Romanticism and Realism

3. Goethe was a famous German writer of the well-known book named *The Sorrows of Young Werther*. He was one of the leaders in the German Sturm und Drang movement, pioneering the Romanticism in German. During his life, he had only one wife but was romantically entangled with many women, leaving us many romance stories. He loved at first sight Charlotte Buff who but was engaged and his romantic relationship with her prompted him to write *The Sorrows of Younger Werther*. His second romance with Charlotte von Stein, thirty-three years old married mother of seven children, lasted twelve years. The woman becoming his wife finally was Christiane Vulpius. Their love lasted twenty-eight years.

Section A Romanticism in Europe
Task 1 Reading Comprehension
1. A 2. B 3. D 4. C 5. C
Task 2 Vocabulary
1. C 2. E 3. I 4. L 5. O 6. J 7. G 8. B 9. M 10. A
Task 3 Translation
1. Although the term "Romanticism" was coined in the 1840s in England, the publication of Wordsworth and Coleridge's *Lyrical Ballads* marked the emergence of English Romanticism.
2. Unlike the Age of Enlightenment, which focused on rationality and intellect, Romanticism placed human emotions, feelings, instinct, and intuition above everything else.
3. Goethe, the German Romantics who praised emotion and feeling, declared, "Feeling is everything."
4. Romanticists desire to follow their inner drives, which leads them to resent and rebel against middle-class conventions.
5. Romantic architects were inclined to replicate Gothic style in both private and public buildings.
Task 4 Further Development
Sample Answer:

  This is a lovely Romantic poem! Shelley regards love as a philosophy because it plays a significant role in driving our life. Philosophy is a theory or an attitude that acts as a guiding principle for our behavior. People do things for love every day. What makes the poem distinctively romantic is Shelley's ways to describe love and liken it to nature. As we have learned in the text about Romanticism, respect for and love of nature is one of the distinctive Romantic features. When examining this poem, we find that Shelley embodies this feature in the

poem by comparing the personal love to the love among natural entities, such as the fountains and the river, the mountains and the heaven, etc. For him, everything in this world is inter-linked and inter-dependent and everything seems to have a spirit. I really appreciate Shelley's enthusiasm for love and nature. He is a great Romantic poet.

Section B Romanticism in America

Task 1 Reading Comprehension

1. F 2. T 3. T 4. T 5. T 6. T 7. NG 8. F 9. F 10. T

Task 2 Vocabulary

1. self-reliance   2. permeated with   3. restorative   4. omnipresent
5. omnipotent   6. essential   7. commune with   8. self-perfected
9. condemned   10. regeneration

Task 3 Translation

1. Just twenty-two years before Emerson was born, the United States had been independent from Britain, only politically not culturally.
2. Emerson was disconcertingly unsatisfied with the materialism-oriented life of his time.
3. Nature was, to them, not purely matter but was alive and filled with God's overwhelming presence.
4. Transcendentalists stressed the importance of the individual, self-reliance and self-purification.
5. Emerson's words shaping the Romanticism in America has had a lasting impact on American life.

Task 4 Further Development

B-C-D-F

Section C Realism in Europe

Task 1 Reading Comprehension

1. In the 19th century and in Russia.
2. Contemporary life and society as it was.
3. *War and Peace*.
4. Because of his masterpiece *La Comédie Humaine* that keenly observed and panoramically depicted French society.
5. Dickens's novels such as *Oliver Twist* encouraged people to push Parliament to change laws to protect the poor.

Task 2 Vocabulary

1. remarkable   2. witnesses   3. emerging   4. profit from   5. domination

Unit 6　Romanticism and Realism

6. prosperity　　　7. aspiration　　　8. panoramic　　　9. corrupted, anti-corruption
10. satirize, invasion

Task 3　Translation

1. are eagerly calling on/appealing to　　　2. characteristic national landmark
3. gripping, funny portrait/portrayal/ depiction　　　4. epidemic disease
5. the traditional cultural classics(canons)/ the traditional classic culture

Task 4　Further Development

Exercise A　Oral Practice

　　Sample Answer: Oliver Twist, the protagonist of Charles Dickens's novel *Oliver Twist* was nine years old, kind and good-hearted. He was an orphan and he lived in a parish workhouse where he felt very sad. In the workhouse, the children ate porridge for breakfast, lunch and dinner. One day, Oliver was so hungry that he took his bowl and asked for some more porridge. Mr. Bumble, who was the master of the workhouse, was very angry and took Oliver in a cold, dark room. After one week Mr. Bumble told Oliver that he had to leave the workhouse immediately. Therefore he had to live with Mr. Sowerberry and work in his shop. At Mr. Sowerberry's house, Oliver was mistreated. There he met a boy called Noah who always said terrible things about Oliver's mother. One day, Oliver hit him and Mr. Sowerberry was so furious with Oliver that he threw him in a cold dark room. Oliver decided to run away from Mr. Sowerberry's house. He ran to the main road, from where he saw the sign for London so he went there. Near London Oliver met the Artful Dodger, a pickpocket who invited him to go and live in Fagin's house. Fagin who was an ugly old and villainous-looking man, the leader of a gang of boy thieves, taught the children to steal with colored handkerchiefs. At the market the Dodger and Charley stole a handkerchief from a gentleman's pocket. The Dodger and Charley ran away, but Oliver was taken to the police station. Mr. Brownlow a very respectable-looking gentleman helped bail Oliver. He invited Oliver to live with him and his housekeeper, Mrs. Bedwin. When Oliver lived at Mr. Brownlow's house he was very happy. But Fagin was furious because Oliver knew about the special box where he put the stolen jewelry. Fagin told Bill Sikes (a hefty vicious housebreaker and thief in his thirties) and Nancy (a young prostitute) to find Oliver immediately. They found Oliver and took him back to Fagin's. Fagin wanted to burgle a rich mansion and he forced Oliver to do that. Bill, Toby and Oliver went to the mansion, but when Oliver entered it the servants shot him. The two boys ran away but Oliver stayed in the road all night. As he was bleeding, he couldn't run. Mrs. Maylie, a dignified, stately old lady and her niece Rose lived in the mansion. They called a doctor to visit Oliver. The boy told Mrs. Maylie and her niece his story and they took Oliver to their house in the countryside. Oliver went to live with Mr. Brownlow, a kind-hearted elderly gentleman who adopted him. One day,

Rose paid a visit to them and saw a painting in their house. It was Oliver's mother. Rose told that she was her sister. The story ends with Fagin being captured and dying in prison, and Olive living happily.

Exercise B Writing Practice

Thesis Statement/Claim/Recommendation: In pursuit of the increase of members and popularity of the Association of World Literature in University Q, the best way that the recruiting director thinks is to institute a "Honoré de Balzac" program this semester.

Evidences:

a. Over the past five years, there has been a 15 percent decline in the size of the average students enrolling in the Association of World Literature.

b. In spite of increased advertising, we are attracting fewer and fewer students to enroll, causing the popularity of our Association to decrease significantly.

c. Two years ago the nearby University P started a "Charles Dickens" program, and its size of members has increased 20 percent since then.

Sample Writing:

Surely, it may be true that the Association of World Literature in University Q need to devote more heart and soul to pursuing its increase of members and popularity, but the recruiting director does not make a cogent case for his or her recommendation which is merely based on the three unconvincing evidences. Thus his or her argument is rife with holes and questions, and thus, not strong enough to support his or her claim that the size of members and the popularity will increase by starting a "Honoré de Balzac" program in University Q.

Building upon the unscientific analogy that the nearby Univerisity P started a "Charles Dickens" program, and its size of members has increased 20 percent since then, the recruiting director hastily recommends that by instituting a "Honoré de Balzac" program this semester, the size of members and the popularity of the Association will increase as well. As we know, different students in different universities have different literary tastes and interests. Even the same students in different periods of time may have different literary attitudes. Thus, such an analogy is chronologically and longitudinally unpersuasive. For example, students in nearby University P are exposed more to British Realist figures as there are many professors proficient at British Realism. It's also possible that students are forced to enroll in "Charles Dickens" program by University P for the enrollment could earn their credits. It's possible that students in University P more like Dickens because of his famous works such as *Oliver Twist* and *David Copperfield*. But two years later, the mimicking of such a program by the Association of World Literature in University Q by establishing "Honoré de Balzac" program this semester may be practically successful or may not, because students are different, their tastes may vary and the literary atmosphere in University Q is unknown. Although Honoré de Balzac, one of the most noted and popular novelists of all times, by virtue of his well-known and multivolume panoramic *La Comédie Humaine* comparable enough to Charles Dickens will be attractive to many students, yet such a single figure is not powerful enough to shoulder such a big responsibility to attract all the students in University Q, because other students may prefer other programs of world literary figures such as Victor Hugo, Lev Tolstoy, Emily Dickinson, William Faulkner, T.S. Eliot, Dylan Thomas, R.S. Thomas, Lu Xun, Ba Jin, Mo Yan, Haruki Murakami etc. Unless the recruiting director makes a fully cogent survey of students' literary needs, and the literary atmosphere in University Q, it would be hasty to recommend instituting a "Honoré de Balzac" program this semester which is believed to lead to increasing the size of members and the popularity of the Association.

A colorful, meaningful and instructive program often adds to an association's literary values, leads to increased members and popularity, and enriches students' university life. To this end, the recruiting director of the Association of World Literature in University Q can recommend instituting a "Honoré de Balzac" program this semester. However, he or she should address the questions listed above, or else his or her argument will not be significantly persuasive, and his or her recommendation will be hasty.

(注：以上三个论据，学生只要选择其中一个，对其中的逻辑错误进行阐述即可。)

Unit 7
Modernism and Contemporary Western Culture

导读

本单元旨在通过对现代主义和以美国文化为代表的当代西方文化等知识的介绍,使学生对19世纪末、20世纪初以来影响西方社会文化生活各个方面的现代主义运动的特征、意义及代表人物有一定的了解,对当代美国文化的特点、困境有初步的认识,熟悉所学西方文化知识及相关的英语表达方式,并为下一步的学习和研究奠定基础。

Before You Start

While preparing for this unit, think about the following questions:
1. Could you make a distinction between the terms like *modern, modernism, modernization, modernist, modernity* and *post-modernism*?
2. Do you know any modernist thinkers, poets and novelists?
3. What do you know about Sigmund Freud's theory?

Section A Modernism and Modernist Movement

① The term modernism is widely used to identify new and distinctive features in the subjects, forms, concepts, and styles of literature and the other arts in the early decades of the 20th century, but especially after World War I (1914—1918). ② The specific features signified by "modernism" vary with the user, but many critics agree that it involves a deliberate and radical break with some of the traditional bases not only of Western art, but of Western culture in general. ③ Important intellectual precursors of modernism, in this sense, are thinkers who had questioned the certainties that had supported traditional modes of social organization, religion, and morality, and also traditional ways of conceiving the human self—thinkers such as Karl Marx, Friedrich Nietzsche and Sigmund Freud. Modernist Movement covers a series of revolutionary movements in literature, art, architecture, and music, which emerged during this period.

Modernist Literature

Modernist literature attempts to take into account changing ideas about reality with the developed innovative literary techniques such as stream-of-consciousness, interior monologue, as well as the use of multiple points-of-view.④ Modernist writers sought to leave the traditions of nineteenth-century literature behind in terms of form, content, and expression. They realized that a new industrial age—full of machines, buildings, and technology—had ushered out rural living forever, and the result was often a pessimistic view of what lay before humankind. Frequent themes in modernist works are loneliness and isolation (even in cities teeming with people), ⑤ and a significant number of writers tried to capture that sense of solitude by engaging in stream-of-consciousness writing, which captures the thought process of a single character as it happens without interruption. Some of the most famous modernist authors include Ernest Hemingway, F. Scott Fitzgerald, Virginia Woolf, James Joyce and T.S. Eliot.

Modernist Art

Modernism in art was not an integrated movement, but rather a multiplicity of "isms"—such as Post-Impressionism, Fauvism, Cubism, and later Dadaism and Futurism. What tied modernist artists together was a desire to break away from the conventions of representational art. ⑥ They ditched the old rules of perspective, color, and composition in order to work out their own visions. Their attitudes were reinforced by scientific discoveries of the day that seemed to question the solidity of the "real" world and the reliability of perception. "Reality"—whatever that was—became a far more slippery prospect than it had been a generation earlier.

The Luncheon on the Grass, 1863, Édouard Manet.

Most art historians agree that the French artist Edouard Manet is the first Modernist painter, and that Modernism in art originated in the 1860s. Paintings such as his *Le Dejeuner sur l' Herbe* (*The Luncheon on the Grass* in English) are seen to have ushered in a new era, among the reasons being that its daring subject, a nude woman picnicking with a group of men attired in suits, was so startling. Painters like Vincent van Gogh, Paul Cézanne, Paul Gauguin, Pablo Picasso, and Henri Matisse were also essential for the development of modern art.

Modernist Architecture

Modernist architects and designers believed that new technology rendered old styles of building obsolete. Le Corbusier thought that buildings should function as "machines for living in." Just as cars had replaced the horse, so modernist design should reject the old styles and structures inherited from Ancient Greece or from the Middle Ages.⑦ Following this machine aesthetic, modernist designers typically rejected decorative motifs in design, preferring to emphasize the materials used and pure geometrical forms. The skyscrapers, such as Ludwig

Ludwig Mies van der Rohe's Seagram Building in New York City

Mies van der Rohe's Seagram Building(1956—1958) in New York, became the archetypal modernist building. Modernist design of houses and furniture also typically emphasized simplicity and clarity of form, open-plan interiors, and the absence of clutter.

Modernist Music

New approaches to form and content were also being explored in music. ⑧ As in the visual arts, music also became less "representational" and evocative and more abstract and expressive. The French composer Claude Debussy explored unconventional harmonies, musical sound and tonal quality in his compositions. ⑨ Debussy's pieces were made the basis for the ballet *Le Sacre du Printempts* by the Russian composer Igor Stravinsky, which, in its complex rhythmic structures and use of dissonance, together with radically unconventional design of dances, shocked both conservative critics and the public. The event, though, established the basis for developments of modernism in music.

⑩ Though some critics claim that Modernism is "ceding its predominance to Post-modernism," it will continue to exert its influence on the later generations engaging in a wide variety of cultural movements.

(Based on http://en.wikipedia.org/wiki/Modernism
http://en.wikipedia.org/wiki/Modernist_literature
http://arthistoryresources.net/modernism/artsake.html)

New Words and Expressions (A)

New Words

New Words	Phonetic Symbols	Meanings
archetypal	[ˈɑːkɪˈtaɪpl]	adj. 典型的
attire	[əˈtaɪə(r)]	v. 穿衣
capture	[ˈkæptʃə(r)]	v. 表现, 体现(感情、气氛)
cede	[siːd]	v. 让给
clarity	[ˈklærəti]	n. 明晰
clutter	[ˈklʌtə(r)]	n. 杂乱
dissonance	[ˈdɪsənəns]	n. 不谐和音
distinctive	[dɪˈstɪŋktɪv]	adj. 与众不同的, 有特色的

Unit 7 Modernism and Contemporary Western Culture

ditch	[dɪtʃ]	v. 抛弃
evocative	[ɪˈvɒkətɪv]	adj. 唤起情感的,引起共鸣的
geometrical	[ˌdʒiːəˈmetrɪkl]	adj. 几何形状
harmony	[ˈhɑːməni]	n. 和声
monologue	[ˈmɒnəlɒɡ]	n. 独白
morality	[məˈræləti]	n. 道德(规范)
nude	[njuːd]	adj. 裸体的
obsolete	[ˈɒbsəliːt]	adj. 废弃的,过时的
open-plan	[ˈəʊpən plæn]	adj. 开敞式的,无隔断的
perception	[pəˈsepʃn]	n. 感觉;认知
perspective	[pəˈspektɪv]	n. 透视画法,视角
pessimistic	[ˌpesɪˈmɪstɪk]	adj. 悲观(主义)的
precursor	[priːˈkɜːsə]	n. 先驱
predominance	[prɪˈdɒmɪnəns]	n. 主导地位
render	[ˈrendə(r)]	v. 使……成为
representational	[ˌreprɪzenˈteɪʃnl]	adj. (绘画)具象风格的,写实的,表现的
slippery	[ˈslɪpəri]	adj. 不可靠的
solidity	[səˈlɪdəti]	n. 可靠性
solitude	[ˈsɒlɪtjuːd]	n. 孤独
specific	[spəˈsɪfɪk]	adj. 特有的,具体的
teem	[tiːm]	v. 充满
tonal	[ˈtəʊnl]	adj. 音调的

Expressions

a multiplicity of	许多
break away	脱离,放弃
in terms of	在……方面
stream-of-consciousness	意识流
take... into account	重视,考虑

Proper Names

Cubism	立体派,立方主义,20世纪初的一种艺术流派
Claude Debussy	克劳德·德彪西(1862—1918),法国作曲家
Dadaism	达达派,达达主义
Edouard Manet	爱德华·马奈(1832—1883),法国画家,19世纪印象派奠基人之一

Ernest Hemingway	欧内斯特·海明威(1899—1961),美国作家和记者,1954年度诺贝尔文学奖获得者
Fauvism	野兽派
Friedrich Nietzsche	弗里德里希·尼采(1844—1900),德国哲学家
F. Scott Fitzgerald	弗朗西斯·斯科特·菲茨杰拉德(1896—1940),美国作家,20世纪20年代"爵士时代"的发言人和"迷惘的一代"的代表作家之一
Henri Matisse	亨利·马蒂斯(1869—1954),法国著名画家,野兽派创始人和主要代表人物
James Joyce	詹姆斯·乔伊斯(1882—1941),爱尔兰作家和诗人,20世纪最重要的作家之一
Karl Marx	卡尔·马克思(1818—1883),德国无产阶级革命家、经济学家、哲学家、马克思主义创始人
Le Corbusier	勒·科比西埃(1887—1965),诞生于瑞士,成名于法国,建筑师、都市计划家、作家、画家,现代建筑运动的激进分子和主将
Le Dejeuner sur l'Herbe	(法语)草地上的午餐
Le Sacre Du Printempts	《春之祭》,俄罗斯作曲家斯特拉文斯基于1913年创作的芭蕾舞剧
Ludwig Mies van der Rohe	路德维希·密斯·凡·德·罗(1886—1969),德国建筑师,现代主义建筑大师之一
Paul Cézanne	保罗·塞尚(1839—1906),法国后印象派画家中的代表人物,"现代绘画之父"
Pablo Picasso	巴勃罗·毕加索(1881—1973),西班牙画家、雕塑家,现代艺术创始人,西方现代派绘画的主要代表
Seagram Building	西格拉姆大厦(美国纽约)
Sigmund Freud	西格蒙德·弗洛伊德(1856—1939),奥地利医生,心理分析的创始人
T.S. Eliot	托·斯·艾略特(1888—1965)生于美国的英国诗人、剧作家、文艺评论家,诗歌现代派运动领袖,曾获1948年诺贝尔文学奖
Vincent van Gogh	文森特·梵·高(1853—1890),荷兰后印象派画家
Virginia Woolf	弗吉尼亚·伍尔芙(1882—1941),英国女作家、文学批评家和文学理论家,意识流文学代表人物,被誉为20世纪现代主义与女性主义的先锋

Difficult Sentences

① The term modernism is widely used to identify new and distinctive features in the subjects, forms, concepts, and styles of literature and the other arts in the early decades of the 20th century, but especially after World War I (1914—1918).

Unit 7　Modernism and Contemporary Western Culture

现代主义一词被广泛用来表述20世纪初期,特别是第一次世界大战(1914—1918)后在文学和其他艺术领域中主题、形式、概念和风格上与众不同的新特征。

② The specific features signified by "modernism" vary with the user, but many critics agree that it involves a deliberate and radical break with some of the traditional bases not only of Western art, but of Western culture in general.

"现代主义"的具体特点因使用者的不同而变化,但很多评论家认为它具有一种有意识地与西方艺术,甚至整个西方文化传统根基完全背离的特征。

③ Important intellectual precursors of modernism, in this sense, are thinkers who had questioned the certainties that had supported traditional modes of social organization, religion, and morality, and also traditional ways of conceiving the human self....

就此种意义而言,现代主义重要的思想先驱是那些思想家们,他们对传统的社会组织形式、宗教和道德的确定性以及传统的人类自身认知方式提出了质疑。

④ Modernist writers sought to leave the traditions of nineteenth-century literature behind in terms of form, content, and expression. They realized that a new industrial age—full of machines, buildings, and technology—had ushered out rural living forever, and the result was often a pessimistic view of what lay before humankind.

现代主义作家试图在形式、内容和表达方式上摆脱19世纪文学传统。他们意识到一个新的充斥着机械、建筑和科技的工业时代已经使人们永远远离了田园生活,其结果通常就是对人类前景持悲观态度。

⑤ ...and a significant number of writers tried to capture that sense of solitude by engaging in stream-of-consciousness writing, which captures the thought process of a single character as it happens without interruption.

许多作者试图通过意识流的手法,一种不间断记录思维进程的手法来表现这种孤寂感。

⑥ They ditched the old rules of perspective, color, and composition in order to work out their own visions. Their attitudes were reinforced by scientific discoveries of the day that seemed to question the solidity of the "real" world and the reliability of perception. "Reality"—whatever that was—became a far more slippery prospect than it had been a generation earlier.

他们摒弃了旧的视角、色彩和构图规则以表现出自己的想象。当时的科学发现进一步强化了他们的观点,这些发现对"现实"世界的可靠性和感知的可信度提出了质疑。无论"现实"究竟如何,较之上一年代都变得更加难以确定。

⑦ Following this machine aesthetic, modernist designers typically rejected decorative motifs in design, preferring to emphasize the materials used and pure geometrical forms.

奉行这种机械美学标准的现代主义设计者们在设计时往往拒绝装饰性主题,而注重所用材料与纯几何形式。

⑧ As in the visual arts, music also became less "representational" and evocative and more abstract and expressive.

与视觉艺术一样，音乐也不再是具象的（写实的）或可以引发情感共鸣的，而变得更加抽象和富于表现力。

⑨ Debussy's pieces were made the basis for the ballet *Le Sacre Du Printempts* by the Russian composer Igor Stravinsky, which, in its complex rhythmic structures and use of dissonance, together with radically unconventional choreography, shocked both conservative critics and the public.

德彪西的作品成为了俄罗斯作曲家伊戈尔·斯特拉文斯基的芭蕾舞剧《春之祭》的基础，而后者因其复杂的节律结构、不和谐音的使用以及激进的、非传统编舞震惊了当时保守的评论界和观众。

⑩ Though some critics claim that Modernism is "ceding its predominance to Post-modernism," it will continue to exert its influence on the later generations engaging in a wide variety of cultural movements.

虽然一些批评家声称现代主义的主导地位正让位于后现代主义，但它必将继续对后世各类文化运动产生影响。

Exercises

Task 1　Reading Comprehension

Directions: *Read the passage and choose the best answer to each of the following questions.*

1. Which of the following words is appropriate to describe the modernist thinkers?
   A. Traditional.　　　　　　　　　B. Uncertain.
   C. Deliberate.　　　　　　　　　D. Revolutionary.
2. Which writing technique could be employed by modernist writers to display the loneliness of an individual character and reproduce his or her thought process according to the passage?
   A. Stream-of-consciousness.　　　B. Interior monologue.
   C. Multiple points-of-view.　　　　D. Not clearly mentioned.
3. Which of the following statements is true according to the passage?
   A. Modernist movement emerged as a clear cut from the traditional values inherited.
   B. Modernist literature adopted new writing techniques to represent the changed ideas.
   C. Modernist artists believed in scientific discoveries and hated the social condition.
   D. Modernist architects thought the function of a building is more important than its form.
4. The most distinctive feature of modernist music is _____.
   A. its use of new approaches to form and content
   B. its emphasis on form more than on content

C. its similarity to the visual arts

D. its complex rhythmic structures

5. Which of the following architectures might not be attractive to modernist architects?

Task 2 Vocabulary

Directions: *Complete the following sentences with proper words or phrases from the box. Change the form if necessary. Please note there are more words and phrases than necessary.*

A) aesthetic	B) authentic	C) conventions	D) emerging	E) ethics
F) expressive	G) horizon	H) innovative	I) isolation	J) motifs
K) radical	L) representative	M) representational	N) stream-of-consciousness	
O) visions				

1. Modernism can be defined as a movement which involves a deliberate and (1)_____ separation with some of the traditional bases of Western civilization, (2)_____ in the early decades of the 20th century and starting a series of revolutionary movements in art, literature, architecture, and music.

2. Very often modernist writers are devoted to exploring themes like loneliness and (3)_____ facing the humankind living in a new industrial age by using literary techniques such as (4)_____, interior monologue as well as multiple points-of-view.

3. One common feature modernist artists enjoy is their desire to break away from the (5)_____ of representational art and to throw away the old rules of perspective, color and composition with the purpose of working out their own (6)_____.

4. Modernist architects, with the guidance of the machine (7)_____, put more emphasis on materials and forms rather than its decorative (8)_____ in design.

5. With the influence of modernism, music also became less (9)_____ and evocative and more abstract and (10)_____.

Task 3 Translation

Directions: *Translate the following sentences into English.*

1. 很多评论家认为现代主义具有一种有意识地与西方艺术，甚至整个西方文化传统根基完全背离的特征。

2. 现代主义艺术并非一场统一的运动，而是多种"主义或派别"的总称。

3. 现代主义作家意识到一个新的工业时代已经使人们永远脱离了田园生活，其结果通常就

是对人类前景持悲观态度。
4. 现代主义作品中最常见的主题是寂寞和孤独,许多作者试图通过意识流的手法来表现这种孤寂感。
5. 现代主义的设计摈弃了古希腊时期或中世纪沿袭下来的古旧样式和结构。

Task 4 Further Development

Directions: *Fill in the blanks with a piece of work for each author mentioned in the passage. You may refer to Background to Western Culture to find the answers.*

Author	Works
Ernest Hemingway	
F. Scott Fitzgerald	
Virginia Woolf	
James Joyce	
T. S. Eliot	
Vincent van Gogh	
Paul Cézanne	
Paul Gauguin	
Henri Matisse	
Claude Debussy	

Section B The Distinct Character of Contemporary American Culture

What makes contemporary American culture distinct from previous eras of U.S. history? What makes American culture distinct from other cultures?

Undoubtedly, the most important contemporary cultural change for not only Americans but everyone on the planet has been the revolution in telecommunications. ① It has eliminated many of the gatekeepers through which news (information) previously was filtered and now vast numbers of people can witness and interpret information raw and unfiltered. ② People from all over the world can register their own views on events, as well as report on their own personal experiences as witnesses to many important events, providing different perspectives as well as context.

But it still begs the question what is distinctive about American culture and what does it mean to be an American?

③ Being an American means more than living within the boundaries of the 50 U.S. states and its territories. It means associating one's outlook with the outlines of the American dream:

where you have the right to life, liberty and the pursuit of happiness. Included in that dream is the right to own property, to follow your own vision of religion without fear of government interference, to be rewarded for your labors and have the opportunities to advance economically based on your own efforts.

④ There are many other things that go into defining what an "American" is, good and bad, but the American self-image is that they are a people who try to be fair and just, try to work for what is right and good, try to uplift those less fortunate by their own example and story.

Elsewhere, what is "American" often is defined by what is portrayed in the movie theater and what is seen on the television screen, as well as what is written in foreign as well as domestic print media.

⑤ We have no "Official Secrets Act" and despite wails of anguish from those who oppose the current administration, the freedom of the press and expression and religion remains vibrant and unchanged. This freedom is alien to most of the world and therefore is not understood.* When the television news reports something (either the broadcast networks or the cable news outlets) to many it is taken as being government sanctioned. It isn't.

In newsrooms around the country, there is no hidden hand at work. ⑥ It is the effort of ordinary people, who may view the world from a common perspective, playing gatekeeper and filtering the news. With every word written or spoken, a decision is made on whether that word is worthy of being said. Whatever you read, hear and see is the result of the choices these journalists and editors make: good, bad or indifferent.

Whether it is George Lucas' or Steven Spielberg's or Oliver Stone's latest effort, there is no hidden hand behind the production or marketing of the work. It merely is a collaboration of people who have come together to produce a vision, an interpretation, of some story.

⑦ So, what makes American culture, even the current culture, so different? In my humble opinion, it is the acceptance of this basic set of freedoms—in the marketplace, in the town square, in church/temple/mosque, in the halls of government, in the press and over the airways—as a given. It is our God-given right as Americans to be free and different, allowed to express ourselves in a multitude of ways, free from government restrictions.

⑧ The American dream—which has remained the same for more than two centuries—now challenges not only Americans but others to expand their horizons as the ability to exchange thoughts and views has been expanded through all the various new media.

⑨ There are so many factors impinging on contemporary American culture today that it would be difficult to define it clearly. Certainly I would have to say that the information revolution, primarily led by the Internet and the global access inherent in that is a large factor. A related factor is globalization itself, which is a mixed blessing. On the one hand, we have access to information from all over the world nearly instantaneously. On the other hand, globalization also means losing jobs to cheaper labor in other countries.

(714 words)

Notes: This passage is written by Bob Trowbridge, an American writer, whose self-perception of his country does not verify its truth. Nevertheress, it serves as a good example of critical reading, being in contrast to the third passage of this unit, which illustrates a rather negative image of America.

New Words and Expressions (B)

New Words

New Words	Phonetic Symbols	Meanings
airways (=airwaves)	[ˈeəweɪz]	n. (美)无线电或电视广播
administration	[ədmɪnɪˈstreɪʃ(ə)n]	n. 管理;行政;实施;行政机构
alien	[ˈeɪliə]	adj. 陌生的 n. 外星人
anguish	[ˈæŋgwɪʃ]	n. 痛苦;苦恼
collaboration	[kəlæbəˈreɪʃn]	n. 合作
context	[ˈkɒntekst]	n. (想法、事件等的)背景
define	[dɪˈfaɪn]	v. 界定,阐释
domestic	[dəˈmestɪk]	adj. 家庭的,国内的
distinct	[dɪˈstɪŋkt]	adj. 不同的
filter	[ˈfɪltə]	v. 过滤
given	[ˈgɪvən]	v. 假设事实
impinge	[ɪmˈpɪn(d)ʒ]	v. 影响
indifferent	[ɪnˈdɪf(ə)r(ə)nt]	adj. 不一般的;漠不关心的
instantaneously	[ˌɪnstənˈteniəsli]	adv. 即刻;突如其来地
inherent	[ɪnˈhɪərənt]	adj. 固有的
interference	[ɪntəˈfɪər(ə)ns]	n. 干扰;干涉
interpret	[ɪnˈtɜːprɪt]	v. 说明;解释
mosque	[mɒsk]	n. 清真寺
multitude	[ˈmʌltɪtjuːd]	n. 多数;大量
portray	[pɔːˈtreɪ]	v. 描绘;扮演
previous	[ˈpriːvɪəs]	adj. 以前的
restriction	[rɪˈstrɪkʃ(ə)n]	n. 限制;约束;束缚
sanction	[ˈsæŋ(k)ʃ(ə)n]	v. 批准;准许

Unit 7　Modernism and Contemporary Western Culture

telecommunication	[ˌtelɪkəˌmjuːnɪˈkeɪʃn]	*n.* 电信,通讯
undoubtedly	[ʌnˈdaʊtɪdli]	*adv.* 确实地,毋庸置疑地
vibrant	[ˈvaɪbrənt]	*adj.* 充满生机的
vision	[ˈvɪʒn]	*n.* 幻想
wail	[weɪl]	*v. & n.* 哀嚎;悲叹

Expressions

a multitude of	许多
associate...with...	把……与……联系在一起
as well as	也,还有
be distinct from	与……不同
free from	不受……影响的
beg the question	引起疑问;绕过正题
go into	被用在
have access to	有权使用;可以利用

Proper Names

George Lucas	乔治·卢卡斯(1944—),美国著名电影导演、制片人和编剧,其最著名的作品是《星球大战》系列(导演)和《夺宝奇兵》系列(编剧)。
Official Secrets Act	官方保密法
Oliver Stone	奥利弗·斯通(1946—),美国著名电影、电视剧导演。他执导的著名电影有《生于七月四日》《刺杀肯尼迪》《尼克松》《华尔街》等。
Steven Spielburg	史蒂文·斯皮尔伯格(1946—),犹太血统的美国著名电影导演、编剧和电影制作人,曾两度荣获奥斯卡最佳导演奖。他执导的著名电影有《大白鲨》《侏罗纪公园》《辛德勒的名单》等。《时代》杂志将他列入世纪百名最重要的人物。

Difficult Sentences

① It has eliminated many of the gatekeepers through which news (information) previously was filtered and now vast numbers of people can witness and interpret information raw and unfiltered.

它(信息革命)清除了以前对新闻或信息进行过滤的多重审查机制,从而使得越来越多的人现在可以直接接触到原始的、未经过滤的信息并对之进行诠释。

② People from all over the world can register their own views on events, as well as report on their own personal experiences as witnesses to many important events, providing different perspectives as well as context.

世界各地的人们都可以发表对某些事件的看法，也能以重要事件目击者的身份讲述个人经历，提供不同的视角和背景。

③ Being an American means more than living within the boundaries of the 50 U.S. states and its territories. It means associating one's outlook with the outlines of the American dream...

作为美国人不仅意味着居住在美国五十个州和海外领土之内，更意味着个人观点与美国梦基本原则的契合……

④ There are many other things that go into defining what an "American" is, good and bad, but the American self-image is that they are a people who try to be fair and just, try to work for what is right and good, try to uplift those less fortunate by their own example and story.

还有许多其他要素可以用于界定何为"美国人"，无论其好与坏。但美国人的自我形象是：他们是这样一个民族——努力坚持公平、正义，追求正确和美好的事物，力图用自己的榜样或经历去鼓舞那些不如他们幸运的人。

⑤ We have no "Official Secrets Act" and despite wails of anguish from those who oppose the current administration, that freedom of the press and expression and religion remains vibrant and unchanged.

我们没有"国家机密法"，尽管反对本届政府的人士发出不满的悲叹，但新闻自由、言论自由和宗教自由仍然充满活力，一如既往。

⑥ It is the effort of ordinary people, who may view the world from a common perspective, playing gatekeeper and filtering the news. With every word written or spoken, a decision is made on whether that word is worthy of being said. Whatever you read, hear and see is the result of the choices these journalists and editors make: good, bad or indifferent.

正是那些以平凡视角观察世界的普通人充当着新闻审查者和过滤者的角色。写的每一个字，说出的每一句话，都有人对其是否有意义做出判断。你的所读、所闻、所见都是这些记者和编辑选择的结果：无论是好的、差的或是一般的。

⑦ So, what makes American culture, even the current culture, so different? In my humble opinion, it is the acceptance of this basic set of freedoms—in the marketplace, in the town square, in church/temple/mosque, in the halls of government, in the press and over the airways—as a given.

那么，美国文化，甚至今天的美国文化的不同之处究竟何在？依本人拙见，美国人把在市场、乡镇广场、教堂/庙宇/清真寺、市政大厅、出版和广播电视等方面享有一系列基本自由视为理所应当，正是对这种观点的普遍认同构成了美国文化之特征。

⑧ There are so many factors impinging on contemporary American culture today that it would be difficult to define it clearly. Certainly I would have to say that the information revolution, primarily led by the Internet and the global access inherent in that is a large factor. A related factor is globalization itself, which is a mixed blessing. On the one hand, we have access to information from all over the world nearly instantaneously. On the other hand, globalization also means losing jobs to cheaper labor in other countries.

当代美国文化受诸多因素影响,难以精确定义。当然我得说,互联网及其在全球范围使用所引发的信息革命是一个重要影响因素。另一个与之相关的因素是全球化本身,此进程有利有弊。有利的是我们几乎可以随时获取世界各地的信息,不利的是全球化进程也意味着美国的就业机会落到了其他国家廉价劳动力手中。

Exercises

Task 1 Reading Comprehension

Directions: *Read the passage and judge whether the following statements are true (T), false (F) or not given (NG).*

True　　　　if the statement agrees with the information mentioned in the passage
False　　　 if the statement contradicts the information mentioned in the passage
Not Given　if there is no information on this in the passage

1. This passage is about American culture and its distinctive historical relationship with other cultures.
2. Gatekeepers have lost their jobs because telecommunications filtered news of employment.
3. Thanks to the development of telecommunications, people nowadays can give their opinions on events and tell their personal experiences freely.
4. American dream is an inclusive idea about the basic right of life, liberty and pursuit of happiness.
5. Americans believe that they are in the pursuit of just, right and good, but their international image is more defined by movies and TV programs.
6. According to this passage, there are some misunderstandings about American people's belief of freedom.
7. The image of American government and the image of American people are not the same thing.
8. The newsrooms usually pretend to give the voice and opinions of ordinary people.
9. George Lucas or Steven Spielberg or Oliver Stone has been trying to hide their production and marketing strategy.
10. The special feature of American culture lies in its acceptance of the basic understanding that freedom is a given right.

Task 2   Vocabulary

Directions: *Complete the following summary of the passage with proper words from the box. Change the form if necessary.*

| global | with | acceptance | raw | effort |
| pursuit | portray | witness | indifferent | eliminate |

What makes American culture different is its _____(1) of the basic set of freedom. The idea of freedoms is very much associated _____(2) the notion of American dream, which suggests that people have the right to life, liberty and the _____(3) of happiness. But American image in other parts of the world is often _____(4) via Hollywood movies and not rightly understood. In America, news from the media is usually the _____(5) of ordinary people, the result of selection by journalists and editors: good, bad or _____(6).

Nowadays, American culture also faces the _____(7) cultural change: information revolution, which has _____(8) many of the supervisions and provides an opportunity for people to (9)_____ many important events in the (10) _____ form.

Task 3   Translation

Directions: *Complete the following sentences by translating the Chinese in brackets into English.*

1. Undoubtedly the revolution in telecommunications has been _____（当代最重要的文化变化）.
2. It is the notion of freedom that makes American culture _____（与……相比具有鲜明特色）other cultures.
3. The special idea of freedom in American culture _____（对……还很陌生）people in other parts of the world and therefore misunderstood.
4. People in the 21st century are able to _____（用多种方式来表达自己）via internet.
5. Learning the culture of others can _____（开阔你的眼界）when your ability to exchange thoughts and views has been improved.

Task 4   Further Development

Directions: *Discuss the following questions in groups, and report your answers to the whole class.*

1. Do you agree or disagree with the author in saying "the American dream has remained the same for more than two centuries"? Give your reasons.
2. What influences can you predict the globalization may have on American culture?

Section C How Contemporary American Society Tramples on Principles of Integrity

By Tracy A. Moore

One day I was discussing with my daughter a lie her then fiancé had told her. Her reply was, "Oh, Mom, everyone lies!" Wow, what an eye-opener for mom. ① My child, who has been raised that honesty is important in everything, has bought into the cultural lie that it's alright to lie in certain situations. What really worries me is that if my overly honest daughter can feel this way, what about the rest of the world?

All you have to do is turn on a television and you will get a view of the "integrity" of American society. Whether TV reflects our culture or creates it is a debate for another time. Either way, the shows are full of people who have absolutely no integrity. They hop in and out of bed with one another. They lie to serve their own purposes. They have no problem with cheating on a loved one. In other words, they have no moral and ethical principles and they have no integrity.

We have a rise in sexual activity among younger kids every year. We have a rise in STDs (Sexually Transmitted Disease) and pregnancies despite "education" and supplied birth control. ② Cheating is rampant in the education field as well as in the corporate world. Integrity, it seems, is something we claim when we need it, but abandon when we don't.

How do we expect our children to have integrity when adults do not? All we have to do is read or watch the news to see the lack of integrity in our public figures, whether they be celebrities or politicians. The only ethic they adhere to is the ethic of their own choice. ③ That the end justifies the means seems to be the mantra of many. Even our highest elected officials are often found guilty of lack of integrity. What message does this send to our kids?

Situational ethics abound in the US today, but what good are ethics if you can change them at will? Integrity comes in when we do what's right no matter what the consequences are. We adhere to a value system that is good for all, not just good for self. We make choices based on a moral code rather than what we need for the moment. Integrity is something you either have or don't have. It is not situational. It is not bendable. It is not fluid. ④ It is what it is, and it is being trampled on every day by those unwilling to stand for what's right no matter what the cost.

⑤ While you can still find pockets of people with integrity, it seems they are few and far between. ⑥ As this country attempts to push God and truth and other restraints to morality out, there has been a rise in morals based on a person's "own" truth which can be twisted to meet his or her own agenda. ⑦ Moral debauchery abounds. The line between right and wrong has been fatally blurred. Is there hope for a turnaround in the United States or the world? I hope so, ⑧ but it will only come when we again embrace absolute truth and integrity with no exceptions.

(523 words)

New Words and Expressions (C)

New Words

New Words	Phonetic Symbols	Meanings
abound	[əˈbaʊnd]	v. 大量存在, 富于, 充满
adhere	[ədˈhɪə(r)]	v. 遵守
blur	[blɜː(r)]	v. (使)模糊, (使)难以区分
celebrity	[səˈlebrəti]	n. 名人
code	[kəʊd]	n. 准则、规范
corporate	[ˈkɔːpərət]	adj. 公司的, 法人的
debauchery	[dɪˈbɔːtʃəri]	n. 道德败坏
embrace	[ɪmˈbreɪs]	v. 热切的接受, 信奉
ethical	[ˈeθɪkl]	adj. 道德的, 伦理的
eye-opener	[ˈaɪˌəʊpnə(r)]	n. 令人大开眼界的事物
fatally	[ˈfeɪtəli]	adv. 严重地
fiancé	[fiˈɒnseɪ]	n. 未婚夫
fluid	[ˈfluːɪd]	adj. 可变的
hop	[hɒp]	v. 跳
integrity	[ɪnˈtegrəti]	n. 诚实, 诚信
justify	[ˈdʒʌstɪfaɪ]	v. 证明(决定、行为或想法)正当
mantra	[ˈmæntrə]	n. (尤指认为并不正确或只是部分正确的)准则
overly	[ˈəʊvəli]	adv. 极度地
pregnancy	[ˈpregnənsi]	n. 怀孕
rampant	[ˈræmpənt]	adj. 猖獗的, 盛行的
restraint	[rɪˈstreɪnt]	n. 约束
sexual	[ˈsekʃuəl]	adj. 性的
trample	[ˈtræmpl]	v. 践踏, 踩蹒
twist	[twɪst]	v. 歪曲

Expressions

at will	任意,随意
few and far between	稀少,罕见
pockets of	一些

Proper Names

situational ethics	境遇伦理学
STD (Sexually Transmitted Disease)	性病

① My child, who has been raised that honesty is important in everything, has bought into the cultural lie that it's alright to lie in certain situations.

诚实是最重要的品德,这是我女儿一直以来接受的教育,但现在她竟然也能够接受这种谎言文化,即在某些特定的情景下撒谎是可以原谅的。

② Cheating is rampant in the education field as well as in the corporate world. Integrity, it seems, is something we claim when we need it, but abandon when we don't.

欺诈行为在教育界和商界盛行。人们似乎只在需要时才主张诚信,不需要时则弃之不用。

③ That the end justifies the means seems to be the mantra of many.

为达目的不择手段似乎已成为很多人的行为准则。

④ It is what it is, and it is being trampled on every day by those unwilling to stand for what's right no matter what the cost.

诚信就是诚信。但如今它却被不愿为正确的事付出高昂代价的人所践踏。

⑤ While you can still find pockets of people with integrity, it seems they are few and far between.

虽然你仍可以找到少数诚实的人,但那不过是凤毛麟角而已。

⑥ As this country attempts to push God and truth and other restraints to morality out, there has been a rise in morals based on a person's "own" truth which can be twisted to meet his or her own agenda.

这个国家正试图将上帝、真理和其他约束乃至道德排斥在外,而兴起一种基于个人"自身"真实情况的道德标准,因而会根据个人需求而扭曲。

⑦ Moral debauchery abounds. The line between right and wrong has been fatally blurred. Is there hope for a turn-a-round in the United States or the world?

道德败坏，是非不分，这种在美国乃至全世界都存在的状况还有可能逆转吗？

⑧ ...but it will only come when we again embrace absolute truth and integrity with no exceptions.

但只有当我们重新坚持绝对真理和诚信时，这一愿望才有可能实现。

Exercises

Task 1 Short Answer Questions

Directions: *Work in pairs to answer the following questions.*

1. What really worries the author according to Para. 1?
2. How do you understand the sentence "That the end justifies the means seems to be the mantra of many" in Para. 4?
3. What message can be inferred from Para. 4?
4. How can people retain integrity according to the author?
5. What can be concluded from the passage?

Task 2 Vocabulary

Directions: *Complete the following sentences with proper words or phrases from the box. Change the form if necessary. Please note there are more words and phrases than necessary.*

A) embrace	B) trample	C) rampant	D) overly	E) abandon
F) corporate	G) twist	H) celebrity	I) justify	J) abound
K) teem	L) integrity	M) blur	N) restraint	O) eye-opener

1. The line between fact and fiction is becoming _____, which is one of the distinctive characteristics of the success of novels.
2. For me, this number was a real _____, as I began to realize how much of my time really is taken up by my chase for more money.
3. The president is calling for spending _____ in some areas, which is sure to be an item on the agenda next week.
4. When they set up the company, they all agreed that adhering to the fair and just principles should be made as vital part of _____ strategies.
5. The countryside _____ in wild life of every kind, which is overly appealing to some biologists.
6. Perhaps most dangerous for our nation now is the official corruption which is _____ in nearly every field of our society.

7. If you cannot stop the comparisons, stay away from big triggers like TV and _____ magazines.
8. Nobody should buy into the assumption that good reasons can _____ a war.
9. I have always regarded him as a man of _____ and showed my due respect to him.
10. They say loggers are destroying rain forests and _____ on the rights of natives.

Task 3　Translation

Directions: *Complete the following sentences by translating the Chinese in brackets into English.*

1. Nowadays the lack of _____(学术诚信) among postgraduate students is rampant.
2. All members of the student union must _____ (遵守一套严格的行为规范).
3. There is no doubt _____ (跳槽) has its drawbacks as well as merits.
4. While you can find pockets of women students with an interest in mechanical engineering , it seems they are _____ (凤毛麟角).
5. No one is allowed to _____(随心所欲地违反规章制度).

Task 4　Further Development

Directions: *Read the passage again and summarize how and why American society tramples on principles of integrity, then compare your answer with your partner's.*

	How	Why
1		
2		
3		
4		
5		

Adages and Proverbs

1. There is no royal road to science, and only those who don't dread the fatiguing climbing of its steep paths have the chance of gaining its luminous summits.
　　　　— Karl Marx (1818—1883), German philosopher and thinker
　在科学上没有平坦的大道,只有不畏劳苦沿着其崎岖之路攀登的人,才有希望到达它光辉的顶点。
　　　　——卡尔·马克思

2. Many are stubborn in pursuit of the path they have chosen, few in pursuit of the goal.
　　　　—Fredrick Nietzsche (1844—1900), German philosopher
　许多人在追求他们选择的道路时固执,却很少在追求目标时固执。
　　　　——弗里德里希·尼采

3. Most people do not really want freedom, because freedom involves responsibility, and most people are frightened of responsibility.
—Sigmund Freud (1856—1939), Austrian doctor, psychologist and psychiatrist

大多数人并非真的想要自由,因为自由牵涉到责任,而大多数人害怕责任。
——西格蒙德·弗洛伊德

4. The man who has begun to live more seriously within begins to live more simply without.　　—Ernest Hemingway (1899—1961), American novelist

心灵愈加严谨,外表愈加简单。　　——欧内斯特·海明威

5. Begin to act boldly. The moment one definitely commits oneself, heaven moves on his behalf.　　—F. Scott Fitzgerald (1896—1940), American novelist

大胆行动,全心全意地投入,连上苍也会受感动。　　——弗·司科特·菲茨杰拉德

6. Thought and theory must precede all salutary action; yet action is nobler in itself than either thought or theory.　　—Virginia Woolf (1882—1941), British writer

思想和理论指引着有益的行动,但行动本身却比思想或理论都要高尚。
——弗吉尼亚·伍尔芙

7. Mistakes are the portals of discovery.
—James Joyce (1882—1941), Irish writer and poet

错误是通向发现之入口。　　——詹姆斯·乔伊斯

8. Only those who will risk going too far can possibly find out how far one can go.
—T.S. Eliot (1888—1965), American born British poet

只有那些敢冒险走向远方的人才会发现一个人到底可以走多远。
——托·斯·艾略特

9. No one can be a painter unless he cares for painting above all else.
—Edouard Manet (1832—1883), French artist

如果不酷爱绘画,他不可能成为画家。
——爱德华·马奈

10. We never really know what stupidity is until we have experimented on ourselves.
—Paul Gauguin (1848—1903), French painter

只有亲身实验过我们才能懂得什么是愚蠢。　　——保罗·高更

11. If one is master of one thing and understands one thing well, one has at the same time, insight into and understanding of many things.
—Vincent van Gogh (1853—1890), Dutch post-impressionist painter

如果一个人能够精通一事且成为大师,他同时就获得了洞察许多事物的能力。
——文森特·凡·高

12. The awareness of our own strength makes us modest.
　　　　　　　　　　　　—Paul Cézanne (1839—1906), French painter
　了解自己的实力才会更谦虚。　　　　　　　　　　　——保罗·塞尚
13. There are always flowers for those who want to see them.
　　　　　　　　　　　—Henri Matisse (1869—1954), French painter
　花朵总是为想看到它们的人而绽放。　　　　　　　——亨利·马蒂斯
14. If there were only one truth, you couldn't paint a hundred canvases on the same theme.
　　　　　　—Pablo Picasso (1881—1973), Spanish painter and sculptor
　如果真理只有一种，你不可能针对同一主题绘出一百幅油画。　——毕加索
15. Everybody has talent; it's just a matter of moving around until you've discovered what it is.
　　　　　　　　　　　　　—George Lucas (1944—   ), American director
　人人都有自己的才华，只是不经过磨练你无法发现而已。　——乔治·卢卡斯

Key to Unit 7 Exercises

导读答案

1. "Modern" is a temporal term, which means relating to the present time, for example the present decade or present century; Modernism was a movement in the arts in the first half of the twentieth century that rejected traditional values and techniques, and emphasized the importance of individual experience; Modernization is a movement which aims to improve a factory, system, a city, a society, etc. by means of science and technology; Modernist means relating to the ideas and methods of modern art; Modernity typically refers to a post-traditional, post-medieval historical period, one marked by the move from feudalism (or agrarianism) toward capitalism, industrialization, secularization, rationalization, the nation-state and its constituent institutions and forms of surveillance; Post-modernism is a late twentieth century approach in art, architecture, and literature which typically mixes styles, ideas, and references to modern society, often in an ironic way. Their Chinese equivalents are respectively "现代的""现代主义""现代化""现代主义的""现代性""后现代主义"。

2. The pioneering modernist thinkers worth mentioning include Karl Marx, Fredrick Nietzsche and Sigmund Freud, whose radical and original thoughts have inspired and exerted great influence on western culture; modernist poets are T. S. Eliot, Ezra Pound, William Carlos Williams, W. B. Yeats and W. H. Auden, whose poems are credited for the best embodiment of modern society; modernist novelists are James Joyce, Virginia Woolf, D. H. Lawrence,

Ernest Hemingway, Joseph Conrad, etc., who experimented with new writing techniques, such as stream of consciousness, inner monologue and narration of multiple points-of-view, to portray the changing reality.

3. Sigmund Freud was born in Austria in 1856 and died in London, England in 1939. Regarded as the founding father of psychoanalysis, Freud is best known for his tendency to trace nearly all psychological problems back to sexual issues. His most significant writings are *The Interpretation of Dreams, The Psychopathology of Everyday Life, Totem and Taboo,* and *Civilization and Its Discontents.* Freud's theory of the Oedipus Complex has become a cultural icon. Other now-famous Freudian innovations include the therapy couch, the use of talk therapy to resolve psychological problems, and his theories about the unconscious—including the role of repression, denial, sublimation, and projection.

Section A

Task 1 Reading Comprehension

1. D   2. A   3. B   4. A   5. C

Task 2 Vocabulary

1. radical   2. emerging   3. isolation   4. stream-of-conscious   5. conventions
6. visions   7. aesthetic   8. motifs   9. representational   10. expressive

Task 3 Translation

1. Many critics agree that Modernism involves a deliberate and radical break with some of the traditional bases not only of Western art, but of Western culture in general.
2. Modernism in art was not an integrated movement, but rather a multiplicity of "isms."
3. Modernist writers realized that a new industrial age had ushered out rural living forever, and the result was often a pessimistic view of what lay before humankind.
4. Frequent themes in modernist works were loneliness and isolation, and a significant number of writers tried to capture that sense of solitude by engaging in stream-of-consciousness writing.
5. Modernist design rejected the old styles and structures inherited from Ancient Greece or from the Middle Ages.

Task 4 Further Development

Author	Works
Ernest Hemingway	*The Old Man and The Sea*, 1952
F. Scott Fitzgerald	*The Great Gatsby,* 1925
Virginia Woolf	*Mrs. Dalloway,* 1925
James Joyce	*Ulysses,* 1922

Unit 7 Modernism and Contemporary Western Culture

T. S. Eliot	*The Waste Land*, 1922
Vincent van Gogh	*The Starry Night*, 1889
Paul Cézanne	*Still Life Paintings*, 1879—1898
Paul Gauguin	*Where Do We Come From? What Are We? Where Are We Going?* 1897—1898
Henri Matisse	*Harmony in Red Room (or Red Room)*, 1908
Claude Debussy	*Pelleas and Melisande*, 1903

Section B

Task 1 Reading Comprehension

1. F 2. F 3. NG 4. T 5. T 6. T 7. T 8. F 9. F 10. T

Task 2 Vocabulary

1. acceptance 2. with 3. pursuit 4. portrayed 5. effort
6. indifferent 7. global 8. eliminated 9. witness 10. raw

Task 3 Translation

1. the most important contemporary cultural change

2. distinct from

3. is alien to

4. express themselves in a multitude of ways

5. expand your horizons

Task 4 Further Development

1. Sample Answers

FOR

I couldn't agree more with the author in saying "the American dream has remained the same for more than two centuries." *Declaration of Independence* proclaims that "all men are created equal" and that they are "endowed by their Creator with certain inalienable Rights" including "Life, Liberty and the pursuit of Happiness." Based on this idea, American dream can be interpreted as "everyone has the right to be successful and everyone can." Central to the American dream is that everyone can get success if he works hard. Since the founding of the United States, this dream has inspired American people of generations, regardless of their backgrounds, to pursue success with hard work, independent and optimistic spirits. The idea of the American dream is deeply rooted in American culture and serves as the guiding standard of behavior for American people. As such, I agree with the author.

AGAINST

The author may have his reason to say so but I won't buy his story. The words or addressing of American dream is the same, but the meaning of American dream can't remain the same as it was first put forward two hundred years ago. As is known to all, the world has changed dramatically since then and people's opinions and ideas have also changed with the changing reality. Take the central idea of the American dream that everyone can get success. In the 18th century, people's interpretation of being successful was home ownership and decent living without worrying about food and clothes, but in the 20th century, possessing a house and having sufficient food and clothes are just the basic requirements. Now to be considered as successful, one has to be materially luxurious, which can't be ensured by working hard alone. Therefore, the meaning of the "American dream" has changed over the course of history.

2. Possible answer

Globalization is the process of international integration arising from the interchange of world views, products, ideas, and other aspects of culture. The process will undoubtedly bring along with it the influence to American culture. With the advance of globalization, American culture might become more inclusive, open-minded and compatible with other cultures. But it is likely that globalization would promote American culture to the status of hegemony, dominating the world culture, strong as it is now. Of course there is still chance that globalization might erase the distinct characteristics of American culture.

Section C

Task 1   Reading Comprehension

1. People's attitude toward lies.
2. Many people accept the ethics that to achieve the desired end one can resort to any means, fair or foul.
3. The adult world lacks integrity and thus sets a bad example for kids.
4. By sticking to a value system good for all at any cost.
5. The author believes that taking up absolute truth and integrity at any time is the only way to change America for better.

Task 2   Vocabulary

1. blurred   2. eye-opener   3. restraints   4. corporate / corporation   5. abounds
6. rampant   7. celebrity   8. justify   9. integrity   10. trampling

Task 3   Translation

1. academic integrity
2. adhere to a strict code of practice
3. job-hopping

Unit 7　Modernism and Contemporary Western Culture

4. few and far between
5. violate rules and regulations at will

Task 4　Further Development

Sample Answer

	How	Why
1	Overly honest people like her daughter shows understanding to lying.	The whole society has bought into the cultural lie that it's alright to lie in certain situations.
2	People hop in and out of bed with one another, lie to serve their own purposes, or cheat on a loved one.	The society is full of people who have no moral and ethical principles and have no integrity.
3	Cheating is rampant in educational field as well as in the corporate world.	Integrity is something people claim when they need it but abandon when they don't.
4	Public figures, including celebrities, politicians and highest elected officials are often found guilty of lack of integrity.	That the end justifies the means seems to be the mantra of many.
5	Situational ethics abound in the US today.	There is no absolute truth and people are unwilling to stand for what's right no matter what cost.

Supplementary Reading

Passage 1 The Toxic Individualism of Pandemic Politics

There are countless studies showing that wearing a mask is an effective way to lessen the spread of Covid-19. It's a simple, inexpensive precaution we can all take when we're out in public to help keep each other safe. ① Yet some people have embraced the mentality of "toxic individualism," rejecting science-based health guidelines and refusing to wear masks instead of looking out for each other. They refuse to do so on the grounds that it infringes on their personal liberties.

② Our culture teaches us to define ourselves by what makes us unique and sets us apart from others. There's a lot of room for us to think and act independently, as autonomous individuals, and that freedom is one of the pillars of our society. Sadly, this pandemic has exposed some of our culture's greatest weaknesses. We are so focused on our own liberties and rights that we've forgotten how to cooperate, how to put others first, how to act in the interest of a common good instead of only looking out for our own. The consequence of prizing personal liberty above all else is that we can become extremely selfish and blind to the impact of our actions on other people. It isn't that we mean to hurt others, necessarily; it's that we place a higher premium on the idea of our individual freedom than we do on taking care of one another.

Many people seem to think that "being free" means that we can literally do whatever we want, regardless of the consequences or how it affects the people around us. ③ I can relate to this mindset because I was 15 years old once. I remember when I thought all rules existed to oppress me. ④ I got a giddy thrill out of breaking them and doing what I wasn't supposed to do just for the hell of it. Nobody was going to tell me how to live my life! I was convinced I knew better. Luckily, I outgrew that phase a long time ago. But it seems like a lot of us in America remain stuck in that teenage mentality of doing whatever we want just because we can. And when we live in a society with other people, at some point, our freedom to do what we want is going to run up against other people's rights and freedoms. What then? Whose freedom matters more? Who gets precedence?

⑤ We may not feel like a whole right now because of how divided we are, but we are all more interconnected than we realize. Maybe we can draw lessons from collectivist cultures. Maybe we can learn how to prize ourselves a little less and act with a little more consideration for the greater whole that we are all a part of. I just hope we start acting before it's too late.

New Words and Expressions

New Words

New Words	Phonetic Symbols	Meanings
toxic	[ˈtɒksɪk]	adj. 极其有害的
individualism	[ˌɪndɪˈvɪdʒuəlɪzəm]	n. 个人主义
pandemic	[pænˈdemɪk]	n. (疾病的)大流行,广泛传播; adj. 大范围流行的
mask	[mɑːsk]	n. 口罩;面具
precaution	[prɪˈkɔːʃn]	n. 预防措施
embrace	[ɪmˈbreɪs]	v. 信奉;欣然接受
mentality	[menˈtæləti]	n. 心态;思维方式
infringe	[ɪnˈfrɪndʒ]	v. 侵犯;侵害(某人的自由、权益等)
define	[dɪˈfaɪn]	v. 下定义;阐明
autonomous	[ɔːˈtɒnəməs]	adj. 独立自主的;有主见的
prioritize	[praɪˈɒrətaɪz]	v. 优先考虑
mindset	[ˈmaɪndset]	n. 观念模式,思维倾向,心态
giddy	[ˈɡɪdi]	adj. (高兴或激动得)发狂的
precedence	[ˈpresɪdəns]	n. 优先
collectivist	[kəˈlektɪvɪst]	adj. 集体主义的

Expressions

on the grounds that	基于这样的理由
in the interest of	为了(……的利益)
just for the hell of it	只是为了捣乱;只是为了寻求刺激

Proper Name

Covid-19	新型冠状病毒肺炎	COVID-19 is the abbreviation(缩略词) for the full name coronavirus(冠状病毒) disease of 2019. CO for corona(冠状物),VI for virus, D for disease, and 19 for the year the outbreak was first recognized, late in 2019.

Difficult Sentences

① Yet some people have embraced the mentality of "toxic individualism," rejecting science-based health guidelines and refusing to wear masks instead of looking out for each other. 然而，有些人却抱有一种"极为有害的个人主义"心态，排斥科学的健康指南，拒绝戴口罩，也不为他人着想。

② Our culture teaches us to define ourselves by what makes us unique and sets us apart from others. 我们的文化教导我们要有个性，以彰显自己的与众不同。

③ I can relate to this mindset because I was 15 years old once. 我能理解这种心态，因为我 15 岁的时候也是这样。

④ I got a giddy thrill out of breaking them and doing what I wasn't supposed to do just for the hell of it. 我也曾因为做了出格的事儿而兴奋不已。

⑤ We may not feel like a whole right now because of how divided we are, but we are all more interconnected than we realize. 由于人与人之间存在着差异，我们现在或许感觉不到我们是一个整体，但实际上，人与人之间的相互关联比我们所意识到的更为紧密。

Passage 2 False Values Conveyed by American Entertainment and Cultural Industries

① Societies, especially ones in which choices can be freely expressed, methodically sort out their values through systems of rewards. It is easy to establish our hierarchies through a simple analysis of the reward system. Who are our most exalted and best-rewarded, among whom we shower treasure, celebrity, and status? Who are scorned and laid aside? Our icons are our sports and entertainment heroes, and our discarded are the keepers and transmitters of values, including ministers and teachers. Our rewards are mainly with cash.

In its search for pleasure, the nation's idols became those who entertain us—movie stars, rock singers, athletes, and stand-up comics. These are our celebrities. These are the rich and powerful. These are the examples we seek to follow. ② America has become a nation that went from baseball to football as our sports-obsession-of-choice. That shift embodied our transformation from the aesthetic, passive, and cerebral to regimented violence, for which we recruited ever faster, bigger, stronger participants. By Super Bowl XXX, on January 28, 1996, advertisers were paying $1.2 million for each of 58 30-second TV commercials.

③ Television was replacing words with images, making us less literate, less discriminating

Supplementary Reading

in thought, as clever marketers devised new persuasions. It was also inviting us to materialism, consumerism, and hedonism as well as making us hungry for simple answers.

Our movies prove an accurate reflection of modern life. We have, indeed, become a society in which the strong do what they can, and the weak suffer what they must. ④ The profound nihilism of films in which evil triumphs, or in which death is the only sensible way out, contributes to the cheapening of such concepts of virtue as honour, patriotism, devotion to an idea, or selflessness and altruism.

⑤ Shrinking newspaper markets speed up the development of quick-read, multi-coloured papers that seek to emulate the superficial glare of the TV screen. There are incredible accounts of the supermarket tabloids and their reports of alien sightings, after-death experiences, and other carnival aberrations.

In sports, fan rowdiness is increasingly expressed in street riots following a championship, assaults on visiting players, violence in the stands, objects thrown from the seats, or the search for celebrity on the field by interrupting contests.

Yet it has to be admitted that American culture sweeps all before it in the world. Planet Earth eats our burgers, sees our movies, squeezes into our jeans, sings our songs, and reads our books. ⑥ The power of American culture cannot be denied, nor can its variety or its breadth, which can encompass the lofty as well as the banal. The question is: what does it reveal and what can we predict about our future from its content?

A healthy society is altruistic; a sick one, hedonistic. The task is to make the reality of the threat vivid enough to make America realize the danger it faces. The problems ahead are disheartening, but America retains the energy and skill to meet them, if it recognizes the danger and retains the will to combat it.

Based on: Tony Bouza. *The Decline and Fall of the American Empire.* Da Capo Press, 2003.

New Words

New Words	Phonetic Symbols	Meanings
methodically	[məˈθɒdɪkli]	adv. 有方法地；有系统地
hierarchy	[ˈhaɪərɑːki]	n. 等级制度；统治集团
exalted	[ɪgˈzɔːltɪd]	adj 地位高的；显赫的
celebrity	[səˈlebrəti]	n. 名誉
scorn	[skɔːn]	v. 轻蔑；藐视
icon	[ˈaɪkɒn]	n. 偶像

discarded	[dɪˈskɑːdɪd]	adj. 丢弃的
transmitter	[trænzˈmɪtə(r)]	n. 传送者；传播者
idol	[ˈaɪdl]	n. 偶像，受到热爱和崇拜的人（或物）
aesthetic	[iːsˈθetɪk]	adj. 美学的；审美的
cerebral	[səˈriːbrəl]	adj. 大脑的；理智的
regimented	[ˈredʒɪmənt]	adj. 组织化的
literate	[ˈlɪtərət]	adj. 有读写能力的；有文化的
discriminating	[dɪˈskrɪmɪneɪtɪŋ]	adj. 有识别力的；有鉴赏力的
hedonism	[ˈhedənɪzəm]	n. 享乐主义
nihilism	[ˈnaɪɪlɪzəm]	n. 虚无主义
patriotism	[ˈpætrɪətɪzəm]	n. 爱国主义，爱国精神
altruism	[ˈæltruɪzəm]	n. 利他，利他主义
emulate	[ˈemjuleɪt]	v. 仿效，模仿
tabloid	[ˈtæblɔɪd]	n. 小报，通俗小报
aberration	[ˌæbəˈreɪʃn]	n. 失常；反常现象
rowdiness	[ˈraʊdɪnəs]	n. 吵闹；粗暴
banal	[bəˈnɑːl]	adj. 陈腐的；平庸的
disheartening	[dɪsˈhɑːtnɪŋ]	adj. 使人沮丧的

Expressions

sort out	挑选出；分类
lay aside	把……搁置一边
in its search for…	在寻找……
stand-up comic	单口喜剧/脱口秀演员
TV commercial	电视广告
it has to be admitted that	必须承认

Proper Name

Super Bowl	超级碗（美国橄榄球超级杯大赛）	The Super Bowl is an American football game that is held each year in the United States between the two best professional American football teams.

Supplementary Reading

Difficult Sentences

① Societies, especially ones in which choices can be freely expressed, methodically sort out their values through systems of rewards. It is easy to establish our hierarchies through a simple analysis of the reward system. 社会通过奖赏机制系统化地确定其价值观，言论自由的社会尤为如此。大致分析一下奖励系统，我们就很容易管窥到等级体系的确立。

② America has become a nation that went from baseball to football as our sports-obsession-of-choice. That shift embodied our transformation from the aesthetic, passive, and cerebral to regimented violence, for which we recruited ever faster, bigger, stronger participants. 美国的国民运动已经从棒球转变为橄榄球。这一变化表明人们已经逐渐忽略了体育运动美感、非暴力和机智的一面，从而转向了崇尚暴力的一面。这就是为什么我们总是想拥有速度更快、块头更大、体格更壮的运动员。

③ Television was replacing words with images, making us less literate, less discriminating in thought, as clever marketers devised new persuasions. 随着营销商的手段越来越高明，视讯时代正以图像取代文字，这就使得我们的文化水平下降、思辨能力减弱。

④ The profound nihilism of films in which evil triumphs, or in which death is the only sensible way out, contributes to the cheapening of such concepts of virtue as honour, patriotism, devotion to an idea, or selflessness and altruism. 某些影片的结局总是邪恶势力获胜或者死亡。这种虚无主义的创作手法严重地贬低了人类本应崇尚的诸如荣誉感、爱国主义、坚守理想、无私奉献等美德。

⑤ Shrinking newspaper markets speed up the development of quick-read, multi-coloured papers that seek to emulate the superficial glare of the TV screen. 报业的萎缩加速了碎片化阅读和彩色刊物的发展，促使人们追求电视节目肤浅的光怪陆离。

⑥ The power of American culture cannot be denied, nor can its variety or its breadth, which can encompass the lofty as well as the banal. 美国文化的影响力不可否认，其多样性和广泛性也毋庸置疑，既包括高尚的文化，也存在陈腐的习俗。

Passage 3 What Is the Bamboo Ceiling and How Do We Break It?

Most, if not all of us, are familiar with a concept called the Glass Ceiling. It refers to the barrier women face when trying to advance in their respective professions. Here we'll discuss a similar issue: the Bamboo Ceiling.

"Bamboo ceiling" is a term that has been around since the 1980s but rose to prominence with a 2005 book, *Breaking the Bamboo Ceiling: Career Strategies for Asians*, by senior Forbes writer Jane Hyun. If you are familiar with the term "glass ceiling," then you can probably guess what the bamboo ceiling is. The bamboo ceiling is, according to Jane Hyun, a "combination of individual, cultural, and organizational factors that impede Asian Americans' career progress inside organizations." ① We see it as the ugly truth of the model minority myth.

② A "model minority" is a minority demographic perceived to be high-achieving and successful. In the United States, it historically refers to Asian and Jewish Americans. It is often used against African and Hispanic Americans. However, if we, the US, collectively perceive Asian Americans as high-achieving and successful, why don't the statistics reflect that? In the recent *South Asian Voices* episode with Paurvi Bhatt a local professional and philanthropist, we approached an answer to that question. Paurvi Bhatt, describes her memories of childhood in the 1960s, recalling some of the efforts her family made to integrate into the Minnesota community. The traditional Indian clothes were largely confined to Indian events. English was the primary language in their home. Paurvi adjusted her name because it was difficult for her classmates and teachers to pronounce. Other friends had anglicized their names entirely.

As the new folks in the neighbourhood, they felt it was important to blend into the community and social crowd. Yet, looking back on it, Paurvi recalls that being a model minority had a lot more to do with not being seen. The less different you are, the greater your chances of success. ③ There was even a point where, for all their efforts to make themselves a little more invisible, their upwards social mobility seemed to grind to a halt. Paurvi, like many others, found that finding success as a South Asian, as a person of colour, often meant doing what she could to minimize her differences. However, many have found such efforts to be rewarded with finding the bamboo ceiling.

When one examines the model minority and the bamboo ceiling together, there's a disconnect. Asians are simultaneously believed to be hardworking and successful, and yet also increasingly underrepresented in positions of leadership and influence. ④ Furthermore, the myth and the bamboo ceiling work together to artificially create competition among Asian Americans, further dividing the community.

How can we break the bamboo ceiling? The first thing we need to do is to abandon our embrace of the model minority myth. The occasional benefit or compliment it affords us does not outweigh the harm it has done. How many of us need help but are afraid to ask for it? How many of us feel unworthy of our accomplishments because of the ever-present pressure to maximize our success? We need to recognize that we are not competing with each other for a seat at the table, and we don't need to suppress our culture to make it there.

⑤ As Paurvi explained, we need to reframe the scarcity mentality into an abundance mentality. The opportunities are there. When we start to collectively view opportunities as abundant, we can create more opportunity for ourselves and others.

Finally, we need to have courage. A 2009 article in *Science* journal quoted an interesting statistic. ⑥ Despite over 30% of Asian Americans facing workplace discrimination (the highest of any demographic), only 3% of formal complaints were filed by Asian Americans. Sometimes it's about having the courage to stand up for ourselves and ask for opportunity. When we band together in support and abandon the myth, our community can achieve true success on our own terms.

New Words and Expressions

New Words

New Words	Phonetic Symbols	Meanings
prominence	[ˈprɒmɪnəns]	n. 出名；突出
impede	[ɪmˈpiːd]	v. 阻碍；阻止
demographic	[ˌdeməˈɡræfɪk]	n. 人口统计数据
philanthropist	[fɪˈlænθrəpɪst]	n. 慈善家，乐善好施的人
integrate	[ˈɪntɪɡreɪt]	v. 加入；融入
anglicize	[ˈæŋɡlɪsaɪz]	v. 使英语化
invisible	[ɪnˈvɪzəbl]	adj. 看不见的，隐形的
mobility	[məʊˈbɪləti]	n. 流动能力；流动性
halt	[hɔːlt]	v. 停止
disconnection	[ˌdɪskəˈnekʃn]	n. 分开，分离
simultaneously	[ˌsɪmlˈteɪniəsli]	adv. 同时
underrepresented	[ˈʌndə(r)ˌrepriˈzentɪd]	adj. 未被充分代表的
artificially	[ˌɑːtɪˈfɪʃ(ə)li]	adv. 人为地
ever-present	[ˈevəˌprezənt]	adj. 总是存在的，始终存在的
maximize	[ˈmæksɪmaɪz]	v. 使（某事物）增至最大限度
suppress	[səˈpres]	v. 镇压，压制
reframe	[rɪˈfreɪm]	v. 再构造
scarcity	[ˈskeəsəti]	n. 稀缺
abundance	[əˈbʌndəns]	n. 大量；充裕
mentality	[menˈtæləti]	n. 心态；思想状况
file	[faɪl]	v. 提起（诉讼）

Expressions

be confined to	局限于，限制在
grind to a halt	慢慢停止；陷入停顿
on one's own terms	按自己的方式
band together	联合；携手

Proper Names

Bamboo ceiling	"竹子天花板"一词源自 Jane Hyun 在 2005 年出版的《打破竹子天花板：亚洲人的职业战略》一书，类似于"玻璃天花板"(glass ceiling)一词的仿造。她在书中谈到了许多亚裔美国人职业领域的障碍，包括个人、文化和组织因素等，这些因素共同构成所谓的"竹子天花板"，阻碍着亚裔美国人的职业发展。	The term "bamboo ceiling" refers to the racial bias that can limit the ability of some Asians to succeed in Western industries, especially the job markets of the United States.
Model Minority	20世纪60年代，以加州大学社会学教授威廉·皮特森在《时代》杂志发表《日裔美国人的成功》一文为标志，"模范少数族裔"理论问世。到20世纪80年代，该理论再次升温。该理论实际在于借夸张宣扬亚裔族群在经济方面的成功实例，影射美国黑人的惰性和对联邦政府的经济依赖。这不仅掩盖了亚裔族群遭受的种族歧视，也煽动了其他种族对亚裔的不满情绪。	The concept of the "model minority" was first established by sociologist William Petersen in an article, "Success Story, Japanese American Style," published in the 1966 *New York Times Magazine*.
Forbes	福布斯，美国出版及媒体集团，旗下有同名杂志(Forbes Magazine)。	Forbes is a global media company, focusing on business, investing, technology, entrepreneurship, leadership, and lifestyle.

Difficult Sentences

① We see it as the ugly truth of the model minority myth. 我们看到了模范少数族裔神话背后丑陋的现实。

② A "model minority" is a minority demographic perceived to be high-achieving and successful. "模范少数族裔"是指在人口统计中被视为取得非凡成就的成功群体。

③ There was even a point where, for all their efforts to make themselves a little more invisible, their upwards social mobility seemed to grind to a halt. 无论亚裔美国人如何低调，但总会有那么一块天花板，阻碍了他们社会地位的上升。

④ Furthermore, the myth and the bamboo ceiling work together to artificially create competition among Asian Americans, further dividing the community. 亚裔美国人人为竞争的根源是模范少数族裔神话和竹子天花板，而这又进一步分裂了这个群体。

⑤ As Paurvi explained, we need to reframe the scarcity mentality into an abundance mentality. 正如保罗维所说，我们需要把这种"机会匮乏心态"调整为"机会富余心态"。

⑥ Despite over 30% of Asian Americans facing workplace discrimination (the highest of any demographic), only 3% of formal complaints were filed by Asian Americans. 尽管有超过百分之三十的亚裔美国人遭受了职场歧视（这是所有人口统计数据中最高的），但正式提起诉讼的却只有百分之三。

Passage 4 White-collar Crime

① White collar crime is criminal behavior undertaken by individuals or corporations employing indirect techniques that require skills and education and frequently involve complex financial transactions. It involves men and women in shirts, ties, suits, or tailored business attire. ② The image must inspire trust if that trust is to be violated successfully.

If the judge recognizes the defendant, either personally or as a familiar type from his own circle, it's a good guess that the prisoner is a white collar criminal. This sense of identification is not a trivial matter. ③ Empathy implies both understanding and sympathy, which are important psychic forces in determining the outcomes. The ability of the authorities to identify with the defendant is likely to contribute to lenient treatment. In addition, white collar criminals often command impressive resources, wealth, power, celebrity, status, which can help to bring out the desired result—exculpation.

In a very real sense, white collar criminals are part of the class/race warfare increasingly raging between the rich and the poor, white and black. ④ A poor, illiterate and unemployable defendant, who is bombarded with media reports of the struggles of the mighty while conscious of his own insignificance, cannot help but resent the appeals the rich white defendant is able to make.

Every study of white collar crime shows hugely greater monetary losses than in crime caused by street criminals. ⑤ In terms of total human suffering occasioned by the different crimes, it can be said that the economic loss by bankers, lawyers, doctors, and other trusted, educated types far exceeds the damage done by our admittedly large and swelling tide of street criminality. But it is easier to hate and fear the black, the poor, and the ghetto dwellers. These cannot be excused, but it is imperative that the link be understood. The levers of power are pulled to aid the former and to punish the latter. The resulting alienation produces the nightly horror show on TV news, while white collar criminals continue their cunning and stealthy conducts.

⑥ Our response to white collar crime could become a final validation of our commitment to a justice that is, at least theoretically, blind to race, class, or condition. Thus, if we were willing to treat white collar criminals as we do street criminals, the Constitution could be validated.

Based on: Tony Bouza. *The Decline and Fall of the American Empire.* Da Capo Press, 2003.

New Words and Expressions

New Words

New Words	Phonetic Symbols	Meanings
transaction	[trænˈzækʃn]	n. 交易, 业务
tailored	[ˈteɪləd]	adj. 定制的
attire	[əˈtaɪə]	n. 服装
violate	[ˈvaɪəleɪt]	v. 违反, 违背
defendant	[dɪˈfendənt]	n. 被告
trivial	[ˈtrɪvɪəl]	adj. 不重要的
empathy	[ˈempəθi]	n. 感同身受; 共鸣
psychic	[ˈsaɪkɪk]	adj. 精神的, 心灵的; 超自然的
lenient	[ˈliːnɪənt]	adj. 宽大的, 仁慈的
exculpation	[ˌekskʌlˈpeɪʃən]	n. 无罪释放
bombard	[bɒmˈbɑːd]	v. 大肆抨击; 大量提问
occasion	[əˈkeɪʒn]	v. 导致, 引起
monetary	[ˈmʌnɪtri]	adj. 货币的, 钱的
lever	[ˈliːvə(r)]	n. 杠杆; 手段
alienation	[ˌeɪlɪəˈneɪʃn]	n. 疏离感; 失去支持
validation	[ˌvælɪˈdeɪʃn]	n. 确认; 批准; 生效

Expressions

identify with	认同; 同情
contribute to	有助于; 促成
be likely to	很有可能
cannot help but	不禁
in terms of	依据; 按照; 在……方面
be blind to	对……视而不见

Supplementary Reading

Proper Name

white-collar crime	白领犯罪	White collar crime tends to refer to crimes committed at a business by a businessman or woman. Such crimes might include embezzlement or fraud. Criminology expert and sociologist Edwin Sutherland came up with the term in a 1939 speech. This type of criminal is sometimes considered less likely to commit another crime, and punishment may be softer than for crimes involving violence.

Difficult Sentences

① White collar crime is criminal behavior undertaken by individuals or corporations employing indirect techniques that require skills and education and frequently involve complex financial transactions. 白领犯罪是指个人或公司的一种隐形的犯罪行为，其手段涉及到技术和高学历，通常还涉及到复杂的金融交易。

② The image must inspire trust if that trust is to be violated successfully. 白领阶层的形象容易使人产生信任感，从而有利于他们犯罪。

③ Empathy implies both understanding and sympathy, which are important psychic forces in determining the outcomes. The ability of the authorities to identify with the defendant is likely to contribute to lenient treatment. 同理心意味着理解与同情，这是决定审判结果的重要心理因素。当局对被告的同情可能会导致对其进行从宽处理。

④ A poor, illiterate and unemployable defendant, who is bombarded with media reports of the struggles of the mighty while conscious of his own insignificance, cannot help but resent the appeals the rich white defendant is able to make. 面对媒体铺天盖地报道有钱白人的上诉，穷困潦倒、目不识丁和失业的被告便会意识到自己的微不足道，从而不自觉地产生怨恨和不满。

⑤ In terms of total human suffering occasioned by the different crimes, it can be said that the economic loss by bankers, lawyers, doctors, and other trusted, educated types far exceeds the damage done by our admittedly large and swelling tide of street criminality. 论及不同犯罪行为，银行家、律师、医生和其他可信赖的、受过教育的人所造成的经济损失远远超过大家所公认的、已泛滥的街头犯罪。

⑥ Our response to white collar crime could become a final validation of our commitment to a justice that is, at least theoretically, blind to race, class, or condition. 对白领犯罪的处理方式能够最终验证我们是否追求司法正义——我们所奉行的司法体系至少在理论上应该是没有种族、阶层或社会地位的歧视的。

Reflection Questions Exercises

1. According to Passage 1, why did some American people reject science-based health guidelines and refuse to wear masks during the COVID-19 pandemic?
2. What is the development tendency of American media? What are the dangers of this development direction?
3. How does America's entertainment and culture industry convey wrong values and make Americans less sensible? What should Americans do first if they want to change this situation?
4. What causes the bamboo ceiling? Who does it affect most? Is it possible to break it? And how to break it?
5. What are the factors contributing to the white collar crimes?

Glossary

New Words

A

abandon	[əˈbændən]	v. 放弃	1-C
abound	[əˈbaʊnd]	v. 大量存在，富于，充满	7-C
absolute	[ˌæbsəˈluːt]	adj. 完全的，纯粹的	3-B
access	[ˈækses]	v. 访问，进入	1-A
accomplishment	[əˈkʌmplɪʃm(ə)nt]	n. 成就，技艺	2-B
acknowledge	[əkˈnɒlɪdʒ]	v. 承认	6-C
adhere	[ədˈhɪə(r)]	v. 遵守	7-C
administration	[ədmɪnɪˈstreɪʃ(ə)n]	n. 管理；行政；实施；行政机构	7-B
admonish	[ədˈmɒnɪʃ]	v. 告诫；劝告	4-C
adorn	[əˈdɔːn]	v. 装饰，使生色	6-A
adultery	[əˈdʌlt(ə)ri]	n. 通奸	4-C
adventurer	[ədˈventʃərə(r)]	n. 冒险家	1-A
airways (=airwaves)	[ˈeəweɪz]	n. (美)无线电或电视广播	7-B
alderman	[ˈɔːldəmən]	n. 市府参事，市议员	5-C
alliance	[əˈlaɪəns]	n. 同盟	1-B
all-out	[ˈɔːlˈaʊt]	adj. 全部的；竭尽全力的	4-C
all-pervading	[ˈɔːl pəˈveɪdɪŋ]	adj. 普及的，普遍传播的	6-B
alter	[ˈɔːltə]	v. 改变，更改	4-A
ample	[ˈæmp(ə)l]	adj. 宽敞的；足够的	4-C
anguish	[ˈæŋgwɪʃ]	n. 痛苦；苦恼	7-B
annul	[əˈnʌl]	v. 宣告无效；废除	4-C
antiquary	[ˈæntɪkwəri]	n. 研究/收藏、出售/古物的人	5-C
approach	[əˈprəʊtʃ]	v. 接近，着手处理	6-A
apt	[æpt]	adj. 恰当的；有……倾向的	6-B
archetypal	[ˈɑːkɪˈtaɪpl]	adj. 典型的	7-A
architecture	[ˈɑːkɪtektʃə(r)]	n. 建筑；建筑风格	1-B
aristocratic	[ˌærɪstəˈkrætɪk]	adj. 贵族的，贵族政治的	1-C
arithmetic	[ærɪθˈmetɪk]	n. 算术	3-C
ascetic	[əˈsetɪk]	adj. 苦行的；禁欲主义的	4-A
aspiration	[ˌæspəˈreɪʃn]	n. 渴望，抱负	6-C
astronomy	[əˈstrɒnəmi]	n. 天文学	3-C
attire	[əˈtaɪə(r)]	v. 穿衣	7-A
Austrian	[ˈɒstrɪən]	adj. 奥地利的	1-A
authority	[ɔːˈθɒrəti]	n. 权威，权力	6-B

B

barbarian	[bɑːˈbeərɪən]	n. 野蛮人	1-B
		adj. 野蛮的	2-A
bard	[bɑːd]	n. 诗人	4-B
barrack	[ˈbærək]	n. 军营	1-B
battlefield	[ˈbætlfiːld]	n. 战场	6-C
beckon	[ˈbek(ə)n]	n. 召唤	4-C
behead	[bɪˈhed]	v. 砍头	4-C
bloc	[blɒk]	n. 团体,联盟	5-A
blur	[blɜː(r)]	v. (使)模糊,(使)难以区分	7-C
bookend	[ˈbʊkend]	v. 放在末尾,置于两端	4-B
boundary	[ˈbaʊndri]	n. 边界	6-A
bourgeois	[ˈbʊəʒwɑː]	adj. 资产阶级的	3-B
brash	[bræʃ]	adj. 无礼的,傲慢的	4-C
brutal	[ˈbruːt(ə)l]	adj. 残忍的;不留情面的	4-C
buggery	[ˈbʌɡəri]	n. 鸡奸,兽奸	5-C
Byzantine	[ˈbɪzəntiːn]	adj. 拜占庭式的	3-A

C

calamity	[kəˈlæməti]	n. 灾难	3-A
calculus	[ˈkælkjələs]	n. 微积分	5-B
campaign	[kæmˈpeɪn]	n. 战役,运动,活动	2-A
captivate	[ˈkæptɪveɪt]	v. 迷住	2-C
capture	[ˈkæptʃə(r)]	v. 表现,体现(感情、气氛)	7-A
cathedral	[kəˈθiːdrəl]	n. 主教堂; adj. 天主教的	3-C
cede	[siːd]	v. 让给	7-A
celebrity	[səˈlebrəti]	n. 名人	7-C
chaotic	[keɪˈɒtɪk]	adj. 混乱的	6-A
chapel	[ˈtʃæp(ə)l]	n. 小礼拜堂,小教堂	4-C
chaplain	[ˈtʃæplɪn]	n. 牧师	5-C
characterize	[ˈkærɪktəraɪz]	v. 表现……的特色	3-C
chariot	[ˈtʃærɪət]	n. 二轮战车	2-B
charisma	[kəˈrɪzmə]	n. 非凡的领导力;魅力	2-C
charm	[tʃɑːm]	v. 迷住 n. 魅力	2-C
charter	[ˈtʃɑː(r)tə(r)]	n. 许可证,执照	3-C
Christendom	[ˈkrɪstndəm]	n. 基督教世界;基督教王国	3-A
chronicle	[ˈkrɒnɪkl]	v. 按事件发生顺序记载	4-B
civilian	[sɪˈvɪlj(ə)n]	n. & adj. 百姓(的),平民(的)	2-B
clarity	[ˈklærəti]	n. 明晰	7-A
clutter	[ˈklʌtə(r)]	n. 杂乱	7-A
code	[kəʊd]	n. 准则、规范	7-C
coexist	[kəʊɪɡˈzɪst]	v. 共存;和平共处	4-A
coin	[kɔɪn]	v. 创造,杜撰(新词、新语等)	1-A

Glossary

collaboration	[kəlæbəˈreɪʃn]	n. 合作	7-B
collapse	[kəˈlæps]	n. & v. 倒塌，瓦解	2-A
colloquially	[kəˈləʊkwiəli]	adv. 用通俗语，口语地	4-B
colony	[ˈkɒləni]	n. 殖民地	1-B
commit	[kəˈmɪt]	v. 犯罪，做错事	4-C
commoner	[ˈkɒmənə]	n. 平民，普通人	4-B
complexion	[kəmˈplekʃn]	n. 肤色	4-B
conclude	[kənˈkluːd]	v. 结束	3-A
confederation	[kənˌfedəˈreɪʃn]	n. 邦联，联盟	1-B
confer	[kənˈfɜː(r)]	v. 授予	3-C
conjugal	[ˈkɒndʒəgl]	adj. 婚姻的，夫妻之间的	5-C
conquer	[ˈkɒŋkə(r)]	v. 战胜	1-B
conqueror	[ˈkɒŋkərə(r)]	n. 征服者，胜利者	2-A
conscience	[ˈkɒnʃəns]	n. 良心	1-C
consolidate	[kənˈsɒlɪdeɪt]	v. 巩固，加强	3-B
conspicuous	[kənˈspɪkjuəs]	adj. 显著的，显而易见的	6-C
constantly	[ˈkɒnst(ə)ntli]	adv. 不断地，时常地	2-B
constitution	[ˌkɒnstɪˈtjuːʃn]	n. 体质	1-C
consul	[ˈkɒns(ə)l]	n. 古罗马的执政官	2-A
contemplative	[kənˈtemplətɪv]	adj. 沉思的；冥想的	4-A
contemporary	[kənˈtemprəri]	adj. 当代的，同时代的	6-C
context	[ˈkɒntekst]	n. （想法、事件等的）背景	7-B
contrive	[kənˈtraɪv]	v. (常指用欺骗手段) 策划	4-C
convention	[kənˈvenʃn]	n. 惯例	6-A
conversion	[kənˈvɜːʃ(ə)n]	n. 皈依	3-B
corporal	[ˈkɔː(r)p(ə)rəl]	adj. 肉体的，身体的	3-C
corporate	[ˈkɔːpərət]	adj. 公司的，法人的	7-C
corrupted	[kəˈrʌptɪd]	adj. 腐败的	6-C
corruption	[kəˈrʌpʃn]	n. 腐败	1-C
cosmic	[ˈkɒzmɪk]	adj. 宇宙的	4-A
courageous	[kəˈreɪdʒəs]	adj. 勇敢的	1-C
crowned	[kraʊnd]	adj. 像王冠的（文中指路中间比两边高的）	2-B
crucial	[ˈkruːʃ(ə)l]	adj. 极其重要的	3-B
cult	[kʌlt]	n. 宗教崇拜，宗教信仰	1-A
curiosity	[ˌkjʊərɪˈɒsəti]	n. 好奇心	1-A
curriculum	[kəˈrɪkjʊləm]	n. （全部）课程	3-C

D

debauchery	[dɪˈbɔːtʃəri]	n. 道德败坏	7-C
deceased	[dɪˈsiːst]	adj. 已故的	4-C
dedication	[ˌdedɪˈkeɪʃn]	n. 奉献	1-B
deem	[diːm]	v. 认为，视作；相信	4-C
define	[dɪˈfaɪn]	v. 界定，阐释	7-B

189

word	pronunciation	meaning	ref
deity	[ˈdeɪəti]	n. 神祇	1-A
democratic	[ˌdeməˈkrætɪk]	adj. 民主的	1-B
depopulation	[ˌdiːpɒpjʊˈleɪʃ(ə)n]	n. 人口下降	3-A
deposit	[dɪˈpɑːzɪt]	n. 矿床,矿藏	2-B
descend	[dɪˈsend]	v. 下降	2-C
descent	[diˈsent]	n. 下降；血统	5-C
despair	[dɪˈspeə]	n. 绝望	2-C
de-urbanization	[diˈɜː(r)bənaɪˈzeɪʃ(ə)n]	n. 去城镇化	3-A
devise	[dɪˈvaɪz]	v. 设计；想出	4-C
dictator	[dɪkˈteɪtə]	n. 古罗马在紧急情况下任命的有绝对权力的独裁官	2-A
disciple	[dɪˈsaɪpl]	n. 追随者,弟子	1-C
discipline	[ˈdɪsəplɪn]	n. 学科	3-C
discourage	[dɪsˈkʌrɪdʒ]	v. 阻止,使气馁	2-B
disinherit	[ˌdɪsɪnˈherɪt]	v. 剥夺继承权,剥夺特权	5-C
disobedient	[ˌdɪsəˈbiːdiənt]	adj. 不顺从的,不服从的	1-B
disposition	[ˌdɪspəˈzɪʃn]	n. 性情	1-C
dissonance	[ˈdɪsənəns]	n. 不谐和音	7-A
distinct	[dɪˈstɪŋkt]	adj. 不同的	7-B
distinctive	[dɪˈstɪŋktɪv]	adj. 与众不同的,有特色的	7-A
ditch	[dɪtʃ]	v. 抛弃	7-A
divine	[dɪˈvaɪn]	adj. 神圣的	1-C
doctrine	[ˈdɒktrɪn]	n. 学说,教义	1-C
dogmatic	[dɒɡˈmætɪk]	adj. 教条的；武断的；固执	5-A
domestic	[dəˈmestɪk]	adj. 家庭的,国内的	7-B
dominate	[ˈdɒmɪneɪt]	v. 控制,支配	6-C
dot	[dɒt]	v. 星罗棋布于；点缀	4-B
draft	[drɑːft]	v. 起草	1-B
drainage	[ˈdreɪnɪdʒ]	n. 排水,排水系统	2-B
drastic	[ˈdræstɪk]	adj. 激烈的	3-B
dwarf	[dwɔːf]	v. 使相形见绌	2-B
dwindle	[ˈdwɪndl]	v. (逐渐)减少,变小	4-B

E

word	pronunciation	meaning	ref
ellipse	[ɪˈlɪps]	n. 椭圆	5-B
emancipation	[ɪˌmænsɪˈpeɪʃn]	n. 解放	5-A
embody	[ɪmˈbɒdi]	v. 体现,使具体化	6-A
embrace	[ɪmˈbreɪs]	v. 热切的接受,信奉	7-C
emerge	[ɪˈmɜːdʒ]	v. 出现,形成	6-C
emergent	[ɪˈmɜːdʒənt]	adj. 新兴的	3-B
encompass	[ɪnˈkʌmpəs]	v. 包围；包含	5-A
endeavor	[ɪnˈdevə]	n. 尝试 vt. 竭力做到	4-C
endless	[ˈendlɪs]	adj. 无止境的；连续的	2-C
endurance	[ɪnˈdjʊərəns]	n. 忍耐；忍耐力	1-C

Glossary

endure	[ɪnˈdjʊə(r)]	v. 忍受；持久	3-A
engagement	[ɪnˈgeɪdʒmənt]	n. 会战	1-C
enormous	[ɪˈnɔːməs]	adj. 巨大的	6-C
enthusiastically	[ɪnˌθjuːzɪˈæstɪkli]	adv. 热心地，满腔热情地	6-B
entitle	[ɪnˈtaɪt(ə)l]	v. 给予……资格	3-C
epitome	[ɪˈpɪtəmi]	n. 缩影；典型的人或事	5-A
equestrian	[ɪˈkwestrɪən]	n. 骑士阶层	2-A
eradication	[ɪˌrædɪˈkeɪʃn]	n. 摧毁，根除	5-A
escalate	[ˈeskəleɪt]	v. 逐步上升	5-A
essence	[ˈesns]	n. 本质，实质	6-B
eternal	[ɪˈtɜːn(ə)l]	adj. 永恒的，不朽的	2-A
ethical	[ˈeθɪkl]	adj. 道德的，伦理的	7-C
eulogy	[ˈjuːlədʒɪ]	n. 悼词；颂词	5-C
evocative	[ɪˈvɒkətɪv]	adj. 唤起情感的，引起共鸣的	7-A
evolve	[ɪˈvɒlv]	v. 进化，发展	3-C
exceptional	[ɪkˈsepʃ(ə)n(ə)l]	adj. 优越的；异常的；例外的	2-B
exclusively	[ɪkˈskluːsɪvli]	adv. 专门地；排外地	5-C
execution	[ˌeksɪˈkjuːʃ(ə)n]	n. 执行，处死	4-C
exotic	[ɪgˈzɒtɪk]	adj. 外来的，异国情调的	2-B
expand	[ɪkˈspænd]	v. 拓展，发展	5-B
expanse	[ɪkˈspæns]	n. 宽阔，广阔的区域	2-B
extant	[ekˈstænt]	adj. 尚存的	3-A
extensive	[ɪkˈstensɪv]	adj. 广泛的，大量的	1-A
eye-opener	[ˈaɪˌəʊpnə(r)]	n. 令人大开眼界的事物	7-C

F

facilitate	[fəˈsɪlɪteɪt]	v. 促进，帮助，使容易	2-B
facility	[fəˈsɪləti]	n. 设备	3-C
faculty	[ˈfæk(ə)lti]	n. 大学的院，系	3-C
famine	[ˈfæmɪn]	n. 饥荒	1-B
fatally	[ˈfeɪtəli]	adv. 严重地	7-C
federation	[ˌfedəˈreɪʃn]	n. 联邦	1-B
feudalism	[ˈfjuːdəlɪzəm]	n. 封建制度	3-A
fiancé	[fiˈɒnseɪ]	n. 未婚夫	7-C
filter	[ˈfɪltə]	v. 过滤	7-B
flamboyant	[flæmˈbɔɪənt]	adj. 华丽的	3-C
fleshly	[ˈfleʃli]	adj. 肉体的；肉欲的	4-A
flood	[flʌd]	v. 淹没，涌入	2-A
flourish	[ˈflʌrɪʃ]	v. 繁荣，兴旺	6-C
fluid	[ˈfluːɪd]	adj. 可变的	7-C
formalize	[ˈfɔː(r)məlaɪz]	v. 使……正式化；定型	3-C
formulate	[ˈfɔːmjuleɪt]	v. 规划，明确地表达	6-B
foster	[ˈfɒstə(r)]	v. 促进，培养	3-B

单词	音标	词性及释义	位置
Frankish	[ˈfræŋkɪʃ]	*adj.* 法兰克人的	3-B
friction	[ˈfrɪkʃn]	*n.* 摩擦	5-C
frugal	[ˈfruːgl]	*adj.* 简朴的	1-C
frugal	[ˈfruːgl]	*adj.* 节俭的	4-B
furious	[ˈfjʊərɪəs]	*adj.* 狂怒的	2-C

G

单词	音标	词性及释义	位置
garment	[ˈgɑːmənt]	*n.* 衣服	1-C
geometrical	[ˌdʒiːəˈmetrɪkl]	*adj.* 几何形状	7-A
geometry	[dʒiːˈɒmətri]	*n.* 几何学	3-C
Germanic	[dʒɜː(r)ˈmænɪk]	*adj.* 日耳曼的	3-B
gladiator	[ˈglædɪeɪtə]	*n.* 古罗马角斗士	2-B
grandiose	[ˈgrændɪəʊs]	*adj.* 宏伟的	6-A
graphic	[ˈgræfɪk]	*adj.* 图表的,形象的	6-C
ground-breaking	[ˈgraʊndˌbreɪkɪŋ]	*adj.* 独创的,开拓性的	6-B
gutter	[ˈgʌtə]	*n.* 排水沟	2-B

H

单词	音标	词性及释义	位置
halt	[hɔːlt]	*v.* 停止	2-B
harmony	[ˈhɑːməni]	*n.* 和声	7-A
headquarters	[hedˈkwɔːtəz]	*n.* 总部	6-C
hegemony	[hɪˈdʒeməni]	*n.* 霸权	5-A
heir	[eə]	*n.* 继承人;后嗣	4-C
hemisphere	[ˈhemɪsfɪə(r)]	*n.*(地球的)半球	4-B
hemlock	[ˈhemlɒk]	*n.* 毒芹(汁)	1-C
heredity	[həˈredəti]	*n.* 遗传(性)	6-C
heresy	[ˈherəsi]	*n.* 异教,异端邪说:已立誓信教或受过洗礼的教徒对罗马天主教教义的异议或否认	3-A
heritage	[ˈherɪtɪdʒ]	*n.* 文化遗产	1-A
hierarchy	[ˈhaɪəˌrɑː(r)ki]	*n.* 等级制度;层次体系	3-C
historian	[hɪˈstɔːrɪən]	*n.* 历史学家	2-A
honor	[ˈɒnə(r)]	*v.* 盛赞	5-B
hop	[hɒp]	*v.* 跳	7-C
hybrid	[ˈhaɪbrɪd]	*n.* 杂交生成的生物体	1-A

I

单词	音标	词性及释义	位置
iambic	[aɪˈæmbɪk]	*adj.* 抑扬格的	4-B
idealism	[aɪˈdiːəlɪzəm]	*n.* 理想主义	6-B
identity	[aɪˈdentəti]	*n.* 身份	1-B
identity	[aɪˈdentɪti]	*n.* 身份;特征	3-B
ideology	[ˌaɪdɪˈɒlədʒi]	*n.* 意识形态,思想意识	6-A
ignore	[ɪgˈnɔː(r)]	*v.* 忽视	1-A
imagination	[ɪˌmædʒɪˈneɪʃ(ə)n]	*n.* 想象力	2-C
immoral	[ɪˈmɒrəl]	*adj.* 不道德的,邪恶的	6-C

impinge	[ɪmˈpɪn(d)ʒ]	v. 影响	7-B
impressive	[ɪmˈpresɪv]	adj. 可观的	3-B
impressively	[ɪmˈpresɪvli]	adv. 令人难忘地	6-C
imprint	[ɪmˈprɪnt]	v. 使留下印象	6-C
incestuous	[ɪnˈsestjʊəs]	adj. 乱伦的	4-C
incite	[ɪnˈsaɪt]	v. 煽动；激励	2-C
incorporate	[ɪnˈkɔː(r)pəreɪt]	v. 包含；吸收	3-A
incredible	[ɪnˈkredɪb(ə)l]	adj. 难以置信的，惊人的	2-B
incredulity	[ˌɪnkrəˈdjuːləti]	n. 怀疑	5-A
independent	[ˌɪndɪˈpendənt]	adj. 独立的	1-B
indifference	[ɪnˈdɪfrəns]	n. 漠不关心，冷淡	6-C
indifferent	[ɪnˈdɪf(ə)r(ə)nt]	adj. 漠不关心的	7-B
individualism	[ˌɪndɪˈvɪdʒuəlɪzəm]	n. 个体主义	6-A
industrialization	[ɪnˌdʌstrɪəlaɪˈzeɪʃn]	n. 工业化	6-C
inevitably	[ɪnˈevɪtəbli]	adv. 不可避免地；必然地	2-B
infamously	[ˈɪnfəməsli]	adv. 臭名昭著地，声名狼藉地	2-A
infancy	[ˈɪnf(ə)nsi]	n. 婴儿期；初期	4-C
infinite	[ˈɪnfɪnət]	adj. 无限的，无穷的	4-A
influential	[ˌɪnfluˈenʃ(ə)l]	adj. 有影响的，有势力的	2-B
inherent	[ɪnˈhɪərənt]	adj. 固有的	7-B
initiate	[ɪˈnɪʃieɪt]	v. 开始	6-A
innocent	[ˈɪnəsnt]	adj. 无害的	1-A
instantaneously	[ˌɪnstənˈteɪniəsli]	adv. 即刻；突如其来地	7-B
instigator	[ˈɪnstɪɡeɪtə(r)]	n. 煽动者；教唆者	4-C
institution	[ˌɪnstɪˈtjuːʃ(ə)n]	n. 机构，制度	3-B
institution	[ˌɪnstɪˈtjuːʃ(ə)n]	n.(社会或宗教等)公共机构；制度；建立	4-A
integrity	[ɪnˈteɡrəti]	n. 诚实，诚信	7-C
intellectual	[ˌɪntəˈlektʃuəl]	adj. 知识的，智力的，脑力的	3-C
intellectualism	[ˌɪntəˈlektʃuəlɪzəm]	n. 理智主义	6-B
intelligence	[ɪnˈtelɪdʒ(ə)ns]	n. 智力	2-C
interference	[ˌɪntəˈfɪər(ə)ns]	n. 干扰；干涉	7-B
internal	[ɪnˈtɜː(r)n(ə)l]	adj. 内部的，内在的	3-B
interpret	[ɪnˈtɜːprɪt]	v. 说明；解释	7-B
intrigue	[ɪnˈtriːɡ]	n. 密谋	5-C
intuition	[ˌɪntjuˈɪʃn]	n. 直觉(力)	6-A
invade	[ɪnˈveɪd]	v. 侵略	2-C
invalid	[ɪnˈvælɪd]	adj. 无效的；站不住脚的	4-C
invasion	[ɪnˈveɪʒn]	n. 侵略	6-C
Islamic	[ɪzˈlæmɪk]	adj. 伊斯兰教的	3-A

J

jealousy	[ˈdʒeləsi]	n. 嫉妒	1-A
justify	[ˈdʒʌstɪfaɪ]	v. 证明(决定、行为或想法)正当	7-C

 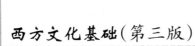

L

lady-in-waiting	[ˌleɪdiɪŋˈweɪtɪŋ]	n. 侍女；宫女	4-C
landmark	[ˈlændmɑːk]	n. 地标，里程碑	6-C
landscape	[ˈlændskeɪp]	n. 地貌	1-B
lavish	[ˈlævɪʃ]	adj. 浪费的；丰富的	4-C
leading	[ˈliːdɪŋ]	adj. 领先的	5-B
league	[liːg]	n. 联盟	1-B
literally	[ˈlɪtərəli]	adv. 字面上，逐字地	6-C
literature	[ˈlɪtrətʃə(r)]	n. 文学	1-B
loyal	[ˈlɔɪəl]	adj. 忠诚的	1-B
loyalty	[ˈlɔɪəlti]	n. 忠诚	1-B
lust	[lʌst]	n. 性欲；强烈的欲望	4-B

M

macadam	[məˈkædəm]	n. 碎石；碎石路面	2-B
mammonism	[ˈmæmənɪzəm]	n. 拜金主义	6-C
manorialism	[məˈnɔːrɪəlɪzəm]	n. 庄园制度	3-A
mantra	[ˈmæntrə]	n. （尤指认为并不正确或只是部分正确的）准则	7-C
manuscript	[ˈmænjʊskrɪpt]	n. 手稿；原稿	4-A
mariner	[ˈmærɪnə(r)]	n. 水手，海员	1-A
mass	[mæs]	n. 质量	5-B
materialism	[məˈtɪərɪəlɪzəm]	n. 唯物主义，物质主义	6-B
medieval	[ˌmediˈiːvl]	adj. 中世纪的	6-A
memoranda	[ˌmeməˈrændə]	n. 备忘录	5-C
migration	[maɪˈɡreɪʃ(ə)n]	n. 迁移，移民	2-A
militaristic	[ˌmɪlɪtəˈrɪstɪk]	adj. 军事主义的	1-B
military	[ˈmɪlətri]	adj. 军事的	1-C
militia	[məˈlɪʃə]	n. 民兵	3-B
miscarry	[mɪsˈkæri]	v. 流产	4-C
misfortune	[mɪsˈfɔːtʃuːn]	n. 不幸；灾祸，灾难	1-B
mob	[mɒb]	n. 乌合之众	1-C
mock	[mɒk]	v. 嘲弄	6-C
monarchy	[ˈmɒnə(r)ki]	n. 君主政体	3-B
monastery	[ˈmɒnəst(ə)ri]	n. 修道院	3-A
monologue	[ˈmɒnəlɒg]	n. 独白	7-A
monopoly	[məˈnɒpəli]	n. 垄断	5-A
monster	[ˈmɒnstə(r)]	n. 怪物，妖怪	1-A
morality	[məˈræləti]	n. 道德（规范）	7-A
mosque	[mɒsk]	n. 清真寺	7-B
mule	[mjuːl]	n. 骡；倔强之人	2-B
multitude	[ˈmʌltɪtjuːd]	n. 多数；大量	7-B
multivolume	[mʌltɪˈvɒljuːm]	adj. 多卷的	6-C

Glossary

mystique	[mɪˈstiːk]	n. 神秘性	2-C
myth	[mɪθ]	n. 神话	1-A
mythology	[mɪˈθɒlədʒi]	n. 神话(总称)	1-A

N

namesake	[ˈneɪmseɪk]	n. 同名者,同名物	1-A
nautical	[ˈnɔːtɪk(ə)l]	adj. 航海的,海上的	2-B
neglect	[nɪˈglekt]	n. 忽略,忽视	1-C
neo-Gothic	[ˌniːəʊˈgɒθɪk]	adj. 新哥特式的	6-A
nevertheless	[ˌnevəðəˈles]	adv. 然而,尽管如此	2-A
nickname	[ˈnɪkneɪm]	n. 绰号,昵称 v. 给……取绰号	2-B
notorious	[nəʊˈtɔːriəs]	adj. 臭名昭著的	1-C
nude	[njuːd]	adj. 裸体的	7-A
numerous	[ˈnjuːm(ə)rəs]	adj. 许多的	2-C

O

obsolete	[ˈɒbsəliːt]	adj. 废弃的,过时的	7-A
oligarchy	[ˈɒlɪgɑːki]	n. 寡头组织	1-B
omnipotent	[ɒmˈnɪpətənt]	adj. 无所不能的,全能的	6-B
omnipresent	[ˌɒmnɪˈpreznt]	adj. 无处不在的	6-B
open-plan	[ˈəʊpən plæn]	adj. 开敞式的,无隔断的	7-A
oracle	[ˈɒrəkl]	n. 神谕;预言	1-A
orbit	[ˈɔːbɪt]	n./v. 轨道;沿轨道运动	5-B
origin	[ˈɒrɪdʒɪn]	n. 起源,出身	2-C
originally	[əˈrɪdʒɪn(ə)li]	adv. 最初,起初	2-B
ostensible	[ɒˈstensəb(ə)l]	adj. 表面上的,貌似的	3-C
otherwise	[ˈʌðəwaɪz]	adv. & adj. & conj. 否则,不然,另外,在其他方面	2-A
otherworldly	[ˌʌðəˈwɜːldli]	adj. 来世的;超脱尘俗的	4-A
outrageous	[aʊtˈreɪdʒəs]	adj. 惊人的;反常的	6-A
outskirts	[ˈaʊtskɜːts]	n. 郊区	1-C
overflow	[ˌəʊvəˈfləʊ]	v. 充满,洋溢	6-A
overlordship	[ˈəʊvə(r)ˌlɔː(r)dʃɪp]	n. 封建君主的权位	3-B
overly	[ˈəʊvəli]	adv. 极度地	7-C
overnight	[ˌəʊvəˈnaɪt]	adv. 通宵,一夜工夫;从夜晚到天明	1-B
Oversoul	[ˈəʊvəsəʊl]	n. 超灵	6-B
overturn	[ˌəʊvəˈtɜːn]	v. 推翻;撤销(判决等)	5-A

P

panoramic	[ˌpænəˈræmɪk]	adj. 全景的	6-C
pantheon	[ˈpænθɪən]	n. 众神	1-A
papacy	[ˈpeɪpəsi]	n. 罗马天主教教皇制度	3-B
parallel	[ˈpærəlel]	v. 与……同时发生	3-A
parliamentary	[ˌpɑːləˈmentri]	adj. 议会的	6-A
passionate	[ˈpæʃənət]	adj. 热情的	6-A

195

patrician	[pəˈtrɪʃ(ə)n]	n. 古罗马的统治阶层成员，贵族	2-A
peak	[piːk]	n. 山峰，最高点	6-C
peculiar	[pɪˈkjuːlɪə(r)]	adj. 特殊的，独特的	6-B
pederast	[ˈpedəræst]	n. 鸡奸者	5-C
pentameter	[penˈtæmɪtə(r)]	n. 五音步诗行	4-B
perception	[pəˈsepʃn]	n. 感觉；认知	7-A
personality	[pɜːsəˈnælɪti]	n. 个性，品格	2-C
personify	[pəˈsɒnɪfaɪ]	v. 使人格化；赋与……以人性	4-A
perspective	[pəˈspektɪv]	n. 透视画法，视角	7-A
pessimistic	[ˌpesɪˈmɪstɪk]	adj. 悲观(主义)的	7-A
pharaoh	[ˈfɛroʊ]	n. 法老	2-C
phase	[feɪz]	n. 阶段	1-A
philosopher	[fəˈlɒsəfə(r)]	n. 哲学家	1-C
philosophy	[fəˈlɒsəfi]	n. 哲学	1-A
physical	[ˈfɪzɪk(ə)l]	adj. 物质的，有形的	3-C
pit	[pɪt]	n. 深坑	4-A
plague	[pleɪg]	n. 瘟疫	1-B
plague	[pleɪg]	v. 使痛苦，造成麻烦	5-C
planetary	[ˈplænɪt(ə)ri]	adj. 行星的	4-A
playwright	[ˈpleɪraɪt]	n. 剧作家	2-A
plebeian	[plɪˈbiːən]	n. 平民，百姓	2-A
pneumonia	[njuːˈməʊnɪə]	n. 肺炎	5-C
poison	[ˈpɔɪzn]	v. 投毒	2-C
polis	[ˈpəʊlɪs]	n. 城邦；城市国家	1-B
pompous	[ˈpɒmpəs]	adj. 虚夸的，浮华的	1-C
pontificate	[pɒnˈtɪfɪkeɪt]	n. 教皇的职务或在任期间	3-B
populist	[ˈpɒpjəlɪst]	adj. 平民主义(者)的	4-B
portrait	[ˈpɔːtreɪt]	n. 肖像，描写	6-C
portray	[pɔːˈtreɪ]	v. 描绘；扮演	7-B
possession	[pəˈzɛʃn]	n. 属地；领地	2-B
potential	[pəˈtenʃl]	adj. 潜在的	1-B
preach	[priːtʃ]	v. 宣扬；布道；训诫	3-A
precocious	[prɪˈkəʊʃəs]	adj. 早熟的	5-C
precursor	[priːˈkɜːsə]	n. 先驱	7-A
predominance	[prɪˈdɒmɪnəns]	n. 主导地位	7-A
predominantly	[prɪˈdɒmɪnəntli]	adv. 主要地	3-C
pregnancy	[ˈpregnənsi]	n. 怀孕	7-C
premier	[ˈpremɪə(r)]	adj. 首位的，首次的	3-C
prevalent	[ˈprevələnt]	adj. 流行的，盛行的	5-A
previous	[ˈpriːvɪəs]	adj. 以前的	7-B
primal	[ˈpraɪml]	adj. 原始的，主要的	6-A
proclaim	[prəˈkleɪm]	v. 宣称	1-A
prominently	[ˈprɒmɪnəntli]	adv. 重要地	1-A

prosperity	[prɒˈsperəti]	n. 繁荣,成功		6-C
Protestant	[ˈprɒtɪstənt]	n. 新教教徒		3-A
prototype	[ˈprəʊtətaɪp]	n. 标准,蓝本,典型		3-C
protracted	[prəˈtræktɪd]	adj. 旷日持久的		3-B
province	[ˈprɒvɪns]	n. 领域		4-A
provision	[prəˈvɪʒn]	n. 规定,条款		3-C
psalm	[sɑːm]	n. 赞美诗		3-C
pseudo-	[ˈsjuːdəʊ]	comb. 表示"假","伪"		6-A
psychiatrist	[saɪˈkaɪətrɪst]	n. 精神病学家		1-A

Q

quarto	[ˈkwɔːtəʊ]	n. 四开本	4-B

R

radiate	[ˈreɪdieɪt]	v. 辐射,传播,流露	2-B
radically	[ˈrædɪkəli]	adv. 根本上;彻底地	4-A
rampant	[ˈræmpənt]	adj. 猖獗的,盛行的	7-C
rationalism	[ˈræʃnəlɪzəm]	n. 理性主义	6-A
rebel	[ˈrebl]	v. 反叛,反抗	6-A
rebirth	[riːˈbɜːθ]	n. 再生;复兴	4-A
recount	[rɪˈkaʊnt]	v. 讲述	1-A
redemption	[rɪˈdem(p)ʃ(ə)n]	n. 救赎	4-A
reflection	[rɪˈflekʃn]	n. 倒影	1-A
regal	[ˈriːg(ə)l]	adj. 王者的;庄严的	4-C
regeneration	[rɪˌdʒenəˈreɪʃn]	n. 再生,重生	6-B
reign	[reɪn]	n./v. 统治	6-C
reinforce	[ˌriːɪnˈfɔːs]	v. 加强,加固	6-A
religion	[rɪˈlɪdʒən]	n. 宗教	1-B
religious	[rɪˈlɪdʒəs]	adj. 宗教的	1-A
remarkable	[rɪˈmɑːkəbl]	adj. 卓越的,值得注意的	6-C
render	[ˈrendə(r)]	v. 使……成为	7-A
renew	[rɪˈnjuː]	v. 使更新,复兴	2-C
renewal	[rɪˈnjuːəl]	n. 重新开始,恢复;复兴	4-A
repay	[riːˈpeɪ]	v. 报答;付还	4-C
replicate	[ˈreplɪkeɪt]	v. 复制	6-A
representational	[ˌreprɪzenˈteɪʃnl]	adj. (绘画)具象风格的,写实的,表现的	7-A
restorative	[rɪˈstɔːrətɪv]	adj. 有助于复元的	6-B
restore	[rɪˈstɔː]	v. 恢复,修复	2-C
restraint	[rɪˈstreɪnt]	n. 约束	7-C
restriction	[rɪˈstrɪkʃ(ə)n]	n. 限制;约束;束缚	7-B
reversal	[rɪˈvɜː(r)s(ə)l]	n. 逆转,颠倒	3-B
revitalization	[ˌriːˌvaɪtəlaɪˈzeɪʃn]	n. 振兴	3-B
revival	[rɪˈvaɪvl]	n. 复兴,复活	6-A

word	pronunciation	meaning	ref
revive	[rɪˈvaɪv]	v. 复兴；复活	4-A
revoke	[rɪˈvəʊk]	v. 废除；撤销	5-C
revolt	[rɪˈvəʊlt]	n. 暴乱	3-A
revolt	[rɪˈvəʊlt]	n. 起义；叛乱	1-B
rhetoric	[ˈretərɪk]	n. 修辞	3-C
rigid	[ˈrɪdʒɪd]	adj. 刻板的	1-B
ritual	[ˈrɪtʃuəl]	n. (宗教)仪式	1-A
rival	[ˈraɪvl]	n. 竞争对手	1-B
roll	[rəʊl]	v. 卷	2-C
romanticism	[rəʊˈmæntɪsɪzəm]	n. 浪漫主义	5-A
romanticize	[rəʊˈmæntɪsaɪz]	v. 使浪漫化	6-C

S

word	pronunciation	meaning	ref
sage	[seɪdʒ]	n. 智者	1-C
sanction	[ˈsæŋ(k)ʃ(ə)n]	v. 批准；准许	7-B
satirize	[ˈsætəraɪz]	v. 讽刺	6-C
scale	[skeɪl]	n. 规模,范围	3-B
scapegoat	[ˈskeɪpgəʊt]	n. 替罪羊	5-C
scholarship	[ˈskɒlə(r)ʃɪp]	n. 学问,学识	3-C
scholasticism	[skəˈlæstɪsɪzəm]	n. 经院哲学	3-A
sculpture	[ˈskʌlptʃə(r)]	n. 雕刻	1-C
secular	[ˈsekjʊlə(r)]	adj. 世俗的；非宗教的	3-B
secularization	[ˌsekjələraɪˈzeɪʃn]	n. 世俗化	5-A
senate	[ˈsenət]	n. 参议院；古罗马的元老院	2-A
severe	[sɪˈvɪə(r)]	adj. 严酷的	1-B
sexual	[ˈsekʃuəl]	adj. 性的	7-C
shipwreck	[ˈʃɪprek]	n. 海难	1-A
significance	[sɪgˈnɪfɪkəns]	n. 意义	1-A
sizeable	[ˈsaɪzəb(ə)l]	adj. 相当大的	3-A
slippery	[ˈslɪpəri]	adj. 不可靠的	7-A
sneaker	[ˈsniːkə(r)]	n. 运动鞋	1-A
solidify	[səˈlɪdɪfaɪ]	v. 巩固	4-B
solidity	[səˈlɪdəti]	n. 可靠性	7-A
solitude	[ˈsɒlɪtjuːd]	n. 孤独	7-A
sonnet	[ˈsɒnɪt]	n. 十四行诗	4-B
spear	[spɪə(r)]	n. 矛枪 v. 用矛刺	1-A
specific	[spəˈsɪfɪk]	adj. 特有的,具体的	7-A
specifically	[spəˈsɪfɪkli]	adv. 专门地	3-C
speculate	[ˈspekjuleɪt]	v. 猜测	4-B
spontaneous	[spɒnˈteɪniəs]	adj. 自发的,自然的	6-A
spur	[spɜː(r)]	v. 促进；推动	3-B
strategically	[strəˈtiːdʒɪkəli]	adv. 战略性地,战略上	2-B
strike	[straɪk]	v. 猛烈击打	1-A

subdivide	[ˌsʌbdɪˈvaɪd]	v. 再分,细分	3-A
subjectivism	[səbˈdʒektɪvɪzəm]	n. 主观主义	6-A
sublimity	[səˈblɪməti]	n. 崇高,庄严	6-A
substantial	[səbˈstænʃ(ə)l]	adj. 实质的,坚实的	3-A
succeeding	[səkˈsiːdɪŋ]	adj. 以后的	1-C
succession	[səkˈseʃ(ə)n]	n. 连续;继位;继承权	4-C
successor	[səkˈsesə]	n. 继承者	2-C
succumb	[səˈkʌm]	v. 屈服	3-A
supernatural	[ˌsuːpəˈnætʃərəl]	adj. 超自然的	6-A
supremacy	[sʊˈpreməsi]	n. 霸权	3-B
surpassing	[səˈpɑːsɪŋ]	adj. 卓越的,优秀的	2-C
surrender	[səˈrendə(r)]	n. 投降	1-B

T

teem	[tiːm]	v. 充满	7-A
telecommunication	[ˌtelɪkəˌmjuːnɪˈkeɪʃn]	n. 电信,通讯	7-B
theology	[θiˈɒlədʒi]	n. 神学	5-A
three-pronged	[θriː-prɒŋd]	adj. 有三叉(尖)的	1-A
thrilled	[θrɪld]	adj. 非常兴奋的,极为激动的	6-B
thunderbolt	[ˈθʌndəbəʊlt]	n. (诗/文)雷电,霹雳	1-A
tint	[tɪnt]	v. 着色	6-B
tonal	[ˈtəʊnl]	adj. 音调的	7-A
trait	[treɪt]	n. 特性,特点	6-A
trample	[ˈtræmpl]	v. 践踏,蹂躏	7-C
transform	[trænsˈfɔːm]	v. 改变	6-A
tremendous	[trəˈmendəs]	adj. 巨大的	6-B
trident	[ˈtraɪdnt]	n. 三叉戟,三齿鱼叉	1-A
Turk	[tɜː(r)k]	n. 土耳其人,突厥人	3-A
tutelage	[ˈtjuːtəlɪdʒ]	n. 指导;保护;监护	5-C
twin	[twɪn]	n. 双胞胎中的一个	2-C
twist	[twɪst]	v. 歪曲	7-C
tyrant	[ˈtaɪr(ə)nt]	n. 暴君	2-A

U

unauthorized	[ʌnˈɔːθəraɪzd]	adj. 未经授权的,未经许可的	1-A
underworld	[ˈʌndəwɜːld]	n. 阴间	1-A
undoubtedly	[ʌnˈdaʊtɪdli]	adv. 确实地,毋庸置疑地	7-B
unified	[ˈjuːnɪfaɪd]	adj. 统一的	3-A
unique	[juˈniːk]	adj. 独特的	6-A
unkempt	[ˌʌnˈkempt]	adj. 凌乱的,不整洁的	1-C
unmatched	[ˌʌnˈmætʃt]	adj. 无可比拟的	1-C
unsurpassed	[ʌnsəˈpɑːst]	adj. 非常卓越的,未被超越的	2-B
urban	[ˈɜː(r)bən]	adj. 城市的	3-B

| usher | [ˈʌʃə(r)] | v. 迎接；开辟 | 6-A |

V

vast	[vɑːst]	adj. 广阔的,巨大的	2-B
vehicle	[ˈviːəkl]	n. 车辆,工具,传播媒介	2-B
vibrant	[ˈvaɪbrənt]	adj. 充满生机的	7-B
violent	[ˈvaɪələnt]	adj. 强烈的	1-A
vision	[ˈvɪʒn]	n. 幻想	7-B

W

wail	[weɪl]	v.& n. 哀嚎；悲叹	7-B
warrior	[ˈwɒriə(r)]	n. 武士	1-A
watershed	[ˈwɔːtəʃed]	n. 分水岭,转折点	6-B
whence	[wens]	pron. 何处,该处	2-B
witness	[ˈwɪtnəs]	v. 目击；n. 目击者	6-C
woolen	[ˈwʊlɪn]	adj. 羊毛的	1-C
worship	[ˈwɜːʃɪp]	v. 崇拜,尊敬	6-A

Y

| yield | [jiːld] | n. 产量 | 3-A |

Z

| zest | [zest] | n. 热情 | 4-C |

Expressions

A

a multiplicity of	许多	7-A
a multitude of	许多	7-B
adhere to	遵循；依附；坚持	5-A
along with	连同……一起；与……一道	4-A
amount to	共计；达到	5-C
as well as	也，还有	7-B
associate...with...	把……与……联系在一起	7-B
at the expense of	以……为代价	3-B
at will	任意，随意	7-C
attach value to	重视	4-A

B

be alien to	与……相异；违反……	7-B
be crowned with	使圆满；使完美	5-C
be deemed to	被认为	6-C
be distinct from	与……不同	7-B
be driven out of	被赶出	2-C
be fascinated by	沉迷于	1-C
be featured by	以……为特征	6-A
be immune from	不受……的影响	3-C
be named after	以……名字命名	1-A
be sentenced to	被判处……	1-C
be unparalleled in convenience	最为便利	2-B
be vulnerable to	易受伤害的；易受影响的	1-A
beg the question	引起疑问；绕过正题	7-B
break away	脱离，放弃	7-A
break down	发生故障，失败	2-C
break off	断交	5-C

C

call upon	号召；要求	1-C
civic function	公民职责	1-C
cling on to sth.	坚持某事	2-A
come into use	投入使用	5-A
come to an end	结束	2-C
commit suicide	自杀	2-C

commune with	与……谈心,亲密交谈	6-B
compare to	把……比作,比喻为	2-B
coupled with	加上	3-B
culminate in sth	终于获得某种结果	5-A
D		
depend on	取决于,依赖,依靠	2-B
due to	由于	5-C
E		
end up with	以……告终	5-C
entitle sb to do sth	使某人有权或有资格做某事	3-C
F		
fall victim to	成为……的牺牲品	5-C
feature prominently	起主要作用,扮演重要角色	1-A
few and far between	稀少,罕见	7-C
fight off	击退	1-B
flee back to	逃回	2-C
foot soldier	步兵	1-C
free from	不受……影响的	7-B
T		
gain force	得势,赢得力量	5-A
get even with	报复;与……扯平	5-B
give away	放弃;泄露;出卖	2-C
give birth to	产生	3-C
give precedence over	给予优先	5-C
give way to	让位于	5-A
go into	被用在	7-B
go through	通过,经受	1-A
gravity force	重力	5-B
H		
have a profound influence on	对……有极大的影响	3-C
have access to	有权使用;可以利用	7-B
have little say	几乎没有发言权	2-A
have much in common	有很多相似之处	1-B
have no intention of	无意……	2-C
hold on to	坚持;信奉	5-A
I		
in essence	本质上	6-B
in favor of	偏好;支持	5-A
in one's honor	为了纪念;向……表示敬意	2-C

Glossary

in terms of	在……方面	7-A
in the flesh	本人	4-C
in the light of	鉴于,参照,根据	5-A
in turn	依次	3-B
in turn	依次;反过来;转而	4-A
involve in	卷入;参与	3-B
L		
lead to	导致	5-B
lie with	是……的权利/责任,取决于	2-A
look upon as	视为,看作	2-C
M		
make reference to	提到	1-A
more than	不只是	4-A
N		
no more than	不过;只是	3-C
not to mention	更别提……	2-B
O		
of one's time	……时代的	5-B
on and off	断断续续地	1-B
P		
pass on to	传承	1-C
personal secretary	私人秘书	5-C
place emphasis on	重视	1-B
place emphasis on	重视;强调	4-A
play a role in	在……起作用	2-B
pockets of	一些	7-C
profit from	从……获利,获益	6-C
R		
rank as	把……视为	1-C
rather than	而不是	6-A
rebel against	反叛;反抗	6-A
reduce to	还原;降为	5-A
refer to as	把……称作/当作	2-A
refer to	提及,谈到;参考;涉及	4-A
revolve around	围绕	5-A
S		
self-culture	自我修养	6-B
sexual preference	性取向	5-C

so much so that	到这种程度以致	1-A
stay up late	熬夜	3-C
stream-of-consciousness	意识流	7-A
subject... to	使……服从	3-B
T		
take for granted	认为……理所当然	2-B
take on	呈现	6-C
take part in	参与	1-C
take pride in	以……为荣	1-B
take up	从事	5-C
take... into account	重视,考虑	7-A
the three laws of motion	三大运动定律	5-B
think tank	思想库,智库	1-B
tie to	依靠;迷恋;关联	5-A
top student	优等生	5-B
trace...back to...	回溯到	3-C
turn to	向……求助	5-B
U		
usher in	开创;开启	4-A
W		
ward off	阻挡,防止	4-B

《西方文化基础》(第三版)

尊敬的老师:

您好!

为了方便您更好地使用本教材,获得最佳教学效果,我们特向使用该书作为教材的教师赠送本教材配套资料。如有需要,请完整填写"教师联系表"并加盖所在单位系(院)公章,免费向出版社索取。

北京大学出版社

教 师 联 系 表

教材名称	《西方文化基础》(第三版)		
姓名:	性别:	职务:	职称:
E-mail:	联系电话:	邮政编码:	
供职学校:		所在院系:	(章)
学校地址:			
教学科目与年级:		班级人数:	
通信地址:			

填写完毕后,请将此表邮寄或者通过 email 发送给我们,我们将为您免费寄送本教材配套资料,谢谢!

北京市海淀区成府路205号
北京大学出版社外语编辑部　李　颖
邮政编码:100871
电子邮箱:evalee1770@sina.com

邮 购 部 电话:010-62534449
市场营销部电话:010-62750672
外语编辑部电话:010-62754382